The World of Women in Pursuit of Human Rights

The World of Women in Pursuit of Human Rights

Patanjali Nandan Chaturvedi

MD PUBLICATIONS PVT LTD
NEW DELHI
www.mdppl.com

Published by :

MD Publications Pvt Ltd
"MD House", 11, Darya Ganj,
New Delhi - 110 002
Phone : +91-11-45355555
E-mail : contact@mdppl.com
Website: www.mdppl.com

ISBN: 978-81-7533-261-4

Published and Printed by Mr. Pranav Gupta on behalf of MD Publications Pvt Ltd at Times Press, Delhi.

Preface

The human rights of women are an inalienable part of universal human rights. Both the Beijing Declaration and Platform for Action and the Millennium Development Goals, recognize that economic and social development priorities cannot be separated from the promotion and protection of human rights and of gender equality.

Women form half of the human beings inhabiting planet Earth. Since human rights are the rights of all human beings, male and female alike, human rights are women's rights. By the same token, a society in which men are not willing to extend human rights to their mothers, the women who bore and nurtured them; their daughters, products of their own loins; and their wives, the women who bear and raise their treasured sons, is a society in which men are unwilling to extend human rights to men of another family, tribe, language, religion, race, ethnic tradition, or nation. If a society does not hold justice and equality for all women in the highest regard, neither will it hold justice and equality for the many varieties of men in high regard. In a very real sense, women's rights are the basis of all human rights. Women's rights belong to women as members of the human family, and, as such, are not dependent either on a woman's marital status or on the number or sex of the children she has borne.

Since the primary responsibility of any society is to bear and raise future generations of male and female human beings, women's roles in reproduction must be held in the highest esteem and must not be permitted to become the basis for discrimination against women as women. Further, the responsibility for raising and nurturing future generations must fall upon men and women equally.

Women, equal to men in the eyes of the law, shall be subjected to the same laws, no more hand no less, as men. All laws that restrict women as women are null and void. Women have the right to the same access as men to food, clothing, shelter, medicine, an education, job training, and employment. Women, like men, have the right to rest and leisure, including a reasonable limitation on working hours, a living wage for a reasonable number of hours worked, and periodic holidays. Women have the right to equal pay for the same work as men. Just as woman has the right to enter the place of public execution, woman has the right to enter the place of public acclaim for her accomplishments. Indeed, tremendous progress has been made since World War II in codifying women's rights and gender equality within the law at both the international and individual country levels. Unfortunately, limited progress has been made in realizing those rights.

I am very grateful to Mr. Pranav Gupta, Director of MD Publications Pvt Ltd, New Delhi, for his kind cooperation and support for this book.

Patanjali Nandan Chaturvedi

CONTENTS

1

A Global Challenge
Human Rights and Women

The ongoing tragedy in Darfur reminds us every day how enormous the challenge is at the international level to protect human rights of individuals and groups suffering from the excesses of tyrannical regimes. A similar grim situation faces those who live in failed states. The existing international machinery is ill-equipped, inadequate, and ineffective for providing the needed protection. As the U.N. Secretary-General noted in his March 2005 follow-up report to the outcome of the Millennium Summit, "[c]hange is needed if the United Nations is to sustain long-term, high-level engagement on human rights issues, across the range of the Organization's work." He emphasized the need to strengthen the U.N. human rights machinery by providing more resources and staff within the Office of the U.N. High Commissioner for Human Rights (OHCHR). He called for the human rights treaty bodies to be more effective and more responsive to violations of the rights under their mandate, which in turn necessitates the finalization and implementation of uniform guidelines on reporting to all treaty bodies.

Noting that the Security Council is fully authorized under the U.N. Charter to use military force, including preventively, to preserve international peace and security when there exist latent threats, the Secretary-General asked rhetorically, "[a]s to genocide, ethnic cleansing and other such crimes against humanity, are they not also threats to international peace and security, against which humanity should be able to look to the Security Council for protection?" He also took special note of the need to replace the discredited U.N. Commission on Human Rights by a smaller and more effective standing Human Rights Council. Subsequently, Heads of State and Government who met at a World Summit at U.N. Headquarters in New York from September 14-16, 2005, agreed in principle to strengthen the U.N. machinery on human rights.

However, the recommendations were in general terms, leaving the specifics for the General Assembly to decide at a later date. A promising development, however, was the agreement on the responsibility to protect populations from genocide, war crimes, ethnic cleansing, and crimes against humanity. Lets discuss here a few promising new developments that should result in enhancing the protection of human rights. The first such development is the recognition by U.N. member states of a "responsibility to protect their populations; the second is their promise to strengthen the Office of the High Commissioner for Human Rights; and last is the decision by member states to replace the U.N. Commission on Human Rights by an effective Human Rights Council.

THE RESPONSIBILITY TO PROTECT POPULATIONS

FROM GENOCIDE, WAR CRIMES, ETHNIC CLEANSING, AND CRIMES AGAINST HUMANITY

The need to protect victims of civil wars, collapsed states, and repressive state practices resulting in massive violation of human rights is undeniable. However, controversy surrounds the claim that there exists a valid right to intervene by military action against a state on humanitarian grounds to protect peoples at risk in that state. Although the United Nations took coercive action, invoking a Chapter VII determination that the humanitarian crisis was a threat to international peace and security, to protect the Kurds from Saddam Hussein's brutality after the first Gulf War, the shameful inaction of the world community in the face of the Rwandan genocide as the screams of hundreds of thousands of innocent men, women, and children being massacred fell on deaf ears in the Security Council; there was soul-searching the world over on how to protect such victims. Questions were being raised as to whether along with the rights associated with sovereignty there was not also an obligation on a sovereign to protect those under its jurisdiction.

Along with academic writing on the subject, several governments took policy initiatives to consider the question. Among the major initiatives were those by the Danish government, the Dutch government, the Swedish government, and the Clinton administration. The Canadian initiative, that of the International Commission on Intervention and State Sovereignty (ICISS), is the most influential of all these initiatives and was undertaken in response to the challenges posed by Secretary-General Annan in his General Assembly addresses, first in 1999 and then again in 2000. This initiative issued a report, entitled "The Responsibility to Protect." In Kofi Annan's words, "if humanitarian intervention is, indeed, an unacceptable assault on sovereignty, how should we respond to a Rwanda, to a Srebrenica - to gross and systematic violations of human rights that affect every precept of our common humanity?"

The government of Canada had established the ICISS in cooperation with a group of major foundations. It may be recalled that the 1999 NATO intervention in Kosovo had taken place in the face of a seeming paralysis and inaction at the United Nations. After deliberations on legal, moral, operational, and political aspects of the issue, and after wide consultations around the world, the Commission concluded that as an exceptional and extraordinary measure, military intervention for human protection purposes is warranted only when there is:

Serious and irreparable harm occurring to human beings, or imminently likely to occur, of the following kind: A. large-scale loss of life, actual or apprehended, with genocidal intent or not, which is the product either of deliberate state action, or state neglect or inability to act, or a failed state situation; or B. large-scale 'ethnic cleansing', actual or apprehended, whether carried out by killing, forced expulsion, acts of terror or rape.

According to the Commission this was the "just cause" threshold. It outlined four precautionary principles to guide the use of force - right intention, last resort, proportional means, and reasonable prospects of success - in halting or averting the suffering "with the consequences of action not likely to be worse than the consequences of inaction." Earlier, in the mid-1990s, the Special Representative of the Secretary-General on Internally Displaced Persons, Francis Deng, had already advocated the responsibility concept pertaining to sovereignty in his studies - in 1995, *Frontiers of Sovereignty*, and in 1996 (co-authored with others), *Sovereignty as Responsibility: Conflict Management in Africa.*

The Universal Declaration of Human Rights, created in 1948 as an international body of laws, was meant to protect the integrity and dignity of human beings. Those laws, together with the 1979 Convention for the Elimination of All Forms of Discrimination Against Women, have been pivotal in the affirmation and implementation of human rights. At the same time, these instruments have been used to prove the continued existence of violations of rights in both public and private spheres. Conventional international human rights must also be understood as a way of truly living and participating in the world without physical or psychological coercion...

The tenacity and persistence of rights violations, throughout history but especially in the twentieth century, which has been called the century of genocide, have generated a substantial body of work by activists, grassroots leaders, writers, and thinkers. The purpose of these writings has been to bring international attention to the gender-based abuses that cut across cultural, social, and political lines. Many of these violations discriminate against status as equal partners and citizens. Widow burnings and honor killings are just two of the most extreme examples. As one begins to grasp the central issue of human rights, it is important to realize that most governments as well as nongovernmental organizations (NGOs) define human rights in terms of male models and patterns of thinking.

The essays collected here demonstrate that the human rights of women form part of a global landscape in which oppression figures regardless of culture, religion, or levels of education; they show how rights can reflect a systematic and universal pattern of abuse. Although there are multiple cultural differences among women and the societies in which they live, there is also a strong commonality that goes beyond national, economic, and social boundaries. This commonality is the anthology's unifying theme, and its definition of human rights recognizes the rights of women both in the public as well as in the private sphere. Such a definition revises and expands the traditional view of human rights, which has focused on actions such as state-sponsored terrorism, and arrives at a more inclusive view of human rights. It is in the spirit of inclusiveness that this anthology was created. . . From an international perspective, this collection explores issues marked by a regional point of view as well as those that are universal and tries to shed light on the common traits of so many lives.

The essays address the centrality of bodies as objects of punishment, either as trophies of war or as victims in abusive domestic relationships that force women into invisibility, silence, and psychological punishment. The first three essays address the historical development of human rights as well as the international movement of activists working for change in NGOs and grassroots organizations. The first of these is Arvonne Fraser's 'Becoming Human: The Origins and Development of Human Rights,' in which the author traces the history of human rights from the perspective of education. She explores the extent to which women were exposed to a world outside the confining and invisible communities in which many of them have lived. The second essay, by Sheila Dauer, director of Amnesty International Women's programs, addresses developments in the pursuit of human rights and equality for all women since 1979, a year of pivotal importance.

That year saw the creation of the United Nations convention calling upon governments to eradicate discrimination against women; it also marked the height of the human rights movement, a period of intense activity that undoubtedly had a great impact on the convention "In Women, Violence, and the Human Rights System, the anthropologist Sally Engle Merry traces the historical, political, and social development of human rights laws within the framework of the Universal Declaration of Human Rights. Merry addresses the dramatic changes in the concept of human rights since 1948, and specifically in the context of women's rights, in particular relating to private and public violence.

In her essay, 'Mainstreaming a Concern for the Human Rights of Women: Beyond Theory,' Felice Gaer writes of the work that international human rights organizations have undertaken specifically to address women's human rights concerns. An important concept that has emerged in these efforts is 'gender mainstreaming': the term signifies that policies must be examined as to their implications for women and men... The longer women are invisible, the more ground is lost in the struggle to make human rights apply equally to men and women. The second section of this volume addresses issues related to women's health. Sandra P. Levison, a physician, and Julie H. Levison, at the time of writing a student at Harvard's School of Medicine, contribute a significant essay on the subject. Not only the pursuit of health and access to health care but the pursuit of dignity and personal freedom are the authors' themes. They describe the extent of access to and types of health care in several countries and the cultural concepts of health care in different societies.

Julia Chill and Susan Kilbourne, in 'The Rights of the Girl Child', observe that 'horrible things happen to children every day in every corner of the world. Boys and girls alike face unimaginable abuses. For girls, the human rights violations are compounded by gender bias, physical limitations, and traditional social roles.' Girls suffer from a range of abuses: female children are more likely to be the victims of infanticide; girls are more likely than boys to be denied access to education;

and girls are the victims in a vast network of prostitution, pornography, and sexual exploitation... Carola Suarez-Orozco's article, 'Psychocultural Factors in the Adaptation of Immigrant Youth: Gendered Responses,'explores the many factors that influence how well immigrants adapt to their host cultures. She offers a wide context of issues that face immigrants and refugees, from the trauma of border crossings to family destabilization to the challenges of learning a new language and functioning in school and the workplace.

The third section of the volume deals with women as activists fighting for social change... The spirit of Temma Kaplan's essay, 'Women's Rights as Human Rights,' in which Kaplan sets out the ways in which activism, mobilization, and the international struggle for social justice are integral parts of human rights and presents the ways in which women in the international community and at the grassroots level have redefined human rights... In The Forgotten Minority, Jean Trounstine, who worked extensively in the prison system in Framingham, Massachusetts, explores the experiences of women behind bars. She treats specifically the issue of institutionalized violence against women, the mistreatment of their bodies, the erosion of their sense of identity and dignity, and the particular health issues faced by women in prison.

Jane Stapleton Deziel's 'Degrees of Separation' addresses the ways in which rape and domestic violence occur in our midst in places often overlooked, under a veil of silence and indifference. Campus rapes and violence against women are rampant, Stapleton Deziel argues, though ignored by the media and public officials, who view rape strictly as assault by a stranger and fail to recognize that the most common form of rape is acquaintance rape... Mahnaz Afkhami's perceptive essay, 'Gender Apartheid, Cultural Relativism, and Women's Human Rights in Muslim Societies,' addresses women's human rights within the diverse communities of the Muslim world. For a Muslim woman living under a fundamentalist regime, certain central human rights questions are constantly at issue: Why cannot a Muslim woman have the right to determine and organize her own life? What gives another person, simply by virtue of being born a man, the right to intervene in a woman's life? Why is it that a Muslim cleric has the right to place a woman within preordained, prescribed boundaries?

Mary Geske and Susan Bourque, in 'Grassroots Organizations and Women's Human Rights,' show the links that have been established between local and global human rights bodies. The authors showcase Latin American groups such as the Mothers of Plaza de Mayo in Argentina who, in pursuit of a fair civil society, have defied their governments and reigns of political terror. Such women have devised strategies to defy government oppression and have there by fostered new political imaginations to fight for democratic values. "The fourth and final section, Beyond the Mirror: Women and the Cultures of Displacement, begins with Barbara Harlow's essay, 'What was She Doing There: Women as 'Legitimate Targets,' which examines the murders of two women in South Africa. Amy Biehl, an American, and Ruth First, a South African, were human rights activists, engaging in tactics for achieving peace in a society torn by conflict. Biehl happened to be at the wrong place at the wrong time, targeted for being while. First was an antiapartheid activist, murdered by South African security forces when openening an envelope.

The novelist Agate Nesaule, in her elegant and moving piece, *How Long Does Exile Last*?, presents an incident at a Latvian church social hour as a defining moment in her self-definition as a perpetual exile. The theme of inner exile and displacement runs through her images of exiled women...Joseph Slaughter and Jennifer Wenzel in their essay, Letters of the Law, discuss three short stories that make use of the private realm of letters, often associated with 'female writings,' to address issues of human rights. In letters women writers struggle with the dichotomy of private and public, negotiating between the secretive realm of the private self and the external face on the public self.

Christopher Merrill's provocative essay, 'Before the Mirror,' which closes the volume, is a series of portraits of women- an architect, a poet, who remained in the besieged cities of the Balkan war. At the beginning of this new century, we stand in possession of accelerated information and communications. The global society with its global citizens has indeed democratized the landscape of the Western world and much of the non-Western world as well. We have become world citizens, with travel and telecommunications becoming easier and more affordable... the world also comes to us. Refugees, immigrants, travelers all seem to interact in a transnational and transcultural world.

Even as the world converges into a global society, much work remains to be done to improve the condition of women and to support their attempts to achieve justice and equal citizenship rights. Revisions of and additions to international law calling for the elimination of discrimination against women and children show a willingness to achieve a more just society. The purpose of this collection is then to focus on the universality of women's invisibility and the ways we can engage in a human rights movement that will create a new vision and response to issues of women, violence, and their legitimacy in civil societies. These essays lend new visibility to women's human rights.

The affirmation of the dignity of all human beings resides at the center of the Universal Declaration of Human Rights. Yet people everywhere continue to be deprived of their human rights... The resilience of women all over the world, as well as their commitment to their communities, has profoundly changed the meaning of human rights of women's rights..." The Country Reports on Human Rights Practices are published annually the end of February by the Department of State and sent to Congress as required by law. WIN NEWS publishes selected sections on women which have to be included in every report. Initially, the Reports only covered countries that received U.S. assistance, but for over 20 years all countries have been surveyed.

Women at first were only included in a few countries. WIN NEWS pointed out that women are half of each population and lobbied Congressional and pertinent decision makers in the State Department. One persuasive argument WIN NEWS made to have reports on women included was and is that violence against women seriously undermines economic development. As the record shows we succeeded to have women included in all reports. These Reports now provide the most comprehensive and comparative survey of the status of women around the world. The information is gathered all year in each country based on legislation, government initiatives, communication with local NGOs, press reports, from the police and judiciary and more. Each Embassy is required to compile information throughout each year according to specific subject headings.

Given the great diversity of societies, countries, geographic and physical surroundings and economic development, it is astonishing to learn that in every single society - without exception - men rule over women by violence. Men beat, mistreat, rape and exploit women in every country. But what is most depressing is that women have tolerated indeed accepted this treatment for centuries because for centuries it has been hidden in every society. Yet women have supported and taken care of men everywhere. Indeed, male violence in the family was never even discussed: traditionally it was accepted as quite "natural" that men abused women. Win News was one of the first publications to report on violence against women - starting in 1977. It was most difficult to get any information. In the UK reports on wife abuse were published first, followed by the US. Gradually women in other European countries began to publish such information, but it took a long time to get documentation from the developing world. For centuries all information of the ongoing universal abuse of women by men in their families had been suppressed, including by the male-dominated press.

From 1977 on WIN NEWS featured a section on violence. Only in the last few years UNIFEM has started a global initiative to stop male violence against women. Reading these Human Rights Reports on women is a shocking experience: they give a factual account of the horrendous attacks perpetrated by men against women - most often women in their own families. This goes on in every single country - making women and girls into victims, exploited and ruled by unrestrained, vicious male attacks. What is described is a war on women in every single country. Women and girls are attacked, raped and killed in their homes and neighborhoods not by soldiers of an occupying army but most often by their own male family members and husbands.

All this has been going on for centuries with women trying to exist in this violent male jungle - which until quite recently - has been accepted as a "normal" condition of female life and supported by male dominated government institutions including religious institutions such as the Catholic Church and Islam and most other religious organizations -all designed to support male domination.

This year the Reports again confirm the ubiquitousness of male violence. Women everywhere need to organize to resist and stop this horrible scourge by men which is used to support and exert male domination and exploitation and to continue male rule all over the world at enormous costs. UNIFEM is the first global organization that quite recently has begun in an organized way to not only record male violence but to bring together women all over the world to resist and work together against the ubiquitous violation and exploitation of women by men using violence as a means of control.

UNIFEM is still the only international organization that has taken on this challenge to rid the world of male family violence - we all need to join them. To be sure there are by now many local groups in different countries, but there is almost no government support. The male constructed legal systems make it enormously difficult everywhere to send proven rapists to jail anywhere, let alone wife abusers.

The State Department Reports are to be sure a unique source of information as here male violence and control by force is documented in great detail by a male-dominated government institution that no one can call feminist. As stated in the introduction the reports cover a large number of subjects related to human rights: women are only one small sub-section. They are posted on the Internet by February 25 each year. The printed reports don't come out until September; the most recent one of the year 2000 had more than 2,800 pages in 2 volumes. The inhumanity and violence of men against women was again most visibly demonstrated in Afghanistan. Under the guise of religion women were segregated and treated like slaves by the ultra-Islamic Taliban While the Western World has spoken out against this treatment of women (though it still continues by the Saudis and other Islamic Fundamentalists) the opening of schools all over Afghanistan was recently celebrated. But these so-called "schools" are unheated, empty shells barely standing up with no windows and no funding from anyone to make them into functioning schools.

The so-called Ministry of Women in Afghanistan has no budget, no building and no government or international support. All the changes for women in Afghanistan are nothing but a sham by men and the male dominated international community. Worldwide men are continuing to abuse and exploit women in every way and everywhere. A few days ago it was reported by the international press that in Saudi Arabia the "Religious Police of the Commission for the Promotion of Virtue and Prevention of Vice" who are directly controlled by the male rulers of the country, stopped firefighters and rescue squads from helping school girls escape from a burning school building: because the Moslem religion forbids any man to go near a girl or woman: so the girls were left to burn to death.

No political leader or any man in a leadership position has ever effectively spoken against abuse of women and girls. No leader in any European or Western country has ever protested family abuse. by men - though this goes on everywhere. No doubt many of the political leaders themselves engage in wife abuse. As the Human Rights Reports document abuse of girls and women goes on everywhere protected by decision makers and our male "leaders" who often are personally involved. The most vicious and widespread abuse of women occurs in Moslem countries, supported by the male religious leadership: all this is documented in the Country Reports and in WIN NEWS with sources given.

The Hosken Report Genital and Sexual Mutilation of Females has documented the attacks on the genitalia of millions of girls all over Africa and the Middle East: no male political leader has ever taken effective actions to stop it. Because men believe these life threatening painful assaults on the bodies of girl children increase male power and their control of women. All this abuse and violence could not go on without the silent support of our great male leaders all over the world. Not even the leader of the United Nations, Kofi Annan, has ever spoken up, though UNIFEM as part of the United Nations has published extensive documentation on worldwide violence against women by men. Without the silent support of the male leadership in so-called "advanced" societies the attacks, abuse, rape and exploitation of women could not continue - no one can claim ignorance.

Around the world women still get paid only 75% or less for doing the same work as men. The abuse of women in all different forms in all societies could not continue without the silent support by all men everywhere. But the essential question all of us must finally ask is: how can men of good will tolerate such behavior and violent practices against women all over the world? How can any decent man allow so many vicious attacks against women to go on in their communities? Don't you have any shame, don't you understand that all men are implicated in family violence by their failure to speak up and stop it? For centuries a conspiracy of silence and shame has covered it up, but now we know the facts.

UNIFEM has established unequivocally what is going on, everyday everywhere all over the world. The U.S. State Department in the Country Reports is providing the most detailed records of this infamy, Why does no world leader speak up and admonish the heads of State and all United Nations members to stop this senseless brutality that costs each country millions annually in lost work and production, in hospital and health costs (as documented by WHO) and causes so much suffering and death. Where are the international leaders to take on this challenge and demand that men stop these assaults. Shame on men everywhere who are failing to organize nationally and especially internationally to finally clean up their own behavior and control themselves and their fellow men: it would save billions around the world in police and legal work, in hospitalization (as the World Health Organization has pointed out) in work time lost and especially in pain and suffering.

We put this question to men, especially our proud political leaders - are you so weak and morally deficient that you cannot control your violent impulses and those of your male neighbors? The violence by which you control family and community life can no longer be concealed, it is now documented and known all over the world. Where are the male leaders to organize a global initiative to stop violence against women? This would result in huge economic gains especially in developing countries. It is a question of leadership: we challenge all heads of state and world leaders, also those who direct universities, institutions, and businesses, national and international leaders to finally organize a global initiative "To Stop All Forms Of Violence Against Women."

"Cultural capital," Bourdieu taught us, denotes critical and diacritical markings of social status, distinguishing us from them. In 'Human Rights and Gender Violence: Translating International Law into Local Justice,' Merry invites us to rethink culture as capital, with provocative implications. In the new international order, culture, like capital, is at once a resource and the instantiation of complex relationships embedded in time and place. And, in the current global movement to promote human rights and eradicate gender violence, cultures, like different forms of capital, have more or less currency.

Merry begins her analysis with a simple but powerful statement: "In order for human rights ideas to be effective ... they need to be translated into local terms and situated within local contexts of power and meaning. They need, in other words, to be remade in the vernacular". Merry explores the work of creating, exporting, interpreting, and implementing human rights discourse. She begins at the top-at the United Nations (UN) guiding us into the corridors and meeting rooms in which (mostly) women write and debate model legislation (mostly) for nations of the South. The UN officials, nongovernmental organization members, and state representatives involved in this process hold "universal" standards that emphasize personal autonomy, security, and equal rights. In the culture of the human rights activists, these premises are nonnegotiable.

Enter next into this world the complex array of cultures as commodity forms in which different use and exchange values compete. Cultures that protect human and gender rights are highly valued; those that permit gender inequity and ignore gender violence are not. From the UN Merry takes us into the Asia-Pacific region, visiting Hawaii, Delhi, Beijing, Fiji, and Hong Kong, where human rights laws are being implemented. She describes organizations, programs, and networks that promote human and gender rights. She finds common patterns in each place, that the universalizing culture we have encountered at the UN and its human rights discourse homogenizes. Everywhere it carries forward the mantra of the autonomous person, the safe body, and the rights-bearing citizen. Everywhere, too, it uses similar tactics: pressure on states to adopt accords and agreements, surveys to document abuse, training workshops to eradicate violence, hotlines and shelters for victims, counseling sessions for batterers, and T-shirts that advocate freedom from violence.

To be successful, however, local advocates must translate theory into community action. This discussion of the "translators," the people who adapt universal principles to local conditions and institutions, is one of the book's most insightful. How do grassroots activists translate global human rights into a language and praxis that is meaningful to people who are far from the centers where such laws are created? How do they reinterpret local grievances into rights that international agencies and governments will define as worthy of attention and funding? Merry calls this process of appropriation and translation, one that has been largely invisible in the literature on human rights, "vernacularization". Her analysis is astute both in its attention to the contradictory demands placed upon the translators as they move between global and local contexts, and in its consideration of issues of power and agency.

Merry also raises complex concerns in her portrayal of human rights subjects and their multiple and sometimes contradictory subjectivities. For example, battered women in Hawaii, but also indigenous rural women in Hong Kong, often think of themselves primarily as mothers, wives, and sisters whose rights are prescribed in kinship norms. Legislation in the United States to criminalize domestic violence and a social movement in Hong Kong to grant women inheritance rights allow women in both places to "try on" new legal identities. In practice, however, the subject positions of kinswoman and autonomous citizen can be incompatible. If compelled to choose between these identities, women may shed the universalistic robe of human rights in favor of the local wrap of kinship.

This text raises interesting methodological questions as a consequence of its scope of inquiry and reliance upon "deterritorialized ethnography". Merry's examination of the practices and pitfalls of protecting women's rights in different locales is uneven. Researching law and human rights internationally means that the ethnographer spends limited time in many places, raising its own evidence and translation problems. As Merry acknowledges, the study focuses on a transnational movement, without a sustained examination of the long-term meaning and consequences of the translation and implementation of human rights law in any one place. Ungrounded ethnography problematizes our assumptions about the enterprise of fieldwork.

Merry ends on a challenging note that should spark new debates in law and society, anthropology, and political and legal history. Is the discourse of human rights, largely the creation of nations of the North, analogous to imperialism? Like much of the rhetoric that characterized colonialism, the universalistic language of human rights is rendered as part of a "civilizing" process, one in which cultures have more or less currency. There are, as Merry points out, crucial differences between these two projects. Yet the question is unsettling. After all, T-shirts bearing slogans to protect human rights are still T-shirts-and some of them are manufactured in sweatshops.

DEMOCRACY AND THE CHALLENGE

Ten years after Beijing, we see a world in trouble. All this, despite the gains we achieved since Beijing. The historic meeting in Beijing allowed us to ensure a globalized women's movement by bringing women activists and policy makers at the national and international levels together to establish a global consensus on women's rights. Gender equality is on the agenda of bilateral and multilateral institutions through which most of the world's social funds are allocated. Since then, we have had important breakthroughs, particularly in the area of accountability for sexual crimes conducted in the midst of mass conflict. Rape as a weapon of war is now recognized not only as a conceptual construct but also as a crime of war, and a crime against humanity. But, despite all this, the world is in trouble.

- More people than ever-most of whom are women-are displaced and uprooted from their homes and communities because of violence, war and poverty.

According to some figures, 500 million people in the Asia Pacific region suffer chronic poverty. They live with hunger, illness and injury - isolated from adequate public services and social security systems. They have lost their land to war or big capital investments. Or, they continue tilling their land and carry the impossible burden of expensive agricultural inputs, over-dependence on chemical pesticides and the general degradation of the natural resources surrounding them.

If not already forced to flee by violence and war, many must leave their rural communities in order to support their families who stay and become rootless migrants, unprotected by law, desperate for decent work in the most abusive sectors of the economy. A large proportion of those who leave are women, who become migrant workers in the urban centers and in other countries, becoming the easy prey of traffickers. The women who stay behind work long hours for low wages, face what amounts to multiple workdays as they juggle agricultural work and work in the home, without controlling their own resources. In the Asia Pacific region, 70% of women work full time in agriculture, but only 1% hold titles to their land. Young girls who do not leave, are married off by their families as part of a culturally-accepted economic strategy for survival. No one calls this trafficking yet, but there are too many resemblances.

- The world is at the grips of a politics of fear where our ethnic and religious identities are being manipulated in a power struggle that is not ours.

Given the overlap of ethnicity, religion and caste in discrepancies in the divide between the rich and poor, between capital and labor, it is no wonder that the human tragedy of September 11 unleashed the politicization of identity to a global scale. Both the global superpowers as well as radical extremists use terror as their tool and manipulate symbols of religion and culture to mobilize public support from among their own peoples.

The ultimate victims are women. Taken as a symbol of religious and cultural purity, women's sexuality has been put at the center of this globalized battleground of identity-based politics. The scale of the problem is huge, given the fact that 45% of civil wars in the world are expressed in terms of ethnic and national identities. Religious extremism among all the big religions of the world is spreading as fast as the spread of people's sense of disaffection and discontent, and as deep as their sense of insecurity and injustice. The Asia Pacific region has not been spared from this particular trend. For the woman, in countries like Indonesia, this has meant the threat of losing control over the way she dresses, where she goes and with whom, how she behaves-socially, politically, economically and sexually.

- Liberal democracy has shown its limits in preventing and addressing violence (war) and destruction (ecological), and has not produced any major breakthroughs in overcoming chronic poverty and systemic injustice.

In and of themselves, the structures set up for democratic processes by nation-states as well as institutions of global governance do not guarantee people's basic rights, human security and sustainable living. We have seen this happen. The US attack on Iraq was carried out in spite of UN protest, even after democratic deliberations were carried out in this global body. As the fate of the Kyoto Protocols show, many policies which contribute to the further degradation of natural resources and the environment are produced in the very countries with democratic political structures and systems.

A recent survey carried out in another region, Latin America (as reported in the International Herald Tribune recently), found that because democratically-elected governments do not guarantee food on the table, people would accept authoritarian regimes as long as this meant a more decent living for the poor. This is a warning to us all. In Indonesia, the democratization process has been a painful experience filled with mass violence, impoverishment and the destruction of natural resources. The big lesson here is that, without strengthening people's capacity to access and effectively utilize established democratic systems and processes-both at the local, national and international levels-to further the goals of social justice, they risk becoming simply tools of political elites.

There have been no major breakthroughs in overcoming chronic poverty and systemic injustice. Donor-supported poverty alleviation programs are mostly technocratic in their approach, and less focused on the imperative of power sharing with poor and disadvantaged communities. Land titling projects are developed without grounding in genuine agrarian reform. For women, despite getting gender equality on the global agenda, less and less resources are being allocated for women's empowerment. In a recent meeting of Asia Pacific women activists in Malaysia, it was said that "In the name of gender equity, the donors have used our very own words against us and are introducing projects that further entrench the existing disparities and inequities," referring to extensive donor support of projects on micro-credit, gender mainstreaming and gender budgeting.

- There is a bankruptcy in the thinking and practice of sustainable development-so much so that we are no longer clear who is benefitting from this other than state bureaucrats and their cronies.

In the name of development, whole infrastructures of patronage are established, whereby the poor, minorities and non-citizens are left out systematically. People's land is appropriated and wages are kept low. In the name of development, regimes of corruption are built which expropriate people's assists rather than providing resources to those most in need. Indeed, it was in the name of development, that at one time, Indonesian women were physically forced to use contraception, including through military intimidation. How can development be sustainable when the very process is exploitative? Sustainable development is not just a notion of environmental conservation. Development can only be sustainable if it is based on true empowerment of the people, including women.

Given this state of the world, we cannot simply continue to articulate problems without proposing constructive agendas. Where do we locate it, though, in this era of globalization and the so-called 'war on terror'? How do we overturn the exploitative and extractive relations and construct a workable framework for social justice and people's democracy? For our movement, three critical steps may be worth considering:

1. Putting the overcoming of chronic poverty and systemic injustice front and center-not charity nor income generating activities, using the language of development; but, enabling leadership of women among poor and rural communities, in the language of empowerment;
2. Securing women's voice in social movements and engendering critical agendas, while maintaining autonomy of the women's movement;
3. Accessing institutions of global governance and international human rights mechanisms (while aware of the limits) to deal with the risks of challenging deeply-ingrained power structures.

Related to this, two major campaigns are currently in preparation and Asia Pacific women activists are actively engaged: the campaign on food sovereignty and the campaign on human rights defenders. The Campaign for Food Sovereignty is a campaign to assert people's rights to food, land and productive resources. Through a People's Caravan, this campaign is advocating for genuine agrarian reform that gives poor peasants access and control over land, seeds and water; yields which are free of pesticides and genetic engineering; guarantees ecological production for present and future generations; strengthens communities in rural areas; and supports the rights of women.

For Asia Pacific women, food sovereignty can be achieved only through women's empowerment, dismantling patriarchal power relations, and ensuring women's genuine access to and control over productive resources. The Campaign for Human Rights Defenders is a global mobilization to recast the universal claim for human rights, this time focusing on women human rights activists themselves. It is a critical response in the context of increasing criminalization of human rights defenders and the continual undermining of the validity of women's human rights in the face of neo-liberal globalization, militarism and terrorism.

Finally, some closing notes in commemoration of ten years after Beijing:

- The global women's movement needs to:
- Address and increase its capacity to empower women living under chronic poverty and systemic injustice, particularly those who live in rural communities and as migrants;
- Be able to inspire the young and compete with the forcefulness of religious extremism.
- There is an imperative of women's rights activists to enter into the cultural space, including religious space, as in the era of identity-based politics, it is no longer enough to engage solely with state actors, state institutions and international legal regimes.
- Institutions of global governance should become more than an alliance among state actors and be reconstructed based on a genuine 'social contract' built on the principle of global citizenship, where non- governmental organizations and social movements have equal rights to decision making in a global governance system.

We are living in a world in trouble. A women's movement that is strong and fully-engaged, critically-thinking and visionary, may well prove to be the kind of leadership the world needs to get out of its downward spiral.

THE CHANGING STATUS OF WOMEN

Closing the gap between rhetoric and reality of how women are treated by men around the world is not yet a top priority. Although many of the norms on gender relations have found official endorsement in the Convention on the Elimination of All Forms of Discrimination Against Women and the Beijing Plan of Action, many countries still have laws and cultures that make women second-class citizens and expose them to violence. Progress on women getting good jobs in politics and business and equal salaries has been slow. Women in legislatures have increased from 13.8% in 2000 to 18% in 2008. Women account for over 40% of the world's work-force but earn only 25% of the income. It is well documented that countries with smaller gender gaps tend to have better economies, healthier children, and superior welfare in general.

The Scandinavian countries top both gender parity ratings and general quality of life indicators. Improving the political, economic, and educational status of women is one of the most cost-effective ways to address the other challenges in this chapter. Even peace builders in the field agree that women find common ground for peaceful resolutions more easily than men. Women are cutting through cultural hierarchies via Internet access to information about health, finance, S&T, and education programs. Even Web sites like iknowpolitics.org help improve women's political skills. Girls' secondary school enrollments are now about 90% of boys' enrollments. If current trends continue, however, UNICEF estimates that by 2015 over 50 countries will not achieve universal primary education and more than 90 countries will not reach gender parity in primary and secondary education.

The largest war on earth today as measured by death and casualties is men attacking women, especially during armed conflicts. Establishing truth and reconciliation commissions on violence against women in armed conflict would help end this. WHO reports that after diseases and hunger, violence against women is the greatest cause of death among women; one in five women will be a victim of rape or attempted rape in her lifetime. Elementary and secondary school systems should consider teaching martial arts and other forms of self-defense in physical education classes for girls. Since there are more women than men in universities in many countries that limit women's professional work, the "female brain drain" could become an issue in countries as diverse as Saudi Arabia and Japan.

According to Plan International, childhood malnutrition has stunted development of an estimated 450 million women; unsafe abortions and birth complications are the leading causes of death for girls 15 to 19 in developing countries studied; and over 100 million girls, some as young as 12, are expected to marry over the next decade even though international treaties outlaw early marriages. About 80% of the 600,000–800,000 individuals trafficked each year are female, in the "largest slave trade in history." Women should use their role in the family to more assertively nurture mutual respect between men and women. A global gender gap integrated index should be created to show trends of the whole picture as well as trends disaggregated by age, education, political and economic participation, and health. Mechanisms are needed to monitor violence against females and recommend interventions.

Legal rights of women (such as access to credit, land, technology, training, health care, child care, and judicial systems accessible to victims of sexual violence) are also needed, including educating men to fully respect women and working with the media to change harmful gender stereotypes that influence the choice of education, training or employment, participation in domestic and family duties, and representation in decision making. Challenge 11 will be addressed seriously when there is gender parity in school enrollment, literacy, and access to capital, when discriminatory laws are gone, and when there are essentially equal numbers of men and women in parliaments and cabinets.

REGIONAL CONSIDERATIONS

Africa: The percent of women in sub-Saharan African parliaments is 17.5%. One in 22 women in sub-Saharan Africa is likely to die as a consequence of pregnancy, compared with 1 in 7,300 in industrial countries. The dropout rate for adolescent girls in Africa is very high, as are systematic rape during armed conflicts and female genital mutilation. Major cultural changes will have to be made to systematically change the prospects for the average woman in Africa. Uganda eliminated school fees to help close the educational gender gap.

Asia and Oceania: Some 17.3% of Asian national legislators are women and 15.4% in Oceania. At least 60 million girls are "missing" in Asia due to the abortion of female fetuses, female infanticide, and deliberate neglect and starvation of baby girls. China funds pension plans for parents with daughters to counter male-only child preferences. Intimate partner violence in Thailand is the leading cause of death for females between the ages of 15 and 24. Millions of young girls have been sold as sex slaves in Asia. Most Muslim-majority countries scored among the lowest in the Global Gender Gap Index. Women in Australia hold 7% of top corporate positions and are paid half as much as their male equivalents.

Europe: While women represent 59% of university graduates in Europe, their employment rate is only 57.2%, they earn on average 15% less than men for every hour worked, and they represent 32% of managers, 10% of board members, and only 3% of CEOs of large companies. Work/life balance is still deficient, and women want improved support that allows them to continue their professional careers, yet they worry about reduced quality time for family life.

About 500,000 women from Central and Eastern Europe are working in the sex trade in Western Europe. The European Nordic countries top the Gender Gap Index, and the EU pledged to fight discrimination and domestic violence against women and to promote women's participation in political life. Norway requires that the boards of all companies registered at its stock market consist of at least 40% of each sex.

Latin America: Although women's participation in Latin American parliaments increased to 22%, women are still threatened by poverty, rising food and fuel prices, inequity, unemployment, lack of access to health services, and violence due to "machismo" attitudes, institutional weaknesses, and a patriarchal culture. Nevertheless, education is improving, with women 15–24 years old in urban areas reaching 9.7 years of education and women in rural areas reaching 7 years. Governments should change laws about rape, sexual harassment, and equal pay for women.

North America: Women account for 16.8% of legislative bodies in the U.S. and 21.3% in Canada. Women executives in the top 500 companies represent 13.6% in the U.S. and 12% in Canada. Nevertheless, at least 86.4% of the U.S. companies had boards with at least one woman member, versus 48.2% in Canada. In Quebec, Canada, state corporate boards by law will have to be 50% female by 2012.

WOMEN FOR WOMEN'S HUMAN RIGHTS

In our struggle to promote women's human rights, we frequently have to confront the mechanisms of patriarchal control over women's sexuality. These collective mechanisms play a crucial and defining role in the propagation, legitimization and reproduction of gender discrimination and inequality in numerous fields, including the public sphere. With their rules conveniently presented as uncontestable taboos, they legitimize human rights violations and act as some of the most powerful tools for the control of women's sexuality.

SEXUALITY: STILL A CONTESTED DOMAIN

Taboos around sexuality, reinforced by the rise of conservative political forces, continue to generate and maintain oppressive constructs and misconceptions about women's sexuality. This not only prevents many women from having an affirmative approach to sexuality and the opportunity to enjoy positive sexual experiences, but also infringes on fundamental rights and freedoms such as health, education, mobility, hindering equal participation in social, economic and political spheres. Conservative political forces are striving to maintain and reinforce control over women's sexuality with ever increasing resolve. In the last decade we have witnessed women's bodies and sexuality increasingly becoming arenas of intense conflict.

Conservative and religious right political forces are fiercely trying to maintain or reinforce traditional mechanisms of control over women's sexuality and even create new ones. Four UN conferences held in the 1990s –the 1994 International Conference on Population and Development (ICPD) in Cairo, the 1995 Beijing Conference, the 1999 five-year review of the ICPD (ICPD+5) and the 2000 five-year review of the Beijing Conference (Beijing+5)- witnessed the Catholic and Muslim religious right engaging in unprecedented cooperation to oppose and restrict women's right to control their bodies and sexuality. In this context, several traditional cultural practices-such as honor crimes, the stoning of women accused of adultery, virginity tests, FGM-in Muslim societies, including the Middle East, have increasingly drawn the attention of the Western media and public in recent years as human rights abuses.

The lack of information on Islam and the wide diversity of Muslim societies; the parallel rise of the Islamic religious right, which claims such customary practices to be Islamic; and the tendency to "essentialize" Islam have led to the incorrect portrayal of such practices as "Islamic" in the West. This depiction is not only misleading, but also stands in sharp contrast to the efforts of women's movements in Muslim societies, which, in their fight against such practices, are campaigning to raise public consciousness that such practices are actually customary practices that have nothing to do with Islam. In the last decade, Islamic fundamentalist movements have been further propagating such customary practices in the name of Islam to societies, where they were previously unheard of.

CHALLENGING TABOOS AROUND SEXUALITY

In the midst of all this adversity, determined efforts by activists to promote sexual rights as human rights worldwide are spreading and gaining strength, countering global conservative politics and challenging taboos around sexuality. Women at international and national levels, as well as at the grassroots, are vigorously struggling to realize their sexual and reproductive rights, becoming more vocal and advocating on numerous platforms. In the past decade, women's NGOs and women's movements in Muslim societies have been vehemently advocating to eliminate such practices and attitudes related to women's sexuality, such as honor crimes, sexual coercion and violence, marital rape, sexual harassment, restrictions on women's mobility, seclusion, forced/early marriages, "imposed" dress codes or virginity tests.

WWHR-New Ways has been working on issues around sexuality and sexual rights with as holistic approach since its foundation, and since 1999 sexuality in Muslim societies has been a priority program area for us. In 2001, we have co-founded the Coalition for Sexual and Bodily Rights in Muslim Societies, the first solidarity network of NGO representatives, academicians and researcher advocating for sexual and bodily rights as human rights in Muslim societies. Our past activities within the framework of this program include publications, advocacy and lobbying, advocacy at the UN level and organizing of regional and international meetings as well as trainings on relevant issues, all of them geared towards the ultimate aim of consciousness raising and advocacy around sexual and bodily rights and health in Muslim societies.

Around the world, women are uniting to challenge unequal gender relations embedded in tradition, religion and law. For 20 years, the Global Fund has supported groups working to advance women's freedom and their status as equal citizens by organizing, building coalitions, changing laws and advancing transformative agendas to improve their lives, their children's futures and our world. In 1993, Women for Women's Human Rights (WWHR) formed to rally for women's equal participation in Turkish society. WWHR empowers women and women's organizations, especially at the grassroots level, by giving them tools and strategies to confront structures of inequality. The group documents and disseminates information on women's human rights, strengthens networks of women's groups across Islamic countries and advances policy and legal change.

The group started its work by doing research on women's rights in Turkey and violence against women in Ankara, Istanbul, eastern and southeastern Anatolia. "During the course of this research, we came across the fact that women are unaware of the rights granted to them by the law. Another fact was that there was almost no women's grassroots organizing and networking other than those in the big cities of Turkey," explains the group. To change this, WWHR dedicated itself to training Turkish women in legal literacy and reforming civil and penal codes to advance women's rights in Turkey and internationally. WWHR organizing has led to significant revisions to the Turkish Penal Code, including criminalizing marital rape, increasing the severity of punishment for sex crimes and "honor" killings, and abolishing discrimination between married and single or virgin and non-virgin women.

They co-created and currently coordinate the Coalition for Sexual and Bodily Rights in Muslim societies. Since 1995, WWHR has educated over 4,500 women and girls on their legal and economic rights through community centers in 36 Turkish provinces. One example of their effectiveness was revealed during an external evaluation. After participating in WWHR programs, 63 percent of the women who faced violence before the training were able to stop it. In 2007, Pinar Ilkkaracan of WWHR and the Coalition shared the prestigious $500,000 Peter and Patricia Gruber Women's Rights Prize for groundbreaking leadership in reforming Turkish laws and advancing the rights of Muslim women.

The last decade has witnessed major advancements towards the realization of women's human rights in Turkey, largely due to the determined and successful advocacy efforts of the women's movement. Despite the constitutional gender equality principal and numerous international documents Turkey is signatory to, until the late 90's, the national legislation in Turkey contained various discriminatory provisions and an overarching patriarchal perspective, be it in civil, penal, or labor laws. This situation has been undergoing rapid change, however, beginning with the adoption of the law on protection orders aiming to prevent domestic violence in 1998, followed by the reform of the Civil Code in 2001, and most recently the Turkish Penal Code Reform in 2004. Through these reforms, women have attained the legal grounds to exercise their human rights and to demand full gender equality to a large extent.

The legislative system had previously granted men supremacy in marriage and deprived women of their civil, economic, and social rights, thereby restricting women's decision making power within the family; and furthermore regarded women's bodies and sexuality as commodities of men, the family and society. This system which legitimized human rights violations like forced marriages, marital rape, honor killings etc., has been extensively changed with the Civil and Penal Code reforms, to embody principals of gender equality in accordance with global human rights norms. The lack of understanding of women's rights as human rights is reflected in the fact that few governments are committed to women's equality as a basic human right in their laws, domestic and foreign policies.

In Turkey, which is a unique example of confluence of Islam, secularization, and the so called "westernization", woman's role in the society has been one of the heated subjects of political debates. Meanwhile, women's human rights issues were considered to be a marginal debate amongst a marginal group of women. The Civil Code Reform, and the Penal Code Campaign from a Gender Perspective has brought up the fact that women's human rights issues are not the issues of a marginal group of women living in the metropolitans, but are actually the demands of the half of Turkey's population, namely the females.

Through the employment of a holistic approach, women's movement in Turkey has considered women's right to bodily integrity and to control their sexuality as an indivisible part of women's human rights, and defended that without it, women cannot fully realize all their human rights. Thus the debates particularly involved various issues on women's human rights related to sexuality, including the insertion of sexuality in law, women's sexual and bodily autonomy, virginity, honor, sexual violence, sexuality of young people, pre-marital sexuality or sexual orientation. Throughout history, both during the Ottoman Empire period, when the legislation was based on Shari'a, the Islamic law, and after the foundation of the Turkish Republic in 1923, women have always been instrumentalized in laws and policies.

Women have served as "protectors" of family values and the social status quo during the Ottoman Empire period, and were instrumentalized as the "protectors" of secularism and the "new Republic". The legacy of ignoring women as autonomous individuals in the construction of a democratic civil order was carried on for several years. The old Turkish Civil Code of 1926 was translated and adapted from the Swiss Civil Code of the time and included several articles reducing women to a subordinate position in the family.

For example, the husband was defined as the head of the marriage union, thus granting him the final say over the choice of domicile and children. The new Turkish Civil Code, which abolishes the supremacy of men in marriage and thus establishes the full equality of men and women in the family, was approved by the Turkish Parliament on November 22, 2001, and came into effect on January 1, 2002. The new Code sets the equal division of property acquired during marriage as a default property regime, assigning an economic value to women's hitherto invisible labor for the well-being of the family household. It also sets 18 as the legal minimum age for marriage for both women and men (it was previously 17 for men and 15 for women), gives the same inheritance rights to children born outside marriage as those born within marriage, and allows single parents to adopt children.

The Turkish Penal Code of 1926, adapted from the Italian Penal Code of 1889, reflected a notion that considered women's sexuality as a potential threat to the public order and morality thus in need of regulation by laws. The Code was regulating all sexual crimes under the section "Crimes Against Society", sub-section "adab- ý umumiye and nizam-ý aile" (crimes against traditions of morality and family order) instead of under the section "Crimes Against Individuals". Regulations of crimes such as rape, abduction or sexual abuse against women as crimes against society, rather than as crimes against individuals, was not only a manifestation of the code's foundational premise that women's bodies and sexuality are the property of men, family or society, but also reflected of the social anxiety that considered a strict state control of sexuality as a necessity.

Certain articles in the Code assigned less value to single/unmarried women and non-virgins compared to married women or virgins. For instance, if a married woman was abducted, the minimum sentence required was seven years of imprisonment, but if the abducted woman was unmarried, the sentence could be anywhere from three to seven years. The new Turkish Penal Code contains more than thirty amendments that constitute a major step towards gender equality and protection of women's human rights in Turkey. The campaign succeeded in achieving a holistic reform to transform the philosophy and principles of the Penal Code in order to safeguard women's rights, and bodily and sexual autonomy. The reform of the Penal Code has transformed the philosophy of the old Penal Code by acknowledging women's right to have autonomy over their bodies and sexuality.

To this end, sexual crimes are regulated as crimes against individuals/crimes against the inviolability of sexual integrity, instead of as crimes against society, family or public morality. All references to vague patriarchal constructs such as chastity, morality, shame, public customs, or decency have been eliminated and definitions of such crimes against women brought in line with global human rights norms. The new code, which states in the first article that the aim of the law is to "protect the rights and freedoms of individuals," brings progressive definitions and higher sentences for sexual crimes; criminalizes marital rape; brings measures to prevent sentence reductions granted to perpetrators of honor killings; eliminates previously existing discrimination against non-virgin and unmarried women; criminalizes sexual harassment at the workplace and considers sexual assaults by security forces to be aggravated offences.

Provisions regulating the sexual abuse of children have been amended to explicitly define sexual abuse and remove the notion of "consent of the child." Provisions legitimizing rape and abduction in cases which the perpetrator marries the victim have been abolished; the article granting sentence reduction to mothers killing the newborn children born out of wedlock is removed; and the article regulating "indecent behavior" has been amended to include only sexual intercourse in public and exhibitionism.

Mainstreaming human rights in advocacy and accomplishing these reforms have not been easy, ready- made accomplishments for the women's movement in Turkey. Often confronted with a combination of resistant conservative forces from the Parliament, government officials, and the media, women's groups had to overcome the challenge of not only finding effective and diverse strategies of advocacy, but also of making their demands heard and publicizing their agenda in a rather volatile political atmosphere.

INTERNATIONAL HUMANITARIAN LAW

The development in the last 50 years of the principles that comprise human rights law has had a major impact on international humanitarian law and indeed on international law generally. In more recent years, the movement for recognition of the equal rights of women has been exerting its own influence on human rights law and to some effect. In 1979, for example, the international community adopted the Convention on the Elimination of All Forms of Discrimination against Women (CEDAW), to which 155 States are now party. Consideration is currently being given to the adoption of an Optional Protocol that will allow for individual and group complaints to be brought before the CEDAW Committee. Governmental and non-governmental organizations have increasingly focused on women's human rights. As a result, a wide range of studies, reports and recommendations on various aspects of the issue is available.

The topic of women is thus firmly established on the international human rights agenda. So much human suffering in today's world occurs, however, in situations of armed conflict, where to a large extent human rights are in abeyance, leaving individuals to rely solely on the protection offered by international humanitarian law. And women are major victims in these situations. There is now evidence, moreover, that women experience conflict in a different way to men, a phenomenon that is confirmed by those working in the field. This distinctive experience, although its effects differ widely across cultures depending upon the role of women in each society, is related to the particular vulnerability of this group when armed conflict breaks out. War exacerbates the inequalities that exist in different forms and to varying degrees in all societies, and women make up 70 per cent of the world's population living in poverty. They are, moreover, generally disadvantaged in terms of education and are considerably less mobile because of their traditional role in caring for others.

Perhaps most significantly, women are generally excluded from access to power structures and participation in decision-making with regard to armed conflict. They are therefore unable to draw attention to the particular difficulties they experience in conflict situations and, moreover, are powerless to recommend any preventive action. Against that background, the present article considers the extent to which the focus on women's human rights and the advances made in the protection of women under human rights law has had an impact on international humanitarian law. As will become apparent, this impact can be seen primarily in developments regarding the criminalization and punishment of sexual violence against women in armed conflicts. Broader consideration has yet to be given to the question of women, armed conflict and humanitarian law.

THE PROVISIONS OF THE LAW OF ARMED CONFLICT RELATING TO WOMEN

There were occasional references to the protection of women in some of the earliest documents of the law of armed conflict. For example, Article XLVII of the Lieber Code punished those responsible for the rape of inhabitants of a hostile country. Until recently, however, sexual violence against women was never taken seriously. Rape was not listed as a war crime at Nuremberg, despite the high incidence of sexual violence during the Second World War. Indictments before the Tokyo Tribunal did contain charges of rape and some individuals were convicted for their failure to ensure that subordinates complied with the law. Moreover, the occupying powers included rape as a war crime in the charters of their national courts set up to try offences committed in Germany, although no prosecutions were ever undertaken on this basis. Generally, however, rape and sexual violence against women were regarded as an inevitable aspect of armed conflict and seldom if ever prosecuted.

The four 1949 Geneva Conventions, which at the time of their adoption were the major instruments protecting the victims of armed conflict (and with their two 1977 Protocols remain so today), contain some 19 provisions that are specifically relevant to women. The scope of these rules is somewhat limited and many of them are in fact designed to protect children. Overall, the aim of the Conventions is to provide special protection for pregnant women, nursing mothers and mothers in general and to address the vulnerability of women to sexual violence in times of armed conflict. Significantly, Article 27(2) of the Fourth Geneva Convention contains the first provision specifically dealing with rape and requires that "[w]omen shall be especially protected against any attack on their honour, in particular against rape, enforced prostitution, or any form of indecent assault".

Although this chapter constitutes a long overdue recognition that rape is unacceptable in times of armed conflict, the extent and gravity of the practice are not acknowledged since the provision falls outside the system of grave breaches of international humanitarian law (under this system States are obliged to seek out and punish persons responsible for failing to observe certain designated provisions of the Conventions). Article 27(2) has also been criticized on the grounds that, like many of the provisions relating to women, it categorizes rape as an attack on the victim's honour and thus does not reflect the seriousness of the offence of sexual violence. Apart from the protection afforded under such articles, which is clearly valuable as far as it goes, any indication that the difficulties women experience in armed conflicts might be distinctive and encompass wider issues than their roles as mothers and victims of sexual violence is not discernible in the provisions of the Geneva Conventions.

To what extent were the provisions of the 1977 Protocols relating to women influenced by the human rights movement? The movement to bring about further improvements in international humanitarian law that culminated in the adoption by States of the 1977 Protocols owed a great deal to developments in the area of human rights. Gerald Draper wrote that progress in the law of armed conflict "had come perilously close to stagnation before the impact of the movement for a regime of human rights was brought to bear". As early as 1956, the ICRC had completed a set of Draft Rules for the limitation of dangers incurred by the civilian population in time of war. No action was taken on these rules.

The question of further revision of the law of armed conflict was shelved by the international community until the work on human rights in peacetime undertaken by the United Nations Commission on Human Rights and the UN General Assembly began to expand logically into concern for human rights in armed conflict. The International Conference on Human Rights held in Tehran in 1968 can be seen as a watershed in this relationship. The final outcome of these initiatives was the adoption of the two 1977 Protocols, which have a distinct human rights flavour. The Protocols merge the respective principles of the so-called law of The Hague and law of Geneva and focus on the protection of civilians. What is the approach of the Protocols to women victims of armed conflict?

Does the emphasis on protection that underpinned the negotiations leading up to the adoption of these instruments and is reflected in their final text extend to a recognition of the distinctive difficulties women experience in times of armed conflict? Overall, the approach to women remains unchanged in the provisions of the Protocols. The focus continues to be on protection for pregnant women and mothers. In the context of sexual violence, Article 76 of Protocol I contains the important comprehensive provision specifically protecting women against rape, although this practice is still not designated as a grave breach. There is no recognition, either in the *travaux préparatoires* or in the provisions themselves, of the other distinctive problems women face in armed conflicts.

WOMEN AND HUMAN RIGHTS

It would be misleading to represent the existing body of human rights law as a satisfactory regime from the perspective of women. Commentators have convincingly demonstrated the limitations of this law, which does not adequately take into account the reality of women's experience of the world. However, it is in the context of human rights law rather than humanitarian law that more progress has been made in recognizing and attempting to meet the as yet unaddressed needs of women. This attention to women's human rights has had substantial implications for international humanitarian law. Indeed, the fact that violence against women and strategies to contain it have been the focus of much of the work of human rights agencies concerned with this group has led to a consideration of the issue in connection with armed conflicts, where so much of the violence against women occurs. What have been some of the results of this work?

The 1993 Vienna Declaration and Programme of Action, adopted by the United Nations World Conference on Human Rights, confirmed that "violations of the human rights of women in situations of armed conflict are violations of the fundamental principles of human rights and humanitarian law" and that they require a "particularly effective response". The Programme of Action also stressed that "the equal status of women and the human rights of women" should be "integrated into the mainstream of United Nations system-wide activity" and "form an integral part of United Nations human rights activities." This growing movement to address the problem saw the adoption by the General Assembly in

December 1993 of the Declaration on the Elimination of Violence Against Women. The Declaration expressly recognizes that women in situations of armed conflict are especially vulnerable to violence.

Another important development in the context of women and human rights during armed conflicts has been the appointment of Special Rapporteurs with mandates covering certain aspects of women's experience of armed conflict. In 1994 the United Nations Commission on Human Rights appointed Radhika Coomaraswamy as the Special Rapporteur on violence against women, with a mandate covering situations of armed conflict. In January 1998 the Special Rapporteur submitted her report on the subject, in which she recommended, in the context of international wars, that the Geneva Conventions be re-examined and re-evaluated so as to "incorporate developing norms against women during armed conflict".

Additionally, in 1995 the United Nations Sub-Commission on Prevention of Discrimination and Protection of Minorities appointed Linda Chavez as Special Rapporteur on the situation of systematic rape, sexual slavery and slavery-like practices during periods of armed conflict. The Fourth UN World Conference on Women, held in Beijing in 1995, recognized the seriousness of armed conflict and its impact on the lives of women. The Beijing Declaration referred to the determination of the participating States to "ensure respect for international law, including humanitarian law, in order to protect women and girls in particular". The Conference's Platform for Action identified women and armed conflict as one of the twelve critical areas of concern to be addressed by Member States, the international community and civil society.

A remedial strategy identified in the Platform was to "increase the participation of women in conflict resolution at decision-making levels and protect women living in situations of armed and other conflicts or under foreign domination". The process of identifying women's particular difficulties and demonstrating the failure of the law to acknowledge them is thus considerably more advanced within human rights bodies than within organizations focusing solely on armed conflict. Of course action plans, recommendations and proposals need to be implemented if they are to be of lasting value. Progress is slow and at times disheartening.

There are, however, positive signs. Of particular significance in this context is the very effective work at the grass roots level of the UN High Commissioner for Refugees in relation to refugee women. All these efforts, whilst groundbreaking in nature, have focused almost exclusively on sexual violence. The broader context of the problem has been largely ignored. However, an exception to this limited view is evident, for example, in the work of the Economic and Social Council, particularly in relation to Palestinian women and children in occupied territories.

INTERNATIONAL HUMANITARIAN LAW OF DEVELOPMENTS IN WOMEN'S HUMAN RIGHTS

There is no doubt that the work of human rights organizations has had a considerable impact on the approach taken to the protection of women in times of armed conflict. A change of emphasis over recent years can be discerned in the work of the ICRC in this context. The protection of women victims of conflict has always been part of the ICRC's mandate. Traditionally, however, women have been subsumed under the general category of civilians or under the separate category of "women and children". This has occurred despite the fact that the needs of these various categories of victims are not identical. Over the years, the ICRC has been active in attempts to mitigate the horrors of conflict for women. For example, efforts were made during the Second World War to ensure the lawful treatment of women prisoners of war.

In the post-war period as well, from time to time the ICRC made efforts to ensure that women were treated humanely in various conflict situations. However, in the context of sexual violence - the most obvious way in which women experience conflict - the silence was deafening, despite the appalling reality of this practice in all armed struggles. The invisibility of women and sexual violence rapidly came to an end with the events that took place during the armed conflict in the former Yugoslavia. Although sexual violence against women had been on the agenda of human rights bodies for some years, it was this conflict that galvanized the international community into action and led to the most significant development of humanitarian law attributable to the growing emphasis on women's human rights: the inclusion of rape within the system of grave breaches.

In 1993, as a response to the findings of widespread violations of international humanitarian law in the former Yugoslavia, including rape and many other forms of sexual violence against women, the Security Council set up the International Criminal Tribunal for the former Yugoslavia (ICTY) to prosecute persons responsible for such acts. One of the issues to be resolved was the place of rape within the Statute of the ICTY. In 1992, in the context of what constituted a grave breach of international humanitarian law, the ICRC had declared that the phrase common to the Geneva Conventions and their Protocols, "wilfully causing great suffering or serious injury to body or health", obviously covered not only rape but also any other attack on a woman's dignity.

This added weight to the argument that prevailed with the Commission of Experts set up by the Security Council to consider the question of the establishment of the ICTY, namely that rape and other sexual assaults, although not specifically designated as grave breaches in the Conventions and Protocols, constituted "torture or inhumane treatment" and acts that "wilfully caused great suffering or serious injury to body or health" and were thus punishable as grave breaches under the Conventions. In the Statute of the ICTY, however, rape is only specifically punishable as a crime against humanity and, to constitute such a crime, it must be directed against the civilian population as a whole: for it to occur on an individual basis is not sufficient. The practice of the Office of the Prosecutor has nevertheless been to charge defendants with sexual violence as a war crime and a grave breach.

Although the presidential value of the ICTY is limited both by its origin as a Security Council measure and by its geographical scope, the normative effect of these initiatives is much more widespread. Consequently, it will now be difficult to maintain that rape and various forms of sexual violence against women committed in international armed conflicts are not grave breaches of treaty rules. This is a major development of humanitarian law and it can be attributed to the growing recognition that women's human rights call for the prosecution of crimes of sexual violence committed in armed conflicts. Doubts have nevertheless been expressed, in the context of the Rwandan conflict, as to whether the Yugoslav experience indicates a lasting reversal of the long tradition of silence and inaction in relation to sexual violence against women in armed conflicts.

The Special Rapporteur on Violence Against Women, after hearing of the levels of sexual violence in the Rwandan conflict was, in her words, "absolutely appalled that the first indictment on the grounds of sexual violence at the International Tribunal for Rwanda (ICTR) was issued only in August 1997, and then only after heavy international pressure from women's groups". Despite these reservations, the criminalization of sexual violence against women in internal armed conflicts by the Statute of the ICTR is an important development, and owes much to the work of human rights activists and commentators. International humanitarian law has traditionally distinguished between international and internal armed conflicts, concentrating on the former. However, the redrawing of the boundaries of human rights law has been integral to the implementation of women's human rights and the influence of this approach is now being felt in humanitarian law.

Any consideration of violence against women naturally encompasses international and internal armed conflicts without distinction (an increasingly unreal division in any context). The Statute of the ICTR reflects this view by providing both that rape is punishable as a crime against humanity and that the practice falls within the Tribunal's jurisdiction since, in common with enforced prostitution and indecent assault, it is specifically designated as a crime under Article 3 common to the Geneva Conventions. Breaches of Article 3, the so-called "mini code" for internal armed conflicts, have traditionally not been regarded as constituting war crimes. Further developments in humanitarian law relating to the enforcement of the provisions protecting women against sexual violence have their genesis in the Yugoslav conflict and the practice of the ICTY. It has long been recognized in the context of women's human rights that, to be effective, any enforcement regime for prohibitions on sexual violence in armed conflicts must incorporate procedural reforms.

This view is slowly gaining broader acceptance within the international community and some progress has been made in taking into account the particular concerns of women in the prosecution of sexual offences. Such matters as the anonymity of witnesses and victims in trials for sexual assault and provision for their support and counseling have been addressed by the ICTY. However, these changes have not been readily accepted. For example, there is a perceived conflict between the demands of a fair trial and the protection of women as victims and witnesses. The two are not necessarily inconsistent: what is required is an appropriate balance between them. Recognition has also been given to the importance of equal gender distribution in the composition of enforcement tribunals and their support staff. The scrutiny by human rights groups of sexual violence against women in armed conflicts has translated into a new perception that such acts must be addressed by mainstream bodies dealing with the enforcement of international humanitarian law.

The inclusion, within the definition of war crimes and as serious violations of Article 3 common to the Geneva Conventions, of several forms of sexual violence against women was considered during the negotiations of the Statute for the International Criminal Court. Other issues of concern to women in relation to the enforcement process in general were also discussed in this context, such as the gender balance of the Court, protection for witnesses and victims, and the investigation of crimes of sexual violence. The Commission on the Status of Women, at its March 1988 meeting called on States to support these initiatives in relation to the future

International Criminal Court. The ICRC has given increasing recognition to the fact that the situation of women in armed conflicts poses distinctive challenges for humanitarian law. In 1993 the Final Declaration of the International Conference for the Protection of War Victims expressed alarm at "the marked increase in acts of sexual violence directed notably against women and children" and reiterated that "such acts constituted grave breaches of international humanitarian law".

In 1995 the 26th International Conference of the Red Cross and Red Crescent adopted by consensus a resolution dealing separately with sexual violence against women, which condemned this practice, reaffirmed that rape in the conduct of hostilities was a war crime and highlighted the importance of enforcing the relevant provisions and the need to train those involved in such processes. Moreover, there is growing acknowledgement of the broader nature of the problem, which has not previously been apparent in the work of human rights bodies. For example, recent ICRC publications emphasize that armed conflict exacerbates inequalities which already exist in different forms and to varying degrees in all societies.

After years on the fringe of human rights law, the topic of women and human rights is nowadays gaining increasing respect as a separate area of concern within the mainstream of international law. Moreover, although women's human rights are very much in the developmental stage as regards both framework and substance, each passing year sees the further elaboration of their guiding principles. Yet the new concern being paid to women's human rights and the impact, albeit small, that the issue has so far made on humanitarian law have not led to the general acknowledgement that women's human rights warrant a special place within the field of international humanitarian law. This is, however, only a matter of time. Let us hope that such acknowledgement, when it comes, will be accompanied by a reassessment of humanitarian law that takes into account the actual ways in which women experience armed conflict.

2

Anti-discrimination and Pro-equality Measures

ANTI-DISCRIMINATION LAW

Anti-discrimination law refers to the law on people's right to be treated equally. Most developed countries mandate that in employment, in consumer transactions and in political participation people may be dealt with on an equal basis regardless of sex, race, ethnicity, nationality, sexuality and sometimes religion and political views.

Examples of anti-discrimination law include:

- Age Discrimination Act of 1975
- Racial Discrimination Act 1975
- Disability discrimination act
- Anti-Discrimination Act 1977
- Title IX

NOTABLE EXCEPTIONS

One notable exception provided for in many nations is the exclusion of women from holding certain positions in the military, such as serving in front line combat capacities or aboard submarines. The reason given varies, for example, the British Royal Navy cite the reason for not allowing women to serve aboard submarines as medical and related to the safety of an unborn foetus, rather than that of combat effectiveness.

As well, some consider affirmative action to be government-sanctioned reverse discrimination. The Expert Group set up by the Ministry of Minority Affairs "to examine and determine the structure of an Equal Opportunity Commission" submitted its report in February, in which it has proposed a draft Equal Opportunity Commission Bill (EOC Bill).

The group, chaired by Professor Madhava Menon, was set up to suggest a workable institutional structure for an Equal Opportunity Commission as recommended by the Justice Rajinder Sachar Committee's "Report on Social, Economic and Educational Status of the Muslim Community of India". The report, while being rooted in Indian circumstances, has drawn from the experiences of countries that have had anti-discrimination laws for years and is an important and positive milestone in our understanding of strategies to respond to discrimination. Before analysing the features of the proposed Bill, a brief clarification on the meaning of discrimination is needed. Traditionally, discrimination has been criticised because it results in inequality. However, an autonomy-based understanding of discrimination looks at what is wrong with the act of discrimination itself. This is a more persuasive moral foundation for anti-discrimination measures.

We "discriminate" in all aspects of life, and, most of the time, there is nothing wrong with it. We choose not to make friends with bullies or insensitive people. Few of us will want to have a violent person for a partner. Professor John Gardner explains that what sets apart legitimate discrimination from illegitimate discrimination on the basis of caste, sex, race, place of birth, gender identity, nationality, disability, religion or sexual orientation is that the latter unfairly impairs a person's autonomy. A fundamental tenet of liberalism is that human beings are autonomous beings who have the right to shape their lives according to their own wishes so long as they do not impair the autonomy of others. Everyone has to author his/her own life and make lifestyle choices. When these choices are authored by someone else and imposed upon a person, one's fundamental right to autonomy is violated.

All the grounds considered to be illegitimate bases of discrimination have a single thread running through them: they are inextricably linked to one's exercise of personal autonomy. The illegitimate grounds of discrimination are either ordinarily beyond the control of the individual or are such fundamental life choices that a non-consensual, externally enforced change would be imposed only at a very high personal and emotional cost and, therefore, should effectively be treated as beyond the control of the individual. Now, if individuals are discriminated against on any of these grounds, they are being denied opportunities for things beyond their effective control. If one is denied a job because one has a short temper and cannot work in a team, one's autonomy is shaped by choices one has made oneself. However, if one is denied a job because of one's sex or caste or sexual orientation, one's autonomy is violated for no fault of the individual concerned.

Clause 2(g) of the Bill, therefore, correctly defines "deprived group" as "a group of persons who find themselves disadvantaged or lacking in opportunities for reasons beyond their control". While this definition could be interpreted so as to include fundamental life choices that are effectively beyond the control of an individual, the Bill should expressly specify "fundamental choice" in addition to "beyond their control" in order to remove all doubt. Locating illegitimate discrimination in the violation of personal autonomy responds to concerns about prohibiting discrimination in the private sector. When any effort is made to regulate behaviour in the private sector, an equality-versus-liberty debate is raised where the equality of deprived groups seems to be in conflict with the liberty of employers to run their businesses as they wish. However, with the explanation just provided, it is liberty at stake on both sides of the balance, which makes comparison easier.

Should a private employer's liberty to commit an unjust act (by illegitimately discriminating) be held superior to applicants' liberty to author their own lives without being punished for things that are beyond their effective control? Viewed in this manner, the answer is much more obvious. It is worth noting here that all that employers are being asked to do is to not take into account illegitimate factors, which are irrelevant from the business point of view anyway. Race or caste has no relation to one's ability to perform, and the private employer can still rely on the relevant abilities of the candidate. This is not an argument for providing reservation in the private sector although the possibility of such an argument being made cannot be denied either. The Menon Committee report is, correctly, "of the firm opinion that the jurisdiction of this Commission should not be limited to the public sector".

India has grappled with the question of discrimination right from the moment it started making its Constitution. The Constitution clearly prohibits discrimination by the state, and this is enforced directly by the Supreme Court and the High Courts. The success of this constitutional prohibition is a mixed bag, but in comparison with all other efforts, there is no doubt that this has been the best implementation strategy. The Protection of Civil Rights Act, 1955 (CRA), prohibited discriminatory acts in the private sector on the basis of untouchability, on pain of criminal punishment. Similarly, the Equal Remuneration Act (ERA), 1976, prohibited discrimination against women in employment, recruitment and pay. This provision is also backed by criminal sanction. The Persons with Disabilities (Equal Opportunities, Protection of Rights and Full Participation) Act (PDA), 1995, is a much more sophisticated piece of legislation, which drew a lot from global experiences.

The Act prohibits discrimination in the public and private sectors and demands that reasonable accommodation in terms of special facilities (such as wheelchair access) be made for disabled persons. It also provided for a dedicated enforcement agency. In the 21st century, newer claimants to non-discrimination have emerged. A petition filed by the Naz Foundation, demanding that the state be prohibited from discriminating against gay people on the basis of their sexual orientation, is pending in the Delhi High Court. Increasing activism by transgender people has brought to light gross discrimination on the basis of gender identity. The culmination of this historical churning and the immediate catalyst for the EOC Bill was, of course, the Sachar Committee report, which detailed the widespread discrimination in India against Muslims.

This historical review offers several lessons. First, it tells us that discrimination is a socially contingent problem. Identification of groups that are seen to deserve protection depends on the socio-political and moral context of a given time, which usually results in *ad hoc* responses directed at particular groups. A holistic solution must, therefore, transcend this *ad hocism* by putting in place institutions that are resilient enough to adapt to new realities on a principled basis. Secondly, the public-private divide with respect to the prohibition of discrimination is pointless. As the section above explains, discrimination by a private person is as wrong as discrimination by the state.

The need to impose on the private sector the obligation not to discriminate unfairly has been increasingly recognised since the time of the framing of the Constitution-in the CRA, the ERA and the PDA. Thirdly, the limited success of these measures has two further lessons. So far, Indian laws have only recognised direct or intentional discrimination. However, discrimination often works in subtle and unconscious ways. An ambitious anti-discrimination legislation must encompass indirect discrimination in all its complexities. Finally, one has to consider the question of implementation. The CRA and the ERA did not go very far in ending discrimination on the basis of caste and sex. While some of the blame must be laid on the lack of a specialised implementation agency (which exists under the PDA), a more important reason for their failure is that their implementation is not victim-driven.

Contrast this with the constitutional protection against discrimination by the state, which gives agency to the victim of discrimination to take up the matter directly with the Supreme Court and High Courts. The CRA and the ERA are both criminal statutes where the victim has but a secondary role and the proof required is beyond reasonable doubt. So, successful prosecutions are rare, and immediate benefit to the victim is limited. It is a matter of common sense that if implementation is to be ensured, agency must be placed in the hands of those most likely to benefit by it. Any effective anti-discrimination measure has to focus on the most intractable of problems and cannot spread the protection so wide that implementation becomes impossible. Therefore, the EOC Bill has envisaged the concept of a "deprivation index" to identify "deprived groups", those groups that are suffering because of systemic and widespread forms of discrimination.

Although isolated forms of discrimination are also wrong, because they are isolated and not systemic or widespread, the victim usually has other opportunities open with other employers. But deprived groups that are systematically discriminated against have no options because a significant number of employers discriminate against them. Members of these deprived groups must get priority protection, as envisaged by the Bill. The Bill also recognises that the concept of deprivation changes with time. What is today a deprived group may not be so tomorrow. Protection will be dependent not on much-maligned "vote-bank politics" but on a principled demonstration of deprivation through the deprivation index. There is no permanent winner or loser in this game, except the idea of deprivation itself.

The Bill also realises that it cannot correctly predict all future grounds of illegitimate discrimination and, therefore, prohibits discrimination "on the basis of sex, caste, language, religion, disability, descent, place of birth, residence, race or any other...". The final residual clause, "or any other", is a place-holder for other analogous autonomy-infringing grounds that may be filled in later. Although this foresight is commendable, it will be a good idea to expand the list to include currently known analogous grounds, such as "sexual orientation, marital status, food preference, age, dress preference, gender identity, pregnancy", while still retaining the residual clause. Finally, the Bill recognises the multiple identities of people by moving away from focussing on single interest groups and arriving at the generic idea of "deprived groups".

One may be rich, male and able but may be discriminated against nonetheless on the grounds of being Muslim. Again, a Dalit lesbian woman carries several depriving identities, the totality of which cannot be captured by a single-issue-oriented law. This design is not only morally better but also has a more universal appeal-with the rich and complex diversity of human identities, most of us are more likely to see ourselves as potential victims of illegitimate discrimination rather than as perpetual non-beneficiaries. This generates the hope of greater possibility of empathy with victims of discrimination rather than with empathy-failure caused by divisions between "us" and "them". The EOC Bill seeks to prohibit not just direct (or intentional) discrimination but also "indirect" discrimination.

Although the concept of indirect discrimination is well established in countries such as the United Kingdom, the United States (where it is called "disparate impact"), South Africa and Canada, it has been introduced into the Indian discourse for the first time. The Menon Committee report explains that indirect discrimination is an unintentional or unconscious act that results in systematically disadvantaging a deprived group. An example should make the concept clear. Let us take a housing society that does not discriminate (or intend to discriminate) on the grounds of religion or caste. But it has a firm policy of not selling or renting any accommodation to non-vegetarians. Here, the intention may not be to discriminate against certain religious or caste groups, but the result of the policy has a disproportionate impact on certain religious and caste groups. Such a policy will, therefore, amount to indirect discrimination on the grounds of religion and caste.

To take another example, an employer does not intend to discriminate against women but is worried that pregnancy will result in the employee taking leave. With this motivation, he does not hire women of a particular age group. Now, he discriminates indirectly on the basis of sex even though there is no intention to do so because the policy has a disproportionate impact on women. As already discussed, the EOC Bill applies to the public sector as well as the private sector. However, citing resource limitations and other practical matters, the Menon report recommends that the initial focus should only be on the employment and education sectors, whether public or private. While this argument has some currency and the proposed Equal Opportunity Commission should not be overwhelmed with more work than it can handle, there is a strong case for including housing in the priority sectors.

Housing discrimination, especially against Muslims and certain castes, is rampant, especially in some western states. Housing decisions are made very few times in an individual's lifetime and the impact is felt for a long period of time. From the societal point of view, housing discrimination creates ghettos where people only interact with their own kind. This is certainly bad news for social inclusion. Now, to the enforcement model envisaged in the Bill. The proposed Equal Opportunity Commission's main role will be to research and analyse the concept of discrimination, to recommend policy, lobby and advocate reform and to monitor concerns related to equality. It has some limited powers of direct enforcement as well, but the report is clear that grievance redressal shall not be the primary function of the commission.

An enforcement model that does not try to deal with every case of enforcement but rather plans to create sporadic and spectacular examples of enforcement with the hope that the effects will trickle down is not a bad model to start with. This is India's first comprehensive experiment with anti-discrimination. It is a good beginning given the peculiarities of the country, especially when it comes to enforcement. The important thing is to recognise it only as a beginning where lessons should be learnt and improvements made at a later date. However, one important flaw in the Bill is that it gives very little agency to members of the deprived groups themselves. At the most, they can complain (as a group) to the proposed commission. We have seen that except for the constitutional prohibition on discrimination by the state, all other models in India suffer from this flaw.

A good remedy will be to give a limited right to information to citizens against private employers, educational institutions and housing societies only on matters related to their discriminatory policies. This decentralised method of information gathering should complement the task of the commission while ensuring that those discriminated against at least have proper information before they raise their voice. But, most important, if the experience of the Right to Information Act, 2005, is anything to go by, very often a mere demand of information is sufficient to remedy the problem at hand. Many private bodies will be spurred into amending their discriminatory policies by such demands.

The Bill is on the whole a good idea whose time has definitely come. Four minor changes may be considered: (i) including the phrase "fundamental choice" alongside "beyond their control" as autonomy-impinging reasons in clause 2(g); (ii) expanding the list of prohibited grounds in clause 2(k) to include analogous grounds such as "sexual orientation, marital status, food preference, age, dress preference, gender identity, pregnancy"(iii) expressly including the housing sector in clause 22(i); and (iv) providing a limited right to all citizens to demand discrimination-related information from public and private bodies.

Discrimination law may be relevant when an employer considers the issue of flexible work practices. Discrimination on several grounds including sex, race, disability and age is prohibited under federal, State and Territory anti-discrimination legislation.

State and Territory laws dealing with the prevention of discrimination and the promotion of Equal Employment Opportunity continue to apply under Work Choices. These discrimination laws include the *Anti-Discrimination Act 1977* (NSW), the *Discrimination Act 1991* (ACT), the *Anti-Discrimination Act 1991* (Qld), the *Anti-Discrimination Act 1992* (NT), the *Anti-Discrimination Act* 1998 (Tas), the *Equal Opportunity At 1984* (WA) and the *Equal Opportunity Act 1995* (Vic).

A number of federal anti-discrimination laws also apply. For example, the federal *Sex Discrimination Act 1984* makes it unlawful to dismiss an employee on the ground of the employee's family responsibilities. Family responsibilities means responsibilities of the employee to care for or support:

- A dependent child;
- A spouse (including a former spouse, de facto spouse or

a former de facto spouse);

- An adult child;
- A parent;
- A grandparent;
- A grandchild; or
- A sibling.

You can find assistance on understanding caring responsibilities and discrimination laws, including case examples found to have involved discrimination in the workplace, by visiting the websites of the government agencies which administer the legislation. Some examples of cases about flexible work practices which have arisen under discrimination laws include:

- *Application for employment:* An employer unlawfully assumed that a woman with children who had applied for a marketing role would not be able to travel interstate or overseas, so told her she would not be interviewed for the job. The employer failed to keep an open mind, and made assumptions about what the candidate could and couldn't do, based on her family responsibilities.
- *Termination:* An employer had a policy that supervisory positions must be filled by people working full-time. The Tribunal held that the employer unlawfully discriminated against a manager by rejecting her application to work in a job-share position (so that she could care for her child), without investigating whether or not it might work in practice. The Tribunal suggested that the job-share arrangement should have been trialled.
- *Regression*: An employee who worked on a full-time basis requested permission to work three days per week on return from parental leave. Her request was denied, although the employer offered her the option of working three days a week in a more distant office and at a lower level. It was found that the employer had discriminated against the employee on the basis of her caring responsibilities because the employer had failed to give any real or proper consideration to whether the employee could perform her substantive role on a part-time basis.

WORKPLACE RELATIONS LAW

Federal workplace relations law may also be relevant to the provision of flexible work practices. Some of the areas of federal workplace relations law which may be relevant are as follows:

MINIMUM ENTITLEMENTS

The *Workplace Relations Act 1996* (the WR Act) guarantees certain minimum entitlements. An employee cannot be required or requested by an employer to work more than 38 hours per week plus reasonable additional hours. The Act also guarantees eligible employees ten days of paid personal/ career's leave per year and up to two days of unpaid career's leave per occasion. Personal/career's leave includes leave taken by an employee to provide care or support for a member of the employee's immediate family or household who requires care or support due to personal illness or injury, or an unexpected emergency.

An employee can refuse a request to work on a public holiday where the employee has reasonable grounds for doing so. In determining whether an employee has reasonable grounds for refusal, regard must be had to the employee's personal circumstances, including any family responsibilities.

WORKPLACE AGREEMENTS AND AWARDS

Workplace agreements (collective agreements or AWAs) are prohibited from containing terms that discriminate against an employee on grounds of sex, race, disability, family responsibilities or marital status etc. Any such term in an agreement will be void and the Employment Advocate has the power to remove such terms from agreements. An employer that lodges an agreement containing a discriminatory term may attract a penalty. If an employee believes that he or she has been discriminated against on the basis of family responsibilities or marital status under a collective agreement or an award the employee can complain to the Human Rights and Equal Opportunity Commission (HREOC).

On a referral from HREOC the Australian Industrial Relations Commission (AIRC) can vary the instrument to remove the discriminatory provisions. When making an award the AIRC must ensure that the award does not include terms that discriminate against an employee because of, or for reasons including, family responsibilities.

TERMINATION

The WR Act prohibits (subject to limited exceptions) an employer from terminating an employee's employment for reasons including:

- Family responsibilities and pregnancy;
- Absences from work during maternity leave or other parental leave.

EQUALITY ENDANGERED

Large-scale travesties of ideals are hugely damaging to them. And since Soviet-style socialism came to an end in 1989 the fundamental assertion that citizens should share equally in a nation's wealth has been struggling to find backers. They are certainly not to be found among social-democrat 'third way' politicians who have zealously sidelined the idea of the 'citizen' with inalienable rights in favour of the 'consumer' with market choice. Not for nothing does egalitarian thinker Ronald Dworkin comment that equality has become 'the endangered species' of political ideals.

THE AGE OF INEQUALITY

Despite this, many believe that we're far more equal now than in the past-and in some ways it's true. The position of women in the West has improved-though in no country in the world have women achieved equality. Racial and sexist discrimination are less tolerated and are punishable by law. Diversity and multiculturalism are more widely seen as indications of the richness of a society. Yet in one basic way we live in an era of inequality that is historically unprecedented: the gap between rich and poor has never been wider. While the West and Asia have got richer, 54 countries in the world-mainly in sub-Saharan Africa and the former Soviet states-saw average income decline in the 1990s and the number of people living on under one dollar day increase.

Some 21 countries went backwards in terms of 'human development'-a measure of income, life expectancy and literacy. Today the income of 25 million Americans is the equivalent of almost two billion of the world's poorest people. And if you think it's always been this bad: in 1820 western Europe's per-capita income was three times that of Africa's; by the 1990s it was more than 13 times greater.

Inequality is deepening within countries, too: the rich-poor gap is growing in more than half of the countries for which there is data. It would now take the average US worker 400 to 500 years to earn as much as their Chief Executive earns in one year. Greed-and élite networks of privilege-are partly to blame. It's telling that Nicaragua and Zambia, among the world's most unequal countries in terms of income and consumption, have both recently tried former presidents for corruption. But other factors exacerbate inequality-like the world's continuing trend towards privatization of basic services such as health, sanitation and education, which put vital services beyond the reach of the poorest. UN economists now recognize that the Millennium Goals to halve world poverty between 1990 and 2015 have no chance of being met unless inequality is drastically reduced.

The brutality of inequality is clear to see. In Norway 4 children in 1,000 will die before the age of 5. In Sierra Leone a staggering 363 per 1,000 won't make it. But does that mean the ideal of equality is the answer? No and yes. At this point it's best to admit that the ideal of equality as an absolute principle is an impossibility. Try to imagine it. Think of all the natural differences between human beings in terms of size, shape, colour, strength, talents, desires, health, physical or mental attributes. Think of all the things that make up a life in terms of social differences such as class, gender, race, wealth, religion, sexual orientation. What kind of accounting method could measure all these against each other and come out with a plausible balance sheet? Even if it could, how could you apply such a measure to the deep diversity of human nature and human experience, let alone the shifting nature of human relationships?

Lack of respect, though less aggressive than an outright insult, can take an equally wounding form. Often political ideas are fine in theory but do not work in practice. With equality it may well be the other way around. The theory does not work-but building equality into political practice and institutions yields tremendous humanitarian results:

- It alleviates the suffering of the worst off.
- It increases a sense of citizenship and trust.
- It provides the basis for policies like universal public education and health.
- It promotes self-respect and respect for human dignity.
- It's an essential element for reducing world poverty.

For many it is the cornerstone of democracy. US academic Elizabeth Anderson argues: 'The point of equality is [to create] a democratic society, in which people stand in relations of equality to one another. Democratic equality entitles all citizens to the goods they need to function as free and equal citizens and to avoid oppression by others.' Democratic equality also, she adds, obliges citizens to promote equality. If you were to judge the health of equality in terms of the numbers of democracies in the world today you would be greatly encouraged. In 1900 no country in the world had universal suffrage. By 2000 most countries had democracies and multiparty elections.

But it's not that simple. German socialist Rosa Luxemburg warned of 'the hard core of social inequality and lack of liberty that lies hidden under the sweet shell of formal equality and freedom'. This is not to say that formal equality is unimportant. As post-apartheid South Africans know, having the vote and a constitution that guarantees equality are precious first steps. But it's getting under that 'sweet shell' and changing the 'hard core of inequality' inside that's the really difficult part.

SHARING THE PIE

So how do we create more equality in a society-or at any rate reduce the injuries of inequality? Most people can agree with the 'formal' equality that holds that everyone above a certain age is entitled to vote and all citizens are equal before the law. Much trickier is creating 'substantive' equality. This involves sharing out resources so that all may benefit. Those resources might be land or industry or mineral wealth or the environment. Reducing inequality almost always requires redistributing wealth from the rich to the poor. Within a country the common way to do this is through taxation on income, capital, inheritance and certain types of consumption.

In a global context, scrapping Third World debt and making trade fair might be effective means of reducing the extreme concentration of wealth and power in the rich world. But what's the goal of redistribution? Is it to ensure that everyone has precisely the same? Probably not. Fairness might require some inequality; a disabled person might need a car more than an able-bodied person. Maybe the aim should be 'equality of welfare' in the sense of providing for equal well-being; equal access to services like health and education being of prime importance. Most egalitarians would agree that people are responsible for certain inequalities resulting from their own decisions-to gamble, for example-and don't deserve to be compensated for this. We can't expect the outcomes of the choices we make in life to be equal, but there should be equality of opportunity at least.

OPPORTUNITY KNOCKS

At its simplest, equality of opportunity means that people should have access to employment or educational advantages based on merit alone. But it does not take account of any previous advantages or disadvantages people may have had. A stronger measure tries to tackle this through affirmative action. For example, universities with a low proportion of working-class students may deliberately encourage children from these backgrounds to apply. Maybe bright students from poor backgrounds will be accepted with lower grades than rich students who have benefited from private education.

The strongest measure of all involves gearing equal opportunities to specific outcomes, perhaps via a quota system, to make sure that the proportion of entrants reflects the population in terms of race, gender, class and so forth. But while equal opportunity policies can do much, they come too late for many people. What's needed is a level playing field right from the start so that all get good healthcare and good education, regardless of social background. Radical? Utopian? Not really, just democratic. As Ronald Dworkin points out: 'In a democracy the rulers have a right to rule only on the basis that they have "equal concern" for the people they rule. This is what legitimates governments.'

Most governments in the world today don't practice this and could therefore be said to be illegitimate. If they cannot show equal concern for children, who can't be accused of having made 'the wrong choices', what kind of claims to democracy can they make?

RESPECT

But repairing the injuries of social inequality will take more than providing good basic services for all. Richard Sennett grew up in Cabrini Green, the working-class, mainly black Chicago project he writes about it in his latest book, *Respect*. Though often ignored, this focus on respect is crucial if you want to understand how inequality plays out at an emotional level-and why formal and social-policy strategies so often fail to counter the harm done by class and race prejudice. 'Lack of respect, though less aggressive than an outright insult, can take an equally wounding form,' Sennett writes. 'No insult is offered another person, but neither is recognition extended; he or she is not seen as a full human being whose presence matters.'

This is the emotional currency of inequality. Sennett remarks how ghetto adolescents 'are highly sensitive to being "dissed", that is, disrespected. In places where resources are scarce and approval from the outside world is lacking, special honour is fragile; it needs to be asserted every day.' He goes on to say that the way to survive in the ghetto is to keep your head down. Not to stand out above the crowd. And definitely not to do too well at school. Adrienne Rich has vividly diagnosed how disregard can affect anyone who does not belong to the majority or to the defining group in society:

'When someone with the authority of a teacher, say, describes the world and you are not in it, there is a moment of psychic disequilibrium, as if you looked into a mirror and saw nothing. Yet you know you exist and others like you, that this is a game with mirrors. It takes some strength of soul-and not just individual strength, but collective understanding-to resist this void, this non-being into which you are thrust and to stand up, demanding to be seen and heard.'

ENERGY FROM BELOW

State policies can do much to foster greater equality. But the energy for change, for getting rid of inequality's tyrannies of sameness, will not come from above. It will come from people organizing at a grassroots level, from people who, in Adrienne Rich's words 'stand up', 'resist the void' and 'demand to be seen and heard'. Brazil has one of the most unequal societies in the world. Less than three per cent of the population owns two-thirds of the country's arable land. While 60 per cent of Brazil's farmland lies idle, 25 million peasants struggle to survive by working in temporary agricultural jobs. The Landless Workers Movement (MST) is a response to these inequalities. Since 1985 hundreds of thousands of peasants have taken it upon themselves to carry out land reform by occupying unproductive land. Today more than 250,000 families have won title to around 60 million square kilometres of land following MST take-overs.

On the other side of the globe another mass movement for equality is building momentum. *Dalits* and Tribals-who make up around a fifth of India's population and who as 'untouchables' have suffered centuries of abuse-are organizing. 'We affirm that every human being has the inherent right to life and dignity and that Black is Beautiful and *Dalit* is Dignified,' they declared in May 2003. Among their demands is equal access to the country's economy and institutions. Meanwhile Afghanistan's women, struggling against extreme gender inequality, are using their own secret networks to fight fundamentalism. When such people's groups get together-for example to protest against the World Trade Organization in Cancún or at the World Social Forum held in Mumbai this year-they become a truly formidable force for equality.

EQUALITY AND LIBERTY

Kurt Vonnegut's short story, with which this chapter began, plays dramatically upon the notion that equality inevitably violates personal liberty. It's a view held mainly-but not exclusively-by conservatives and libertarians who see all pro-equality measures as interference. It's true that at times equality policies will impinge upon a person's ability to do exactly as they please. But there are important ways in which liberty and equality are natural bedfellows. Amartya Sen's proposal that we have equal rights to what he calls the 'capabilities to achieve functioning's' takes a very dynamic and enabling view of equality.

Human beings are deeply diverse and have diverse needs. They have an equal right to the freedom to pursue the goals that are valuable to them. These goals may range from elementary things like being well-nourished to something as complex as happiness. Ultimately, though, what matters most is that a society has equal concern for all its citizens. Feminist Martha Nussbaum agrees, adding that citizens should be conceived 'not as passive recipients of social planning, but as free and dignified beings who shape their own lives'.

One clear reason for the multitude of inequality indices is the lack of a mathematical definition of inequality-if one existed, it would be fairly straightforward to seek an estimator for it. When deriving a measure for inequality, one seeks to quantify a pattern of some resource being shared among individuals. We hence use the general term "resource acquisition" for the currency for which inequality values are derived. The results apply to a wide range of interpretations. Thus, in studying competition between plants, these measures could apply to mass, number of pollinators, light intercepted, or seed number. In the examples considered here, we interpret the resource as mating success of liking males. At this point, one needs to address a semantic confusion that exists in studies of inequality.

Many of the measures that aim to quantify inequalities among individuals, especially in the fields of sexual selection and reproductive skew theory, are called skew measures. Inequality, however, is intuitively more linked to the variance in resource acquisition among individuals (roughly, magnitude of spread around the mean) than to skewness, the statistical definition of which is related to the shape of the spread around the mean. Mathematically, variance is equal to the second moment of a distribution, whereas skewness is related to the third moment. Therefore, a skewed distribution of resource sharing may have smaller variance than a non-skewed distribution, and a non skewed distribution may show pronounced inequality among individuals. This confusion probably arises from the usage of phrases like "skewed male mating success" to describe unequal success.

To avoid confusion, one also needs to realize that the word "distribution" has three very different meanings in this context. Third, the observed data can be shown in the conventional form of a frequency distribution. This will be Poisson if the propensity distribution is even. The graphs of the propensity distribution and the frequency distribution can look very similar, but they describe inequality in very different ways. Many inequality measures attempt to produce a measure from observed data that would correspond to the degree to which the propensity distribution deviates from equal values. However, there are several sensible criteria that should apply to any measure.

Natural requirements are that all observations that arise from the null hypothesis of equal gain propensities-regardless of total resource acquisition R or the number of competitors should ideally be interpreted as indicating no inequality, that all observations that arise from unequal gain propensities should be given positive inequality values (assuming that 0 is chosen as the value of equality), and that the maximum inequality should occur when one individual monopolizes all the resource with propensity.

Practically, sampling error will make it difficult to detect small deviations from equal propensities, and a good measure should have high power in doing so. Preferably, the distribution of the measure value under the null hypothesis should be known; very few of the recently proposed measures satisfy this criterion. Further, the distribution of measure values should shift monotonically upward when the propensity distribution is changed in a way that unambiguously increases inequality.

It is generally agreed that inequality is unambiguously increased if resource units are transferred from an individual with a smaller share to an individual with a larger share. Measures that aim to quantify the inequality of the propensity distribution are focused on the underlying gain propensities of individuals, not on their realized achievements. Proponents of such measures typically state as an additional requirement that changes in the total resource R being divided should ideally not affect the expected mea- sure value. For example, estimates of inequality of male copulatory success in leks should not depend on how many copulations the researcher has been able to observe.

However, a completely alternative view exists, which interprets increases in the measure value with increasing R to have a true meaning: a lek where one male monopolizes all females has, in absolute terms, a bigger evolutionary impact if the male inseminated 20, rather than two, females. One can hence divide measures into two groups, those that quantify relative inequality (by having an upper bound for the inequality value, regardless of R), and those that respond to absolute differences. We do not attempt to judge their relative superiority. A similar requirement is for insensitivity of the measure value to changes in the number of competitors.

Again, counter arguments can be made: a single monopolizing male can be seen to indicate higher inequality if he outcompetes 100 rather than 10 other males, and, of course, the opposite argument of lower inequality can be defended from the viewpoint of the unsuccessful males. In addition, there is no unique way to define how a propensity distribution should change when a new competitor is added, to yield an unchanged level of inequality-unlike in the context of changing R where the propensity distribution can simply be left intact. Hence, we report the behavior of each measure when R and n change, but we focus on the two main criteria mentioned above: ease of recognizing unequal propensities (i.e., ease of obtaining the measure value distribution under the null hypothesis and the power of detecting deviations from it) and the ability of the measure to detect differences between cases where inequality is increased in an unambiguous way.

Measures of Inequality In the following discussion, the terms "measure" and "index" are used interchangeably, although we note that there has been a tendency to use the name "index" for measures that are bounded within a predefined range (usually from 0 to 1). We calculate, where possible, three expected values of the measure: expected value under the assumption that every individual is observed to have the same share (i.e., the variance of the frequency distribution equals 0); under the assumption of equal gain propensities, that is, that each resource unit is randomly assigned to an individual (resulting in a Poisson distribution of resources); and under conditions where one individual completely monopolizes the resource.

We denote the first case by observed resource shares being even and the second case by them being random; one should keep in mind that equal gain propensities result in the second case rather than the first. Measures Based on the Variance of Resource Acquisition Sample Variance and Its Modifications. According to Fisher's fundamental theorem of natural selection (1958), the rate of evolutionary change in a population is proportional to the variance in fitness. It is therefore natural to start by considering variance as a primary measure of inequality. Variance (of the frequency distribution) relates naturally to the spread of individuals around the mean. Also, it has the advantage of having a well-defined distribution (Poisson) under the null hypothesis of equal gain propensities.

IMPLEMENTATION OF THE PLAN

In order to create a gender-equal society, it is necessary that the national machinery for the advancement of women play a leadership role in close cooperation with other concerned administrative bodies in comprehensively and effectively promoting à broad, diverse range of measures, based on trends in the international community and changes in the Japanese economy and society. In addition, it is important that gender equality be reflected in all policy areas in the future.

In addition to national efforts, it is expected that local governments, women's organizations, private companies, management organizations, labor organizations, the media and other groups, as well as all citizens - old, young, male and female - will cooperate as necessary in a systematic way and make independent efforts that reflect their respective positions. For this reason, the following measures must be formulated in order to comprehensively and effectively promote this plan, along with the strengthening of the necessary structure for implementation.

ACTIVE IMPLEMENTATION OF MEASURES AND REGULAR FOLLOW-UP

Encourage the close cooperation of concerned administrative organizations to promote comprehensive, consistent measures toward the achievement of the basic goals and priority goals. Regularly follow up on progress in the implementation of this plan and maintain a constant grasp of the current situation and problems related to gender equality in Japan. Convey the situation to the public in a manner that is easy to understand and reflected in policies and measures. Review the plan whenever deemed appropriate in order to respond to trends in the efforts of the international community or changes in the economic and social situation in Japan.

Reflect gender equality in all measures

Reflect gender equality in all measures that exert a direct or indirect impact on the formation of a gender-equal society.

Ensure that Coordinators for Gender Equality and divisions of each ministry and agency in charge of the promotion of gender equality give due consideration to positively contribute to the planning of such measures. Give measures related to the creation of a gender-equal society an appropriate place in the various plans formulated by the Government, thus promoting the formation of such a society through the efforts of the entire national administration.

Enhance training opportunities for administrative staff

Produce and utilize gender equality guidelines and to enhance training opportunities and information provision in order to raise awareness of women's human rights and foster a gender-equality perspective among all national administrative staff.

RESEARCH AND THE COLLECTION, ORGANIZATION AND PROVISION OF INFORMATION

Research the Creation of a Gender-equal Society

Conduct studies and research on the pioneering efforts of other countries and the possibility of introducing such measures into Japan in terms of comprehensive and basic issues related to the creation of a gender-equal society (including methods to evaluate and analyze the impact on women and men of organizations and functions of national machineries in other countries, legal systems related to gender equality, and various measures and plans). Study and research problems accompanying changes in the economic and social environment as well as new problems proposed by the international community.

Regularly grasp conditions and awareness of gender equality, by utilizing statistical and general awareness studies. Make efforts to make the results of these studies and research mutually available to national and local governments, NGOs, and others through various information networks.

Provide information on trends in the efforts of the international community and other countries

Collect and organize information on trends in the efforts of the international community and other countries at meetings of the United Nations Commission on the Status of Women and the Committee on the Elimination of Discrimination against Women, as well as the next World Conference on Women and its preparatory meetings. Provide this information to local governments, NGOs and others through various meetings, publications and the Internet.

Make Japan's efforts known overseas

Communicate overseas the efforts of Japan for the creation of a gender-equal society and the results of those actions by transmitting via the Internet and other new media. Enhance cooperation with international organizations and the national machineries of other countries.

DEVELOPING AND STRENGTHENING THE STRUCTURE FOR COMPREHENSIVE IMPLEMENTATION

Strengthening the organization and functions of the national machinery

Establish a new advisory council to promote the formulation of a gender-equal society. Continue study on the establishment of a new advisory council to promote the creation of a gender-equal society as proposed in the "Vision of Gender Equality" "a legally based advisory body should be installed that can provide advice and suggestions on government policies for gender equality as requested by the Prime Minister and other Cabinet Ministers. This body should also understand how the policy measures are being executed, and express opinions to the Prime Minister and Ministers from a basic and comprehensive viewpoint."

Consider a fundamental law to promote the creation of a gender-equal society. Study a fundamental law to promote the creation of a gender-equal society. Study and research the possibility of introducing ombudsperson(s) into Japan who resolve problems concerning gender equality, making reference to related activities and legal systems in other countries.

Enhance the support system for the Minister for Women's Affairs. Further enhance the support system to enable the Minister for Women's Affairs to effectively coordinate a diverse range of relevant policies. Flexibly hold Meetings of the Headquarters for the Promotion of Gender Equality and of the Coordinators for Gender Equality. Flexibly hold meetings of the Headquarters for the Promotion of Gender Equality and of the Coordinators for Gender Equality to promote the gender equality measures of concerned ministries and agencies in a unified manner. Ensure that the officials in charge of gender equality in each ministry and agency, who coordinate policy under their respective jurisdictions, make efforts to take advantage of all opportunities to mutually exchange information and further stimulate those activities.

Enhance the divisions of ministries and agencies in charge at the Headquarters for the Promotion of Gender Equality. Further enhance the divisions of ministries and agencies in charge at the Headquarters for the Promotion of Gender Equality to strengthen the structure supporting the activities of the national machinery, and ensure close mutual cooperation with these administrative organizations by holding regular liaison meetings of concerned ministries and agencies. Actively utilize women in administration consultative committees and as Civil Liberties Commissioners.

Actively assign women to positions on administration consultative committees and as Civil Liberties Commissioners and provide more research opportunities and information to increase awareness of gender equality. Study the appointment of regional officers who give priority to gender equality problems and are especially knowledgeable on women's issues. Study the introduction of a mechanism to reflect the lessons learned by these individuals into the planning and promotion of new measures as a way of contributing to more effective measures.

Ensure, via the national government, close cooperation with administrators in charge of women's affairs in local governments in dealing with complaints related to women's problems.

Strengthen cooperation with international organizations and national machinery of other countries. Strengthen cooperation with international organizations and national machineries of other countries through various information exchanges, etc., related to the formation of a gender-equal society. Increase opportunities for mutual exchange in cooperation with the Asia-Pacific region and actively contribute to the various fora sponsored by the Economic and Social Commission for Asia and the Pacific (ESCAP) that are profoundly related to the creation of a gender-equal society in light of Japan's geographical proximity and common cultural roots.

Strengthening cooperation with national and local governments and NGOs; strengthening measures by the entire nation. Strengthen cooperation between national and local governments. Further strengthen cooperation with regard to information exchanges, establishing research opportunities, and carrying out publicity and educational campaigns in order to ensure the effective implementation of national and local government measures. Actively collect and make available information on the adoption, in local governments, of action plans and pioneering efforts that utilize the special qualities of the region.

Appeal to prefectures and designated cities to steadily promote and enhance the content of measures in the future and ask these governments to cooperate to encourage similar action at the municipal level. Actively support the efforts of municipalities to improve and enhance promotional structures, formulate and promote action plans that take full advantage of regional characteristics, implement various publicity and educational initiatives, and provide training to staff. Produce guidelines on drafting procedures and basic points to be incorporated, while giving due respect to the independence of these regions to contribute to the action plans of municipalities. Actively provide information to cities that have declared themselves gender-equal and the National Urban

Conference on Women's Issues and make efforts to support exchanges among cities and to disseminate knowledge on municipal-level measures nationwide.

Deepen understanding on a gender-equal society among heads of local governments, through national governors meetings, national mayors meetings, national municipality meetings, etc.

Enhance facilities that serve as bases for the activities of women

Enhance and encourage cooperation among public and private women's centers and other facilities which serve as bases for the activities of women in various regions by providing information to women, providing a space for the independent activities of women's groups and organizations, offering consultation services, conducting research, and performing a variety of other functions.

Form a network with NGOs

Form a network centered around the national machinery that enables the mutual provision of information on trends in national and local government policy and international conferences, as well as the daily activities of NGOs and information on pioneering action, considering the extremely large role NGOs play toward the creation of a gender-equal society by offering a unique perspective in carrying out volunteer activities in various areas, in order to establish equal cooperative relations among the national government, local governments and NGOs. Upgrade, in this effort, the information network that utilizes new media and to mutually communicate that information in a manner that is suited to the respective medium of communication. Study a mechanism for giving small NGOs working in municipalities and communities access to that information.

Pave the way for the creation of a gender-equal society

Encourage support so that the national government, local governments, NGOs and others will work together toward the creation of a gender-equal society, and so that all levels of the nation take part in the implementation of a variety of measures.

3

From Sex Roles to Sex Industries

Many women earn all or part of their living as sex workers or in other areas of the sex industry, including pornography, nude dancing, telephone sex, and computer pornography. Contrary to the ugly stereotypes of prostitutes as fallen women, dope addicts, or disease carriers, sex workers are women at work - supporting children as single parents, trying to save money to go to school, surviving economically in a job market that underpays women at every economic level.

Once politically voiceless and isolated from other women, sex workers have organized over the past 25 years for support and political action. As adult sex workers speak out, they expose the many forms of violence that they experience:

- Poverty that forces women, especially women of color and runaway teenagers, into work as sex workers
- Sexism in the job market that means that even middle- and upper-class women can earn more in sex work than in most other jobs available
- Intimidation and beatings by pimps, to whom many sex workers must give their earnings in return for protection
- Police harassment and lack of police protection when we are victims of crime such as robbery, battery, and rape
- The arrest and prosecution of prostitutes while clients go free
- The racism and class bias that lead to the arrest and imprisonment of far more prostitutes of color and women

with low incomes than white, middle-class women, even though the majority of sex workers are white and middle-class

As a middle-class white woman, trained as a registered nurse, could work in a private call business instead of hitting the streets was arrested but never did time in prison; the system isn't aimed at putting me in jail. Women of color have less easy access to places like upper-class hotels, where if you're a black woman and alone you're automatically tagged as a hooker. So they're in the streets and in the bars, where they are more visible and more vulnerable to exploitation and arrest - and they're the ones who end up in jail.

Some feminists have been critical of prostitutes for reinforcing sex-role stereotypes by allowing themselves to be sex objects or for participating in the sex industry, which many think contributes to violence against women. Many see sex work as violence in and of itself, especially when children and young girls are involved. Others insist that it is a legitimate way for women to earn money from men. As one prostitute said, "It's my body; why shouldn't I be the one to decide how I should use it?" Some sex workers find that the experience is generally positive, and the negative parts arise from the violence and harassment that they may be more at risk for because of their profession. Others enjoy parts of the work and hate other parts. Still others name their experience as violence.

Prostitutes point out that they are no different from most women in having to sell their services to men. In the words of an ex-prostitute:

I've worked in straight jobs where I've felt more like I was prostituting my being than in prostitution. I had less control over my life, and the powerlessness wasn't even up front. People didn't see me as selling myself, but with the minimum wage so little and my boss so insulting, I felt like I was selling my soul.

Prostitutes have organized in the U.S. and Europe to demand decriminalization, the abolition of all laws against prostitution. With decriminalization, prostitutes would have more control over their work and the money they earn. Most of all, they would no longer go to jail for providing a service that society itself puts in such high demand and for choosing the highest-paying work available to them.

SEX INDUSTRY LAWS IN AUSTRALIA

Prostitution laws in Australia have been influenced by the English Abolitionist approach of the turn of the century that seeks to control or eradicate activities associated with the sale of sex. These activities include organising, operating or managing sex industry businesses or receiving direct financial benefit from the labour of sex workers - usually defined as 'living off the earnings of prostitution'. Under abolitionist influenced laws individual sex workers may or may not be criminalised for the sale of sexual services depending upon the sector of the sex industry in which they work. However, in practice, abolitionist influenced laws do not allow for sex work to be freely practiced since the control of associated activities limits the ability of individual workers to make choices regarding where they can work and in what manner.

Recently, changes have been driven by the need to control the perceived impacts on the broader community and unrealistic, offensive stereotypes. These impacts include ensuring that 'public morality' is not offended, the protection of minors, managing public health concerns with respect to sexually transmitted infections (ACT, 1991), the control of organised crime and illegal drugs and local government planning issues. Another significant influence on the law reform agenda is the equivalence of sex work with violence both towards the women who work in the sex industry and with respect to its impact on women in the broader community.

Those supporting this view wish to eradicate the sex industry whilst claiming to support individual sex workers. Little consideration is given to the role laws regulating the sex industry play in determining occupational conditions. These approaches underpinning sex industry law reform are rejected by sex workers and their organisations who locate discussions regarding sex industry law reform within a framework of work. Recognition that sex work is labour facilitates law reform objectives to focus upon human rights, occupational health and safety, and working conditions. Positioning sex work as a labour issue does not ignore the conditions under which many sex workers operate but challenges assumptions regarding sex work.

The violence and exploitation that sex workers around the world may experience is acknowledged but it is criminal laws regulating the conditions within the sex industry and the stigmatisation of sex workers that creates the conditions for this exploitation. This document sets out the principals that should guide sex industry legislation to ensure a balance of stakeholder needs. It demonstrates through evidence that many of the perceived "problems of the sex industry" are addressed when sex workers' occupational health and safety, working conditions, and their human rights are the primary goals of reform agendas.

Sex industry legislation that fails to address these issues has been shown to fail the world over. This is demonstrated repeatedly by the fact that whilst various jurisdictions have attempted to prohibit certain sectors of the industry and support others, they all continue to exist and in some cases flourish. Current laws in the majority of Australian States and Territories (particularly Tasmania, Queensland, South Australia and Western Australia) are negatively impacting on sex workers' health and safety, undermining public health outcomes and initiatives, setting the conditions for police corruption and control of local industries, failing to regulate working conditions, forcing sectors of the sex industry underground, criminalising sex workers, encouraging discrimination against sex workers, limiting sex workers' access to legal mechanisms to address crimes committed against them and ignoring and denying basic human rights.

That all laws criminalizing the sex industry be removed and the industry be regulated through standard business, planning and industrial codes/laws. Most criminal laws regulating the sex industry reflect a lack of understanding of it, particularly in relation to health measures and the specificities of the various sectors that comprise it. These laws reflect stereotypes of sex workers as deviate, irresponsible victims in need of protection by the state and turned sex workers into a criminal sub-class of people (mostly women). This is demonstrated by police statistics which confirm that women are the most likely targets of police activity to curb sex work. For example, in the year 1992-1993, over 70% of persons arrested in South Australia for sex work related offences were female.

The majority of arrests during this period were for 'living off the earnings of prostitution' - an offence supposedly aimed at the pimps and exploiters, traditionally associated with men. Women accounted for 85% of the arrests under this charge. In Victoria, for the same period, 65% of arrests for prostitution related offences were women, 294 women were arrested for soliciting or loitering, whilst only 2 men were arrested for 'inviting prostitution' or "gutter crawling". In Queensland, laws that came into effect on 1st of July 2000 reflect the construction of sex workers as criminals. Under the Prostitution Act 1999 any person with a criminal record relating to running, organising or managing a brothel will be prevented from holding a licence to operate a brothel.

Given that operating a brothel in Queensland has been illegal over the past century (although tolerated at times), that corruption allegations against police for extorting money from brothels lead to an increase in arrests and that receptionists are often charged for 'assisting in keeping premises', a significant proportion of current sex industry personnel have criminal records which exempt them from applying for a licence. The intention of the law is to exclude undesirable or criminal elements from the sex industry, but the effect it will have is to exclude many sex workers from participating in the organisation or management of their own industry. Since these workers want to continue to work in the industry, they will do so illegally and will be branded criminals.

Being labelled and defined as a 'criminal' has the consequent implication of restricting numerous life choices for sex workers. Some of these include the denial of the right to freely travel (many countries deny entry to known prostitutes) and difficulties in changing jobs (many jobs entail perusal of a person's criminal record and if a person wishes to conceal employment in the sex industry there is often problems in explaining gaps in employment history). The consequence of a criminalised sex industry is that many sex workers are more likely to come in to contact with the police force and are exposed to police harassment, and extortion attempts. Working within a criminalised framework means that many sex workers are denied the same access to workplace benefits that other Australian employees enjoy.

This is particularly relevant with respect to conditions such as sick leave, holiday pay, workers compensation and superannuation entitlements. Even payment for work services provided is not guaranteed as workers must rely upon the honesty of brothel or escort operators to make payment. If the operator chooses not to pay a sex worker, then that worker risks being charged with an offence if s/ he contacts police in order to seek legal redress. The existence of laws that criminalise sex work maintains and promotes false stereotypes about sex workers in the public consciousness. This leads to the stigmatisation of sex workers as deviant and immoral people who represent a health risk to the general community. They are also conceptualised as victims without the skills necessary to obtain other employment.

This stigmatisation and criminalisation has profound impacts on a group of people based purely on an occupational choice. To avoid discrimination and stigmatisation many sex workers maintain a fiction that they do not work in the sex industry that can lead to high levels of stress for leading a 'double life'. This is particularly relevant for women who have children. Sex workers working under criminalised frameworks are also denied the same access to legal remedies to address crimes committed against them, including crimes of violence. This ranges from anti-discrimination protections to judicial remedies relating to rape and other crimes of violence. In the rare cases that crimes of violence against sex workers proceed to court, judicial outcomes have reflected a belief that sex workers are not worthy of the same degree of legal protection as other women.

This dissuades sex workers from utilising these legal remedies and reinforces the assumption that sex work is inherently dangerous and the women who choose to work in the industry accept the risk associated with their work choice. These types of judicial responses send out the message to perpetrators that sex workers are easier targets who may be offended against without redress. The sex industry is the only industry in which laws actually have the effect of minimising occupational health and safety. Laws that regulate the sex industry should support occupational health and safety outcomes and improvements in working conditions. General criminal laws are adequate to address deception, fraud, violence, and exploitation of minors in the industry.

There is no necessity to frame specific legislation within sex industry laws to address these issues. Similarly, sex industry or public health laws should not specifically target the sex industry but should be generalised in relation to the whole sexually active population. Creating special laws that relate to sex workers does not achieve desired public health out- comes because they generally rely upon mandatory testing. This approach cannot guarantee sexual health status as it does not apply to all sexually active people and in particular clients. A more affective approach would be to encourage all sexually active people to have periodic health screening for STIs and become more acquainted with their own bodies through general population education campaigns.

Mandatory health laws framed in sex industry legislation further stigmatises sex workers whilst being largely irrelevant as sex workers have the lowest rates of sexually transmitted disease and enjoy better sexual health than the general community. It is sex workers who require protection from clients and sex industry operators who may seek sexual services without a condom. Sex industry laws are often concerned with regulating all aspects of operation. Sex industry businesses are no different to other service industries and do not require unnecessary and complicated regulations to comply with conditions of legal operation.

The task of law reform is lessened by seeking parallels to other industries and applying similar legislative obligations.

An awareness of the differing requirements of the various sectors of the sex industry allows for work- able and appropriate application of regulations. For example, whilst a registration/legalisation approach may be appropriate for brothels it is unlikely that this approach would be successful for private or street workers. Registration when it occurs within other industries tends to apply to professional associations with the purpose of ensuring that the people practicing in that field have the necessary skills.

For example, doctors, hairdressers, dentists etc. are not controlled by specific government legislation but are members of their own professional bodies. When registration is applied to sex industry businesses or individual sex workers the intention is usually as a form of government surveillance. Registration should never apply to individual sex workers as it is an invasion of basic human rights and perpetuates stigmatisation. Examples of applying standards similar to other service industries relates to restrictions on advertising and alcohol.

Many jurisdictions restrict the advertising of sexual services and for the recruitment of staff within the sex industry. The sale or serving of alcohol is generally restricted in brothels as they are prevented by law from obtaining liquor licenses. In the Australian Capital Territory both advertising and alcohol are not restricted under sex industry regulations and there has been no increase in the prevalence of either people entering the sex industry or alcohol related violence/ consumption. These restrictions are not applied to any other industry and sex industry laws should correlate with standards applicable for other recognised industries. Sex industry laws should assist sex workers to exercise greater control over their work environment by articulating sex industry industrial responsibilities.

Industrial work conditions cannot be implemented in the sex industry under laws that deny sex industry businesses are workplaces. Current available legal remedies and industrial mechanisms are generally unavailable to sex workers who work illegally. It is important sex industry businesses meet their obligations to their employees and that laws regulating the sex industry support this obligation.

CRIMINAL LAWS UNDERMINE EMPLOYERS INDUSTRIAL RESPONSIBILITIES

In an environment where sex work is decriminalised, sex workers take more pride in the work they do and are more likely to challenge unfair and discriminatory practices in the sex industry. Sex industry laws must acknowledge employment in the sex industry as legitimate work rather than being concerned with regulating activities perceived as associated with the sex industry such as organised crime, local government planning concerns, police corruption and public health concerns Public discourses (general public, feminist, political) on the sex industry, and expressed in legislative aims have failed to include industrial rights within the framework of discussion and debate.

Sex industry legislation must acknowledge that prostitution is work and that the workers who work in that industry are entitled to the same industrial rights and protections as other workers. As a consequence of the criminal law's intervention in sex work, contracts made with respect to prostitution may be void for illegality, or for being contrary to public policy. Individual sex workers can make valid contracts with their clients - the provision of private sex work services is not illegal. Sex work, however, invariably involves the worker in numerous commercial arrangements besides the client-worker relationship.

For example, a sex worker may lease or hire out premises for the purposes of conducting her/his business. An escort worker might hire a driver to transport her/him between jobs, providing her/him with a degree of personal security. Even though these arrangements are of an undeniably commercial character, the law may not uphold them if the sector in which the sex worker operates is illegal. The illegality of activities associated with sex work allows workers to be exploited by brothel owners/operators. At the basis of any employment relationship is a contract of service between the employer and the employee. If there is no contract of service, there is no employment relationship.

Without such a relationship, workers must rely on the honesty of their 'employer' to pay them, and to provide reasonable terms and conditions of employment. Also, without such a relationship, workers are not entitled to statutory employment protection, such as non-wage conditions specified in industrial awards, superannuation entitlements, workers' compensation and occupational health and safety. In those jurisdictions where brothel keeping is illegal, rates of pay and other non-wage conditions for brothel workers remain largely at the discretion of brothel owners or operators. Brothel workers often complain of being required to work long hours and of having no control over their clientele. Brothel workers do not receive paid sick leave (even when their condition may be work related) or paid holidays.

While it is true that many other service providers (such as trades people) do not have contracts of employment, other self-employed persons are free to enter independent contracts to insure their income and work related health. Brothel workers do not even have this choice. This situation stands in direct contrast to the ACT and Victoria where sex workers can enter work related contracts as evidenced by a number of successful workers compensation and unfair dismissal claims. On the assumption that at some time in the future, sex workers will negotiate an industrial award with emplcyer groups, then permanent full-time and part-time employees will be entitled to paid sick leave, maternity leave and holiday pay.

This will keep many workers out of the social security system, on which they are presently forced to rely in times of sickness or pregnancy. Acknowledgement of sex work as work has a positive effect on the economy through the collection of the GST and other taxes. In addition, sex workers can benefit by claiming work incurred expenses and legitimises their income. Whilst the payment of tax on income is a requirement under federal statute irrespective of the legal status of the work performed to derive that income, sex workers feel cheated and are reluctant to pay tax when they don't enjoy the same rights as workers and citizens as other taxpayers. The point of view that equates sex work with sexual exploitation (particularly sexual exploitation of women) fails to understand that every area of work is based on utilising some or all parts of the body.

Academics utilise their intellect through their brains and to a lesser degree their hands when they write. Models utilise their entire bodies, naked at times; bus drivers use their hands, legs and brain for concentration. Sex workers utilise their entire bodies including their genitals. It is illogical to construct this as "sexual exploitation" simply because the genitals are involved. Those who work in the industry (and we should not deny or ignore sex workers but listen to what they have to say, given that it is their lived experience!) see it as work.

For some sex work represents other things too (e.g. a means of sexual expression, etc.), but primarily they see it as a job. If the "sex work as sexual exploitation" view is analysed and explored, it follows that at the base of its assumptions is that women are incapable of having and enjoying sex outside of the context of an emotionally committed relationship. Why does sex become "exploitative" simply because money is exchanged for a negotiated service? It can be argued that since the sex that occurs within the context of sex work is so well negotiated that it is the most consensual kind of sex. If prostitution is decriminalised, sex workers working for employers should be treated as such for industrial benefits.

Sex Work is Legitimate Employment

- Sex work should be recognised as work for industrial, and other legal rights as it has already been for tax purposes;
- As participants in the Australian workforce sex workers are entitled to work in healthy and safe environments with appropriate working conditions;
- The police do not control or regulate any other Australian workplaces and the sex industry should be no difference; and
- Sex industry reform debates in various Australian jurisdictions must include sex workers. They are the ones who will work under any legal or administrative changes

and have a right to participate in discussions regarding the regulation of their own industry.

That laws regulating the sex industry include all sectors of the sex industry and not be directed at forcing sex workers to operate in a limited legal framework Laws that limit the sectors of the sex industry in which sex workers can legally work fail to recognise that the various sectors are shaped by market forces, the legal environment and the variety of needs of clients and sex workers. The reasons that sex workers choose a particular work environment include: flexibility of hours, greater personal control over choice of clients and money received, managerial and administrative requirements, types of services provided, skills required, security, fear of a criminal record, privacy issues and general work conditions offered.

Likewise, clients access the sector that meets their particular needs such as speed of service, cost of service, level of privacy offered, likelihood of being seen by someone they know, type of services offered and the surrounds. Therefore, sex workers and clients may ignore laws that restrict their favoured choice of work environment regardless of the consequences and penalties. For example, in Queensland, where between 1992 and 1999 private work (defined as operating alone from your own premises) the only lawful sector in which to work was, did not have the desired effect of eradicating brothels. Since the law limited the mechanisms that private workers could adopt to protect themselves, such as employing support staff or working with another worker, it was perceived by many sex workers (unfamiliar with this work environment) to be too dangerous and it is these workers who continued to work illegally in brothels or in collaboration with other workers.

A direct consequence of forcing Queensland sex workers to operate in one sector of the sex industry has been a significant rise in violence and other crimes against sex workers. In fact, six sex workers have died as a direct consequence of Queensland laws. In addition, there was a substantial increase in street work and whilst the number of brothels was reduced they did not disappear altogether. Generally, sex workers who have chosen private work as their preferred work option have been workers who have had experience in other sectors of the industry (e.g. brothel, escort) and have therefore acquired the skills to "go out on their own". In a sense they have been through an apprenticeship in more supportive sectors of the industry.

Without the choice or ability to do this, sex workers are left isolated and vulnerable to those who seek to cause them harm. The consequences of limiting employment opportunities for sex workers are detrimental not only to sex workers but the broader community. Laws that prohibit work in specific sectors of the sex industry undermine occupational health and safety by forcing sex workers underground as sex workers need to clandestinely stay one step ahead of the law. This limits sex workers access to legal remedies to address crimes of violence, encourages unfair employment practices and conditions, allows unregulated and unenforceable occupational health measures, allows for local police control and local government control in determining how and where sex workers may operate promoting conditions conducive to police corruption, and provides the opportunity for criminal control of the industry.

Criminalising work options for sex workers is also a denial of basic human rights. Australia has an obligation under international conventions to guarantee its citizens the right to work and free choice of employment under favourable conditions (Universal Declaration on Human Rights). Where legislation is deemed necessary it must recognise and incorporate all sectors of the sex industry with the primary aim of supporting occupational improvements in all sectors of the sex industry. Legalisation introduced to tightly regulate or control the sex industry is not necessary and will only act against occupational health and safety outcomes. Further, it has failed in every state where control/licensing models have been introduced.

For example, in Victoria a legal brothel industry operates alongside an illegal industry. Street work remains highly criminalised yet this has failed to halt street work, even though violence against Victorian street workers is apparently increasingly. Alternatively, in New South Wales where street work has been decriminalised violence against street workers remains significantly lower. It is essential that the law does not require individual sex workers to be registered, as sex workers concerned about privacy, confidentiality and discrimination would refrain from registering thus forcing them to work illegally. Workplace reforms cannot be achieved where certain sectors of the sex industry are forced under- ground to avoid criminal charges.

Consequences of Limiting Employment Options in the Sex Industry

- Restrictive laws discourage the application of occupational health and safety standards throughout the sex industry;
- Restrictive laws fail as they force some sex workers to ignore the law in order to work in the sectors of the sex industry in which they feel secure and safe;
- Restrictive laws are detrimental to the broader community as they force illegal sex workers underground thereby setting the conditions for the emergence of police corruption, organised crime and limited access to health services;
- Restrictive laws are detrimental to sex workers as they are less likely to report crimes to police and encourage unfair and exploitative employment practices; and
- Restrictive laws deny sex workers basic human rights and contravene Australia's obligations under specific international treaties.

Areas of the Sex Industry which should be lawful

The following areas should be decriminalised: street, brothel (small and large), escorts, and private work:

There are approximately 25,000 sex workers in Australia, 90% female, 8% male and 2% transgender working in the following sectors: 10%street, 70% brothel, 10% escort, 10% private. Many escort workers also work from brothels; and as in any industry, the sex industry organises in response to market demands and changing technology. For example, escort work did not exist prior to the wide availability of the telephone.

That the priority aim of sex industry legislation be to maximise occupational health and safety provisions for sex workers. Sex industry legislation has a direct impact upon the health and safety of sex workers. Criminal laws have a significant role in shaping unsafe work conditions including violence against sex workers; limiting sex workers' access to legal mechanisms to address crimes of violence; limiting sex workers' access to health information and services; impeding the adoption of safe sex practices; and perpetuate the myth that sex workers are a significant vector of sexually transmitted infections (STI) in Australia. One of the most compelling arguments for decriminalising the sex industry to improve health outcomes is the police use of safe sex paraphernalia to obtain convictions against sex workers.

Currently, in South Australia police routinely confiscate condoms and safe sex literature produced by SASIN (the sex worker organisation in South Australia) to use as evidence of prostitution taking place in court proceedings. The effect of such policing practices is that sex workers are reluctant to carry quantities of condoms and other safe sex paraphernalia. These sorts of police practices endanger sex workers and the general community and are diametrically opposed to achieving stated public health policy objectives. Police should not have any role in the sex industry other than to respond to complaints and investigate the commission of a crime.

The major health and safety concerns for sex workers under criminal laws are as follows:

- Research demonstrates that laws criminalising sectors of the sex industry hinder the implementation of STI education and prevention strategies and occupational health and safety standards in the sex industry. Criminalised frameworks do not support the development of mechanisms and standards to enhance the occupational health of sex workers and hinder public health initiatives;

- Those sex workers most marginalised by their work environment (e.g. street workers), as determined and influenced by legal constraints, are at greatest exposure to health risk;
- Sex workers working illegally are unlikely to disclose their occupation when accessing health care therefore a range of sexual health tests may not be conducted;
- Sex workers are more vulnerable to sexual assault and other violence when they work illegally as they perceive police do not take crimes against them seriously and clients are aware of the propensity for sex workers not to report crimes of violence to the police;
- Criminal laws operate against the development of organisational and industrial safe sex cultures as sex workers and establishments are reluctant to keep material on premises regarding safe sex practices and street workers my not carry condoms or lubricant for fear of seizure by police;
- Occupational health and safety standards can not be implemented in those sectors of the sex industry that remain illegal as they are unenforceable; and
- Increased occupational stress on sex workers due to the necessity to lead a double life to minimise stigmatisation.

In order to maximise occupational heath and safety in the sex industry all that is required is the development of guidelines or a legally enforceable code of practice. This approach has been adopted as the primary means of regulating many industries. The Scarlet Alliance (national forum for sex worker right organisations) has developed model guidelines for OH&S in the industry which covers some of the following issues: condom breakage and slippage, disinfection and cleansing techniques for premises and tools of the trade, safe sex practices, visible check of clients for signs of STIs, drug use policy, etc.

Legislation that requires adherence to inappropriate and coercive practices such as compulsory STI testing should be rejected. An educative approach to health practices is more effective. Further, laws that allow for the introduction of safe sex materials into evidence to secure penalties against sex workers mitigate against health practices in the sex industry and must be repealed as a matter of urgency.

Criminal Laws Undermine Occupational Health:

- Criminal or restrictive laws hinder the implementation of sexual health education and prevention strategies;
- Under criminalised frameworks health priorities are undermined by policing strategies that include seizing safe sex paraphernalia as evidence for prostitution related offences;
- Criminal frameworks force sex workers underground where they are less likely to disclose their occupation when presenting for sexual health testing, thus limiting the types of tests undertaken; and
- Sex industry and public health laws are directed at sex workers not the client rather than encouraging best practice occupational health standards in the sex industry.

CRIMINAL LAWS UNDERMINE OCCUPATIONAL SAFETY

Sex workers are more vulnerable to sexual assault and other violent crimes under criminalised frameworks as they are less likely to report crimes to police. That public health concerns be met through removing criminal sanctions, so that sex workers can confidentially access health services and promote safe sex practices as an industry standard. All states and territories have public health and criminal laws that cover unacceptable behaviour by all citizens in relation to public health concerns including communicable and sexually transmitted infections.

In relation to STIs, they include provisions on "knowingly transmitting an STI", notifying a sexual partner of an infection prior to sex, quarantining people and sanctions for recalcitrant behaviour. Since sex workers are more aware of sexual health and safe sex practices than the rest of the community they should not have special laws targeting them in relation to STIs. Generalist provisions within public health and criminal codes suffice to deal with offences whether committed in the private context or the professional realm of sex work. In addressing the perceived risk of the spread of STIs through sex work, some legislatures have responded by forcing sex workers to be "compulsorily" tested for STIs.

There are numerous inherent flaws in adopting this approach. For one, it has led to a mentality within the sex industry of brothel operators requiring sex workers to present sexual health clearance certificates. In some instances it has led to corruption, such that an operator will require a sex worker to see a doctor of the operator's choice and the results being handed directly to the operator rather than the worker without regard to privacy. Compulsory testing in itself is detrimental to health outcomes as it creates a false sense of security in clients and workers. Clients believe that a sex worker is free of STIs because she/he has been tested and are more likely to request sexual services without the use of prophylactics. Mandatory testing of sex workers does not assist sex workers in avoiding sexually transmitted infections, as a client's sexual health status is unknown.

In addition, test results are unreliable as the 'window period' for each infection varies and an individual's STI status cannot be assured even at the time of testing. For example, someone may have practiced unsafe sex and contracted an STI, go for testing the day after and they will be shown to be free of STIs because it may take a couple of weeks for a disease to produce symptoms for testing. Further, by promoting the use of compulsory testing as a legislative tool to allay community fears only perpetuates stereotypes of sex workers as diseased. This is reflected in high premiums for workers compensation and health insurance. The Insurance Council of Australia has justified their high premiums by relating that they view the sex industry as a high risk for HIV and violence (personal communication).

There are numerous other industries which have a greater impact on public health, yet legislators have not adopted the draconian measures applied to the sex industry. For example, the food industry (restaurants, take-away shops) are responsible for the death and intoxication of large numbers of people every year, yet food handling workers in restaurant kitchens are not required to be compulsorily tested for various communicable diseases (e.g. Hepatitis A and B). Likewise, neither health care workers nor their clients are required to be compulsorily tested for blood borne diseases yet needle stick injuries are an every day occurrence in health care settings and contraction of a blood borne disease occurs far more easily through direct needle contact than through a broken condom through sex.

The pornographic film industry does not have compulsory testing even though the actors in most films do not use prophylactics on a regular basis. Health concerns in relation to the sex industry should be contained within enforceable occupational health and safety codes or guidelines that include the compulsory use of prophylactics, the provision of safe sex tools by employers (include safe sex literature for clients and workers), policies on condom breakage, visual inspection of clients for STIs, etc. The sex industry has shown it is responsible by developing its own guidelines on OH&S (Scarlet Alliance) which should be adopted by parliaments in all jurisdictions. In addition, from time to time general population campaigns should be conducted in order to increase general sexual health knowledge of the community.

These could be done in much the same way as governments deal with smoking, breast cancer, skin cancer, drink driving, etc. Sex workers should not be prevented from working in the sex industry if they have an STI. Prohibition is premised on intercourse being part of every service, when sex workers offer many services which do not expose clients to STI contraction. During the period of treatment, sex workers can provide services that do not expose clients to risk, such as massage and masturbation, massage and oral sex, bondage and discipline and other fantasy scenarios not requiring penetrative sex. If the STI is contracted through work, STIs should be seen as industrial diseases and workers retrained to perform other work.

The IGCA in 1992 examined the public health implications of sex industry laws and concluded that laws criminalising the sex industry reduced the "effectiveness of measures designed to prevent the spread of STDS". The most successful means of achieving health outcomes for sex workers is peer-based education conducted through sex worker organisations. It is therefore imperative that state and territory governments recognise the expertise of peer-based approaches delivered through sex workers community organisations and adequately fund them to continue and expand their work.

This model, initiated in Australia is being replicated the world over with great success.

- Good public health outcomes are best supported through decriminalisation of the sex industry. General public health laws and criminal laws that deal with health issues are sufficient to cover personal or work behaviour;
- Criminal laws force sex workers underground where it is difficult for them to disclose occupational status for fear of discrimination. This may impede sex workers from obtaining a range of sexual health services;
- A public health focus must recognize clients as a sexual health risk to sex workers and support the promotion of safe sex practices as an industry standard rather than promote the myth that sex workers are vectors for the spread of sexually transmitted infections;
- Peer-based approaches to providing health and safety services to sex workers are the most successful means of providing safe sex knowledge which can be converted into safe sex practices; and
- All sexually active people should be educated to have periodical health screening for STIs, given the high levels of herpes, Chlamydia and warts in the general population.

No Mandatory Testing:

- Since sex workers are more aware of sexual care than others, sex industry laws should not contain requirements for mandatory sexual health testing and registration of sex workers;
- As sex workers provide a wide range of services, many which pose little or no risk of STI transmission sex

workers should not be excluded from working with an STI;

- Health related regulations are best served through the development of enforce- able occupational health and safety standards; and
- Occupational health and safety standards should include the compulsory use of prophylactics, provisions of safe sex tools by employers.

Differing local planning laws and zoning provisions apply in various Australian jurisdictions for private sex workers, street workers and brothels. This approach has mainly been adopted in jurisdictions controlling the industry under a legalised or decriminalised model with regulations. In some jurisdictions planning provisions are contained both within state laws and local council laws. In Victoria, to operate a brothel, operators and private workers (defined as one or two sex workers working together) need to register with the Prostitution Control Board (PCB) after they have received a planning permit from their local council.

The brothel must be in an industrial zone, at a distance greater than 100m from a residential area, greater than 200m from churches, schools, kindergartens or places that children frequent and if renting the premises written approval must be sought from the owner of the building. Private brothels can apply for license and license fee exemption. In NSW, different councils have different policies, but the majority have forced brothels (including private workers, as the law defines one person operations as brothels as well) into industrial areas, and in some cases commercial.

In the ACT, where there is no third tier of government, the Prostitution Act 1992 provides for the restriction of brothels to prescribed locations. Current prescribed areas are limited to industrial suburbs. Private sex workers (one worker working from a premise) can be located in residential, commercial or industrial areas as long as they are registered. In the case of private workers, both in the ACT and Victoria, privacy protections are in place so that personal and work details are not available to the general public whereas information relating to brothels is freely accessible. Whilst local councils in most states have legal jurisdiction over the location of brothels, state legislation may also specify brothel location.

This approach reflects the history of sex industry law reform in Australia with governments regulating the sex industry in a highly restrictive manner. This over-regulation is unnecessary as sex industry businesses should be treated in a similar manner to other commercial enterprises. In relation to the location of brothels and private workers, state legislation specific to the industry should either be more prescriptive or leave planning issues to local councils to apply general planning principles. The evidence so far indicates that many local councils have been unable to make consistent and fair decisions regarding applications for brothel locations.

The implications from arbitrary and inconsistent local authority guidelines and policy regarding brothel location has been that many sex industry businesses are unwilling to make applications for permits to legally locate fearing they will be rejected and to avoid closure must embark on expensive and lengthy appeal procedures. For example in NSW, since decriminalisation, the Land and Environment Court heard a total of 93 cases regarding Development Applications (DA's). Local council brought 53 cases to court, winning 40 of these cases - a 75% success rate. This rate must be understood in the context of local councils closing down existing brothels by restricting brothels to industrial zones or severely limiting location sites. In addition, brothel operators took 40 cases to court, winning 37 of these cases - a 92% success rate.

When sex industry businesses have a right under law to seek application and are denied on the basis of a moral objection to their existence the appeal process has generally upheld the law and granted application. Local authorities discretionary powers have favoured big business, contributed to sustaining an illegal brothel sector and do not treat sex industry businesses on an equal footing with other commercial enterprises. Further, they undermine the intention of sex industry legislation where that intention is to legalise sex industry businesses.

This is damaging to sex workers as they continue to work for businesses that are criminalised although a framework for legal operation exists. As a result, the appropriate health and safety guidelines adopted by specific councils cannot be enforced. Sex industry businesses should be subject to consistency and continuity in planning decisions. Sex industry businesses are a commercial enterprise and must integrate into local communities subject to the same regulations as other commercial enterprises. They should not be subject to special provisions that set them apart from other businesses but should be in accord with sensible urban design.

The onus should be upon local authorities to ensure that their urban design visions sensibly address issues that arise not seek to exclude or scapegoat sex industry businesses. Local authorities should not be able to disallow approval for brothel location on other than legitimate planning grounds as subsequent appeals are wasteful of resources. Local Councils must provide evidence that a business is not suitable for that locality based on pre-determined criteria that applies to all commercial enterprises.

Good urban design responds to the public and private domain. It should meet and support its users' needs, be accessible and identifiable to those requiring entry, and meet privacy and amenity requirements both within and without while minimising opportunities for crime. These outcomes should be achieved within a design which is visually and functionally appropriate to its setting. Additional amenity issues such as noise attenuation, traffic regulation, lighting etc. are more easily achieved within the context of good design. An issue of serious concern is where individual sex workers are considered private home businesses and are subject to local authority planning permission. In some local authority jurisdictions whilst individual sex workers are legally permitted under the Prostitution Laws Amendment Act 1992 to work from their own homes they must first seek local permission.

This requires that an individual sex worker place signage out the front of her/his premises advertising that s/he is seeking permission to operate a small business from home and the nature of that business. Such an approval process is potentially dangerous as it publicly identifies the location of a sole operator. It is also unlikely to be a successful means of achieving sensible planning outcomes as individual sex workers are unlikely to comply with such provisions. Zoning or the creation of 'red light' districts for both individual sex workers and brothels has been suggested as a means of 'controlling' the proliferation of sex industry businesses. The relegation of sex industry businesses or sex workers to red-light areas is likely to be in isolated industrial areas that place sex workers at risk.

- As they are generally unpopulated at night, little safety mechanisms exist. They are also unlikely to meet occupational health and safety standards in the sex industry businesses as the buildings and facilities are designed for industrial purposes.
- Under local planning laws sex industry businesses should be treated in a similar manner to other commercial enterprises. This means consistency and continuity in local authority planning decisions.
- Local partnerships which foster a collaborative approach, create opportunities to find mutually acceptable solutions. Local councils should be encouraged and supported to create working partnerships, which engage all the stakeholders, such as members of the sex industry, businesses, residents, health care providers and relevant community organisations in a joint effort to achieve regulation of the industry. Local initiatives need to be supported by strong leadership and clear guidance from state governments.
- Sex industry businesses should not be subject to special provisions that set them apart from other businesses.
- Local authorities' discretionary powers have favoured big business and contributed to sustaining an illegal brothel sector. This is damaging to sex workers as they continue to work for businesses that are criminalised even though a

framework for legal operation exists. Therefore, the appropriate health and safety guidelines adopted by specific councils cannot be enforced.

- Local authorities should not be able to disallow approval for brothel location on other than legitimate planning grounds as subsequent appeals are wasteful of resources.
- Local Councils must provide evidence that a business is not suitable for that locality based on pre-determined criteria that apply to all commercial enterprises;
- Individual sex workers should not subject to local planning laws, and in particular should not be subject to the same laws as large brothels.

Zoning

The creation of 'red-light' areas or zones is not acceptable as it segregates the sex industry into poorly lit, under-resourced and unsafe work areas. One of the greatest myths in politics is that if parliamentarians support sex industry law reform, they will incur voter backlash. There are pockets of voters who through an allegiance to a particular moral agenda will always oppose support for a well-regulated, decriminalised sex industry. Nonetheless, they have not man- aged to influence the outcomes of elections over this issue.

Evidence indicates that voters choose their voting preference on such major issues as the economy, health and education. In order to oppose reforms, politicians from all sides of politics have invoked community moral standards and panic mode polemics such as: "we'll have brothels popping up on every street corner," "What about the children?" etc. However, on the basis of empirical evidence available in Australia, these attitudes are out of step with the community. It has been shown that the community generally supports sex industry reforms and is more realistic about the consequences of attempting to suppress its operation.

Two recent pieces of empirical research have been conducted in Australia to gauge community attitudes to sex industry law reform and are worth reporting. Both studies were conducted in Queensland and employed similar methodology to test for validity over-time and ensure that sample sizes were large enough to provide a reliable indicator of community attitudes. The first was conducted by the Criminal Justice Commission (1991) and the second by Police and Corrective Services (1998).

The sample size for the first report was 1833 and for the 1998 report 2361. The results of both surveys were similar and the following findings from the 1998 report are reported below:

- 59.4% of Queenslanders' agreed or strongly agreed that there is nothing wrong with a person paying for sex;
- 61.9% believed that a sex worker should be allowed to provide services from his or her home;
- 63.5% believed that two or more sex workers should be allowed to work from premises in a non-residential area, including 71.7% of 35-44 year olds;
- The main restrictions that should apply if brothels were allowed to operate related to "restricting the places at which brothels can operate (92.0%), keeping a register of sex workers (89.0%) and restricting the type of people who can own/or operate brothels (88.8%)";
- Only 21.0% of people believed that there were no benefits from allowing brothels to operate. The main reasons given for allowing sex work to operate was that it benefits both sex workers and the community by "providing a healthier work environment".
- The concerns expressed by respondents to allowing brothels to operate related to "The location of brothels", "Spread of STD/AIDS" and Health of prostitutes".

The only sector of the sex industry that the community expressed any significant opposition to was street work with 93.2% of respondents believing that soliciting in a public place should remain an offence. It appears that community attitudes have not changed over-time between the 1991 sample and 1997 sample although the reasons that respondents support sex industry law reform may have changed. Primarily this is because the first survey was conducted in 1990 following a

Commission of Inquiry (1989) had identified widespread police corruption and claims of organised crime in the sex industry.

The second survey was conducted following the murder of a number of sex workers and may have influenced respondents understanding of occupational safety issues at the time. The random telephone sampling method adopted for the survey of community attitudes highlights a high level of support for sex industry reforms. This type of methodology relies upon community perceptions as no educative information is provided to influence the outcome of the survey. It is likely that community support for sex industry law reform would be even higher if the community were educated about the benefits of reform and issues relating to the location of brothels, health and street work.

These results are even more significant when it is considered that sampling was undertaken in a State that is renowned for conservative community attitudes. Interpretation of both pieces of research together suggest that the community supports law reform not only because they fear the consequences (police corruption, organised crime) of continuing to suppress sex work in Queensland but because they also believe that sex work can not be suppressed and should not be subject to criminal laws as such an approach does not benefit the community. Further, increasing support for legalising the sex industry over time is seen in a number of surveys from 1960 to the present.

For example in 1960, in a national newspaper poll of 1,045 people, 45% supported legalising the sex industry. In 1985, in a poll conducted by the Sydney Morning Herald of 2,027 people, 75% agreed with legalising the sex industry. The current levels of community support reported in the Queensland studies are consistently reflected in other states. This increase in support over time can be explained by the formation of sex worker rights organisations who have promoted a number of issues in the public arena, the media has increased the coverage and range of issues covered in relation to the sex industry, the advent of HIV placed greater focus on the industry, and more sex workers are "out".

All these issues have had the effect of educating the community on sex industry issues, and they have responded by showing a greater acceptance of sex work as a work option.

- Government fears regarding potential voter backlash if they support sex industry reforms are unfounded;
- Research demonstrates that most members of the community do not support criminalisation of the sex industry;
- Research demonstrates that most members of the community support brothels, escort and private sex workers;
- Research demonstrates that the community is more concerned that an illegal sex industry sets the conditions for the emergence of police corruption, organised crime and poor occupational health and safety standards; and
- Support education programs to change social attitudes which stigmatise and discriminate against sex workers.

Discrimination harms sex workers in both their professional and personal lives. Professionally this discrimination is apparent in the restrictions on how sex workers may operate and include:

- Restricting sectors of the sex industry in which sex workers can legally obtain employment;
- Lack of occupational health and safety standards;
- Preventing sex workers access to health services;
- An absence of workplace benefits and conditions (e.g. Work Cover, leave entitlements, superannuation, workplace fines for breaching rules);
- Employment on a contract rather than employee status;
- Special local council provisions to approve location of sex industry businesses, including private sex workers;
- Preventing sex workers' access to small business opportunities required to establish successful businesses;
- Mandatory health checks for sexually transmitted infections (STI) as a requirement of employment;
- Discrimination on the basis of health status;

- Fear of public identification or retribution limiting sex workers access to legal remedies to address unfair work practices;
- Police harassment and corruption;
- Restrictive advertising practices (e.g. Pre-payment of advertising, designated area of the paper in which permitted to advertise, the design, size and wording determined by the publisher, higher cost of advertising);
- Difficulties in obtaining goods and services to operate a sex industry business (e.g. higher rent/lease agreements, income protection and business insurance coverage, credit card and other banking facilities such as loans and other credit arrangements); and
- Stigmatisation of the profession.

Personal discrimination may affect sex workers by:

- Limiting sex workers access to legal remedies to address crimes of violence due to a perception that crimes against sex workers are not taken seriously by the police;
- Preventing access to justice and legal remedies to address crimes of violence in a work setting;
- Work affecting personal relationships because friends/ families/partners fear criminal prosecution or police attention for associating with sex workers;
- Exposing friends/family/partners to the risk of prosecution for sex industry offences such as "living off the earnings of prostitution";
- Silencing sex workers from disclosing previous or current work in the sex industry for fear of discrimination when seeking alternative employment, membership of organisations or undertaking study or travel;
- Restricting the purchase of goods or services for personal use (e.g. Home and contents insurance, private health care insurance, personal loans and other consumer items; and
- Limiting sex workers participation in community activities.

The right to freely choose employment is a fundamental human right. The right to work in the sex industry free from discrimination is articulated in a number of International Covenants to which Australia is signatory. The Universal Declaration of Human Rights states that: Everyone has the right to work, to free choice of employment, to just and favourable conditions of work and to protection against unemployment *(UDHR)*. State and Territory sex industry laws consistently infringe this right. Although Australia is bound to honour the UDHR it has largely failed to grant freedom from discrimination to sex workers on the basis of employment.

To varying degrees, existing State and Territory laws regulating the sex industry in Australia fail to provide sex workers with equal treatment and protection under the law. This discrimination is apparent in laws which restrict where and under what conditions sex workers can work in the sex industry, and may prohibit their financial support of partners/families/friends. It acts against implementation of occupational health and safety standards; may perpetuate discrimination on the basis of sex workers' assumed health status through mandatory testing provisions and registration; and limits sex workers confidentially utilising legal remedies to address crimes of violence and to freely travel.

Discrimination:

- Discrimination limits occupational health and safety standards in the sex industry;
- Sex workers are discriminated against in the workplace due to an absence of workplace benefits and conditions such as Work Cover, leave entitlements, superannuation and the imposition by employers of workplace fines for breaching industrially unacceptable workplace rules;
- Discrimination means that sex workers may fear public identification which limits their access to legal remedies to address unfair work practices;
- Discrimination prevents sex workers from using legal remedies to address crimes of violence in a work setting and in their personal lives
- Discrimination means sex workers may be subject to police harassment and corruption; and

- Discrimination perpetuates the stigmatisation of the profession by perpetuating myths about sex workers.
- Criminalisation of the sex industry is a human rights issue;
- Laws criminalizing the sex industry contravene Australia's international obligation as signatory to conventions that enshrine a person's right to free choice in employment.
- The Federal Government should include "occupation/ profession/trade or calling" as an area of discrimination within its human rights laws. This would not only apply to sex workers but to anybody who suffers occupational discrimination.
- State and Territory Governments should amend their Anti-Discrimination laws to cover discrimination on the grounds of occupation.
- National community education campaigns should be conducted to counter discriminatory practices against sex workers.

The term 'sex slavery' (a term often used interchanged with 'trafficking in women') has globally become synonymous with images of generally young women from non-English speaking backgrounds who are kidnapped and trapped into working in the sex industry in developed countries. Unfortunately in Australia the term is increasingly being used to refer to all foreign sex workers who come to Australia to work (whether through force or not). Australian legislation introduced into the Federal Parliament in 1999 enshrines the notion that 'sex slavery' is purely a problem connected to the sex industry, as other manifestations of it (e.g. in forced/arranged marriages, mail order bride system, etc.) are not covered.

It is difficult to estimate precisely the prevalence of 'sexual slavery' due to its covert nature and illegal status. However, former Minister for Justice, Amanda Vanstone's Information Paper on the 'sexual slavery' issue reports that the Department of Immigration and Multicultural Affairs (DIMA) deported 54 people in 1996-97 for working illegally in the sex industry and for the seven months to end- January 1998, DIMA deported 67 persons for illegally working in brothels (Justice Department, 1998: 4).

Not all of these women were necessarily being employed in slave-like conditions. Additionally, many more foreigners are caught illegally working in non-sex industry related employment in Australia. For example, in 1998, 400 foreigners were found to be working illegally in Australia, of these only 14 were found to be working in brothels. Yet the sex industry is singled out for special legislation that does not acknowledge that sex work is work rather than general legislation concerned with 'labour exploitation' applicable to any industry. It appears that if a person's work includes sex, it is not defined as work but rather as a sexual practice related to non-consensual 'sexual slavery'. Arguably, the danger comes from the label 'illegal migrant worker' rather than the nature of the work to be performed.

All illegal migrant workers are potentially subject to exploitation in a variety of contexts that are non-sexual. The important distinction to make in relation to 'sexual slavery' is whether sex workers coming to Australia do so willingly or through trickery or force. Anecdotal evidence from sex worker organisations indicates that most overseas sex workers who come to work in the Australian sex industry are sex workers in their country of origin and know that this is the type of work they will do. There are cases of trickery, deceit and force but they are minimal and both situations require different approaches.

A more sensible approach is to repeal the current definition of sexual slavery and broaden the generalist definition of slavery/servitude in the Criminal Code 1999 (Commonwealth) to include all contexts under which people are recruited, transported and transferred, harboured or received by others, by means of the threat or use of force or other forms of coercion, abduction, fraud, deception, abuse of power or a position of vulnerability or the giving or receiving of payments or benefits to achieve the consent of a person having control over another person, for the purpose of exploitation.

Exploitation at a minimum should include sexual exploitation (wherever it occurs), forced labour or services, slavery or practices similar to slavery, servitude or the removal of organs. This type of definition is broad enough to cover all areas for which people are moved across borders including labour, forced marriages and the large growth area of immigrant smuggling into Australia. Legislation covering these areas rather than singling out the sex industry would comply with Australia's obligations under the recently negotiated Protocol to Prevent, Suppress and Punish Trafficking in Persons, Especially Women and Children, supplementing the United Nations Convention Against Transnational Organised Crime, which Australia is likely to soon ratify. Outreach projects at the Sex Workers Outreach Project in New South Wales and Self-health for Queensland Workers in the Sex Industry have identified that illegal foreign sex workers are difficult to access for a range of reasons.

The specific barriers are:

- Fear of deportation due to the worker's status under Australian migration law;
- NESB sex workers often support family members in their home country and can experience severe financial difficulties if prevented from working;

  Limited language, both oral and written, may hinder effective use of services in Australia;
- Discrimination and stigmatisation of Asian sex workers in Australia, and within their communities, affect access to health services;
- There is an unwillingness to utilises agencies, both community and government, for assistance due to distrust and fear;
- NESB sex workers may be 'protected' by management of sex industry businesses who may not want them to acquire information bout their legal rights.

It is imperative that foreign sex workers are able to confidentially access health and other services. This is unlikely when foreign sex workers fear deportation due to legal or entry status and are regarded as 'trafficked' into the sex industry. A decriminalised sex industry, which allows foreign sex workers to work in the Australian sex industry under an employer sponsored scheme would allow health and other service providers to make contact with sex workers from non-English speaking backgrounds and inform them of health services and their legal rights.

- The incidence of 'sexual slavery' is likely to be highly exaggerated in Australia;
- 'Sexual slavery' legislation is not required as many of the manifestations of it are covered by existing criminal laws, e.g. fraud, blackmail, kidnap, rape and other offences against the person.
- A distinction is required between human rights abuses arising from being forced to work in the sex industry (or any other industry) and seeing foreign sex workers as forced per se.
- Foreign sex workers chose to work in the sex industry;
- Decriminalise the sex industry so that it does not operate underground;
- It is their illegal status as migrants that make overseas sex workers vulnerable to exploitation rather than the work that they do.

Solutions

The Federal Government should adopt a quota system in extending the employer-sponsored scheme to overseas sex workers willing to work in Australia. Additionally a code of practice for the industry could be developed to cover this type of activity. This would enable overseas sex workers to work legally and enjoy the same conditions as local sex workers. The Federal Government should repeal its sexual servitude amendment to the Criminal Code and instead enact legislation that covers all forms of recruitment, transportation and transfer, harbouring or receipt of persons, by means of the threat or use of force or other forms of coercion, of abduction, of fraud, of deception, of the abuse of power or of a position of vulnerability or of the giving or receiving of payments or benefits to achieve the consent of a person having control over another person, for the purpose of exploitation. Exploitation at a mini- mum should include sexual exploitation (wherever it occurs), forced labour or services, slavery or practices similar to slavery, servitude or the removal of organs. Human rights standards of treatment should be incorporated into the Criminal Code 1999 (Commonwealth) to protect any person who has been the victim of any of the practices described above.

These should include: protection of the privacy and identity of the victim, information on any relevant court and administrative proceedings, assistance to enable the views of the victim to be presented and considered at appropriate stages for any criminal proceedings against offenders, in appropriate cases and to the extent possible provide for the physical and psychological recovery of victims, appropriate housing, counselling and information in a language that the victim understands, medical, psychological and economic assistance, employment, education and training opportunities, provide for the physical safety of victims; provide for measures which offer victims the possibility of obtaining compensation for damage suffered, temporary or permanent residency in appropriate cases, facilitate the return of the person to their county of origin if it is safe for them to return.

The often-underground nature of the sex industry combined with a lack of re- search that accurately reflects the realities of sex work has assisted in sustaining a variety of myths about the sex industry. The most enduring of these myths are the prevalence of drugs, pimps, coercion and minors in the sex industry. The perpetuation of these myths is damaging to sex workers as they are often used as the justification for criminal laws or unnecessary restrictions upon sex industry operations.

Drugs

One of the many myths that exist is that the majority of sex workers are intravenous drug users and that this is the reason for working or that the stress of work is so great that workers are driven into taking drugs in order to cope with the work. In Australia, large-scale studies have estimated that less than 2% of the general populations are intravenous drug users (IDUs). Several studies of sex workers, using samples selected by different methods, have estimates of sex workers using intravenous drugs ranging between 10-15%.

These figures need to be taken with caution and understood in context. Research suggests that illicit drug use amongst street workers is higher than among workers in other sectors of the sex industry. However, the small amount of research that has been conducted with the sex industry as a whole indicates that sex workers' use of certain drugs, such as alcohol and amphetamines, may actually be lower than the general community whilst smoking is significantly higher. Further, the higher incidence of heroin use noted amongst street workers may be related to sample selection, since brothel workers are less likely to disclose drug use since penalties may result from disclosure, given the anti-drug practices of many brothel managements.

Research that examines sex workers reasons for choosing to work in the sex industry rarely refers to a need to support a drug habit. Instead, lifestyle factors, freedom, flexibility, good money and a need for money are identified as the primary factors. Most people make decisions about how to generate an income based on a range of factors. These factors may include the ability to maximise income, flexibility of hours and other lifestyle choices.

For some IDUs the benefits of working in the sex industry suit individual lifestyle choices and provide a higher than average income. It must be acknowledged that the majority of sex workers do not use illicit drugs and that in the majority of sex industry businesses drug use is actively discouraged and banned from the workplace. Health issues relating to illicit drug use are only compounded by criminal laws surrounding the sex industry and use of illicit drugs.

Pimps

Pimps - a person who forces a person to work and takes their earnings - are not a feature of the Australian sex industry. Pimps have been dramatised in movies, books and documentaries as their existence serves to reinforce notions of sex workers as controlled, intimidated and victims. Whilst overseas research suggests that pimps are a common feature of the street sector in many countries it must be questioned to what extent this is a reality for the majority of sex workers. In the Australian context, the belief that pimps control sex workers has allowed for laws to be introduced and maintained that infringe upon sex workers' personal lives. Laws relating to "living off the earnings" have been argued as necessary to get at "pimps" but in reality are usually directed against partners and friends of sex workers. Sex workers, like any other Australian worker, have a right to spend their money how they choose. It is not acceptable to control sex workers' associations and spending. Existing non-specific criminal penalties are adequate to address crimes relating to stand-over tactics and other forms of coercion.

The use of these legal remedies is hindered by criminal laws that prevent sex workers from reporting crimes due to the fear of retribution for working illegally. The notion of a "pimp" also enshrines the stereotype of a sex worker who needs to be controlled to do sex work otherwise they would not choose to work in the sex industry. This plays into paternalistic notions of women being in moral danger and needing the protection of the law. Some street, escort and private workers employ a male for security reasons, just as any other worker in a similar situation might. Sex workers need to be viewed as adults who can make decisions for themselves and allowed to be entrepreneurial in their work practices.

Minors

The sex industry is often characterised by images of youth. However, the reality is that in some cases sex workers continue to work in the sex industry until their late 50s. Australian research indicates that most female sex workers start working in the sex industry in their late teens or early 20s. Only a very small minority of sex workers starts work before the age of 15. Legislation directed at the protection of minors in the sex industry is unnecessary and merely perpetuates the myth that many underage workers work in the sex industry. Existing legislation relating to the employment of children and sexual exploitation is adequate to halt underage workers in the sex industry.

Addressing issues such as youth unemployment, housing, family circumstances and education is more likely to assist young people who seek employment in the sex industry out of necessity rather than choice. Unfortunately the response to the visibility of itinerant underage sex workers selling sex on the streets has resulted in responses that involve law enforcement mechanisms as a means of stopping the practice. This approach results in a failure to examine the wider contexts that lead young people to become homeless, particularly the impact of family circumstances on these adolescents. Rather than perpetuating myths about the widespread involvement of young people in the sex industry consideration should be given to the issue of the age at which people are able to work in the sex industry.

A nationally consistent age of lawful entry to work in the sex industry is required. In the international arena there has been an overt focus on the 'commercial exploitation of children'. In spite of international commitment to the eradication of all practices associated with the sexual exploitation of and sale and traffic in children, there is little comprehensive data on the extent, mechanisms or root causes. Research has thus far been largely exploratory, to a great extent generated from secondary sources, most frequently from journalists and non-government organisations.

There is an urgent need for more systematic and global knowledge of the nature and incidence of the problem. This includes developing an understanding of the cultural, social and economic contexts in which it arises and flourishes and the development of typologies and categories that can be of use not only in developing appropriate conceptual frameworks and methods of research but also in guiding policy formulation and programme development by national and international bodies. The stereotypes relating to underage sex workers, pimps and drug use have been used to justify further criminalisation or regulation of the industry. Often these issues are focused upon at the expense of occupational health and safety.

- Sex workers' reasons for working in the sex industry rarely relate to a need to support a drug habit;

- Research shows that sex workers' use of certain drugs is lower than the level of use in the general community;
- Pimps are not a feature of the Australian sex industry. It is not acceptable to control sex workers' associations and spending by enacting laws relating to "living off the earnings of prostitution";
- Legislation directed at the protection of minors in the sex industry is unnecessary as adequate, non-sex industry specific laws already exist to address the sexual exploitation of minors;
- In relation to minors working in the sex industry, wider focus needs to be placed on preventative measures, such as support for "at risk" families, support for young, homeless children, and work options for children;
- Government's (federal, state and territory) should implement the recommendations of the National Action Plan on the Commercial Exploitation of Children.

POLITICAL AND BUREAUCRATIC SKILLS UNDERSTANDING THE POLITICAL SYSTEM

Involvement and liaison with the relevant arms of political power - including the parliament, its committee structures and the bureaucracy - are essential to influencing policy, decision making and legislative changes so that they reflect sex worker needs. The media can also play a role in influencing and reflecting public opinion on sex worker issues and is therefore essential to engage with. It is useful to understand how these structures are established, the interactions between them and the role that sex worker organisations and their advocates can have in influencing decisions. Following is a brief introduction to parliamentary structures and how laws are made.

The Parliamentary structure in Australia is based on the English Westminster system of government called "Responsible Government". It comprises the "Executive" (the Parliament), the "Legislature" which is vested with powers to carry out laws and enforce them (it is independent from the Parliament - generally government departments or independent statutory bodies) and the "Judiciary" (the courts), which has the power to apply and interpret laws.

The Parliaments

All the parliaments in Australia are made up of two houses (bicameral), except for Queensland, The Northern Territory and the ACT which only have a Legislative Assembly (unicameral). The state bicameral houses are made up of the Legislative Council (House of Review, or upper house) and a House of Assembly or Legislative Assembly (lower house), from which the government is formed. Federally, the House of Representatives, from which government is formed is equivalent to a state House of Assembly and the Senate is equivalent to Legislative Councils.

The period between elections varies from three to four years and apart from the ACT which has set terms of parliament, other parliaments vest the power of deciding for a date for an election on the government. As a result of this, elections are called on the date most likely to favour the incumbent (government in power) as indicated by polling. Bills (proposed law) can be initiated in either house but must be sanctioned or approved by the other house. Australia operates under a Cabinet system of government. It is the key decision-making body of the government and comprises senior Government Ministers. Since Cabinet Ministers have more power than an ordinary sitting Member, they are worth targeting as key people to lobby on your particular issue.

Division of Powers between the Commonwealth and the States

Upon federation, state parliaments retained all legislative powers not conferred exclusively on the federal parliament. Those powers that are exclusive to the federal parliament include defence, postal and telephone services, marriage, currency, customs, trade and immigration. States make laws on such things as police, roads, education, health and social welfare. State parliaments can legislate on shared powers, but where there is a conflict, federal law prevails. In relation to laws relating to sex work, they come within state/territory jurisdiction, which is why they vary widely.

Generally a bill is introduced by a Minister or private member. Accompanying each bill is an explanatory memorandum. This is a separate document explaining the reasons for the bill, and giving a general outline of its contents and notes explaining the intention of each clause. At this stage it is only read by the Clerk and is not open to debate. During the second reading, the Minister or member who has proposed the bill elaborates on its principles and opens debate on its provisions, at which point the first amendments are made. The house then moves into "committee" stage or detail stage to consider the bill clause by clause and make further amendments.

This is the most crucial stage of the bill and a valuable time to put extra energy into last minute lobbying if you haven't had any success in getting your points adopted. Bills become "Acts" when passed by both houses and assented to by the Governor-General. The Daily Bills List shows bills currently before the Parliament and the stage reached by each bill.

The text of all current Acts as well as related legislative material can be found on the Internet at parliamentary web sites. The federal parliament web site has links to every parliament in Australia and from there you can find the relevant state/ territory legislation. Australia operates under a Cabinet system of government. It is the key decision- making body of the government and comprises senior Government Ministers, so these Members are particularly important to target as they carry more sway than an ordinary member of the government (e.g. a backbencher).

Parliamentary Committees

A parliamentary committee consists of a group of Members of the House of Assembly (MHA) or Members of the Legislative Assembly (MLA) or both in the case of joint committees. They are appointed by one or both Houses of Parliament. The purpose of parliamentary committees is to perform a range of functions such as carrying out inquiries, hearing witnesses, sifting evidence, discussing matters in detail and scrutinising bills. They also check administrative details relevant to government operations such as the expenditure of public money and public service accountability in relation to the carriage of administrative duties.

Committees provide a public forum for the presentation of the various views of individual citizens and interest groups, such as sex worker organisations. Parliamentarians can use the Committee system as a stalling mechanism, particularly when they do not want to take a position on a controversial matter. It is interesting to note that prior to any sex industry legislation being introduced into any parliament in Australia they all conducted parliamentary committee inquiries into the issue. In the case of Tasmania, it was Scarlet Alliance lobbying efforts that led to a referral to a parliamentary standing committee to examine the issue of sex work law reform.

This was a stalling tactic on our part. At the time it looked like the Attorney General (AG) would introduce legislation based on the Victorian model. We suggested that adopting the Victorian model was not appropriate for Tasmania and recommended the establishment of a parliamentary committee to examine particular local issues. Our aim was to influence the outcome and recommendations of the committee by ensuring our supporters submitted comments. There are various types of committees, including Standing Committees (appointed for the life of a Parliament that are usually re-established in successive Parliaments as they have a continuing role), Select Committees (appointed as the need arises, for a specific purpose, with a limited life), Joint Committees (whose membership is drawn from and reports to both houses).

Membership to committees is derived from the Members of parliament, excluding Ministers. Committee membership normally comprises Members from the various parties or independent Members in proportion to the numerical strength of each group in the House. Committee proceedings are 'proceedings in Parliament', and therefore 'privileged'. Members and others participating, such as expert witnesses, are protected from being sued or prosecuted for anything they may say during such proceedings.

Written evidence received by a committee is similarly protected. After examining the evidence, a report is prepared setting out the committee's conclusions and making recommendations. This report is presented to the House, or to both Houses in the case of a joint committee and government's given a specified period of time to prepare a response. On occasion some members of a committee do not agree to all recommendations in the report and they may add a minority or dissenting report.

Lodging a Submission

Any member of the public has the right to lodge a submission with a committee on the subject of an inquiry. A submission should state the name and address of its author and, if relevant, of the organisation the person represents. A committee's terms of reference are usually advertised at the start of each inquiry. Once a committee has formally received a submission, it becomes the property of the committee and may not be published or disclosed elsewhere without the committee's authorisation.

Any uncertainties in this area should be clarified with the committee secretary. Some committees also hold public hearings. The media may be present so if you are concerned about this you should enquire whether the hearing is privileged and therefore cannot be reported on by the media. Further, you can request a private hearing ('in camera') and for documents submitted to be regarded as confidential. Such requests are usually, but not necessarily, granted.

Question Time

The accountability of the Government is demonstrated most clearly and publicly at question time when questions without notice are put to Ministers. The media in particular pay close attention to this part of the Parliamentary process as the Opposition general use this time attempting to embarrass the government. Question time allows Government members to promote particular policies or programmes. These 'planted' questions are known as 'Dorothy Dixers'. Questions on notice are questions delivered in writing to the Clerk to be placed on the Notice Paper. In this case neither the question nor answer is read to the House but are printed in Hansard.

In addition copies are supplied to the press. There is no time limit by which questions must be answered, but many Parliaments have adopted a procedure where if a reply has not been received after 60 days, the Member concerned can rise in the House and ask the Speaker to write to the Minister involved, seeking reasons for the delay. Question time is an important avenue for sex worker organisation's to use by contacting a member and asking them to put a question. The following example illustrates how successful this procedure can be.

When the ACT Sex Industry Advisory Group was established, the inclusion of a sex worker representative was overlooked. A MLA was contacted to ask a question (i.e. how can you have an advisory group on the industry that excludes the most important player!). Since it was a question on notice (that is, the Minister knew the question was going to be asked), the response was that just that day an invitation letter had been sent to Workers in Sex Employment in the ACT (WISE) for representation on that group.

Petitions

These allow any individual or group of individuals to place grievances directly before the House of Representatives or Houses of Assembly. It is the only direct means of communication between the people and the Parliament. It is basically a request for action. Petitions may ask the House to introduce legislation, to repeal or change existing legislation, to take action for a certain purpose or for the benefit of particular persons.

For example, a sex worker organisation may organise a petition that requests that the Parliament repeal laws against street work given the high level of violence that street workers are subjected to. Certain rules apply to drawing up a petition and the correct format is found on most Parliamentary web sites. It has to be addressed to the Speaker and Members of the House of Representatives (federal) or House of Assembly (state) assembled in Parliament. It must state the facts that the petitioners want to bring to the attention of the Members, conclude with a request for action, and include the signatures and names and addresses of petitioners.

No letters, affidavits or other documents may be attached to a petition. Although a petition only requires one signature to be accepted, it appears more representative of public feeling if signed by as many people as possible. A petition must be presented to the House by a Member of the House. This can be any Member, including a Minister, and does not have to be the petitioners' local Member. Every petition presented is referred by the Clerk to the Minister responsible for the matter which is the subject of the petition.

THE MEDIA

The media play an important role in educating the community on particular issues and in shaping their views. In addition, politicians pay close attention to polls published and views expressed in the "Letters to the Editor". In relation to the sex industry most elements of the media have tended to focus on the negative and visually extreme ends of the industry. Of course, the titillation factor is over depicted, but this is something we can turn around and use to our advantage. Dealing with the various sectors of the media is a skill that is only acquired through practice. It is also worthwhile to nurture relationships with journalists who give you a fair story. Instead of just putting a press release out that targets all media you might contact that particular journalist and provide them exclusive stories. A word of warning - many journalists/ interviewers want to catch you out and others have a particular ideological position and keep on repeating the same question until you answer in the way that satisfies their angle.

A way of over- coming this is to ask the journalist the types of questions they are going to ask before the interview. You can then think about your answers. It is good practice to speak in concise short sentences, as these are easier to edit and therefore are more likely to be used. If you want to make a particular point, repeat the point regardless of the question asked. The journalist has no alternative but to use it (politicians are particularly good at this!). If you make a mistake and wish to withdraw your statement but are concerned it will be edited and run then interrupt the statement half way through so that it is difficult to edit. The best way to ensure that you are not misrepresented through editing is to conduct live to air interviews (this applies to radio and sometimes current affairs programs).

Depending on the issue you want covered you may decide to target a particular sector of the media. If you want an in-depth examination of a particular issue you can contact magazine editors, discuss the angle for a feature article in the weekend papers with the features editor, or the producer of a current affairs program. The best contact resource is, Margaret Gee's Australian Media Guide. This resource is updated every four months and published by Information Australia- Margaret Gee Media. It contains contacts for newspapers, magazines, radio and television in national, metropolitan, regional, country and suburban newspapers, as well as overseas press and media regulatory bodies. It contains the names contact details for chiefs of staff, specialised writers, television news chiefs of staff, etc. It is an expensive resource but some larger community organisations and libraries subscribe.

Press Releases

A media/press release is a short statement provided to the press to attract attention on a particular issue. The measure of success in relation to a release is the media does not contact you but merely reports the release (this of course is very rare!). Press releases can be proactive or reactive. For example, you may run a campaign which focuses on dispelling myths about street workers. A press release may link the laws to an increase in violence against sex workers and as an organisation or group of sex workers call on the Government/Parliament to reform it laws to diminish violence. Alternatively, reacting to inaccuracies reported about the sex industry may be the subject of a press release. The title/header for the press release is very important (the more titillating the better!) as it attracts press attention and encourages them to read the release. Common headers include: "Sex workers Outraged at Government Action on Laws"; "Sex workers Call Government to Action on Laws"; "Sex workers Demand ...".

Timing is essential to the story being run, so check what other stories/issues are in the media and decide whether to delay putting out the release. Making connections to other current media reports may assist in getting the story run. For example, during the Olympics connect industry issues to this, or when taxation is featured in the media connect your story to that. Monday is the busiest media day so it is more difficult to get your story picked up due to the competition with other news stories. Friday is often the quietest day and the media are seeking stories to cover over the weekend. It is easier to get your story covered if you release your statement on a Friday morning. It is general practice to release your press statement in the afternoon or late evening of the day prior to the story being run. Alternatively very early in the morning of the day you want the story to run. You can also embargo the release for a certain period. A release provided on Monday for Tuesday coverage should state: "embargoed until Tues 12th Nov, 2pm EST".

Most Parliaments have press galleries that contain press boxes that are regularly checked. You can place your press releases in parliamentary press releases. The easiest way to distribute a press release is via fax or email to the chief-of-staff of a newspaper, radio or television. If the story has a specific perspective, such as industrial relations or law, you should also send it to the industrial or legal reporter of the newspaper. The ABC has specialist programs such as the Law Report and The Health Report that are worthwhile to send relevant press releases. Fax and email addresses are located in the Media Guide or on web sites of particular media source.

If you are unsure of where to send the release, ring the newspaper, television or radio station and ask for appropriate referral and contact details. The Australian Federation of AIDS Organisations (AFAO) employs a media officer who can assist in sending press releases to all media sources. It is worthwhile contacting the media officer and asking for assistance in distribution. Likewise, the Scarlet Alliance has a database of media contacts for distribution.

Media/Press Alerts

Media or press alerts are usually one-page press releases that put the media on notice in relation to an upcoming event. They are generally short and do not provide much detail so the story cannot be written from the alert. In relation to the sex industry, some of the events which you may want to write a media alert for include launches of reports/resources (e.g. Occupational health and safety guidelines), fund raising events (e.g. raffles, hookers balls), community education events (e.g. World AIDS Day), etc.

The detail required is the date, venue and time of the event and the person launching/presenting the event (as this can create further interest in getting the press to attend the event) and the aim of the event (e.g. fundraising for the industry, or to educate sex workers about a particular issue, etc.). Generally, a media alert is released three to five days before the event. The day prior to or the morning of the event consider providing a comprehensive press release. Consider ringing the media to enquire whether they received your press releases. This provides an opportunity to sell the event or story, provide more information, personally invite the media to attend and therefore strengthens the likelihood of the media turning up.

FEMINIST APPROACHES

Feminists are sometimes represented as a bunch of man hating dowsers who simply make life difficult for men and for those who earn their living in the sex industry. However, I think the real situation is somewhat more complicated than this. Rebecca West had this to say about the label 'feminist': I myself have never been able to find out precisely what feminism is. I only know that people call me a feminist whenever I express sentiments that differentiate me from a doormat.

By this definition most sex workers would have to be called feminists! And, over the last ten years, more than a few sex workers have publicly proclaimed their adherence to a feminist politics. It is probably the case then, that the labels 'feminist' and 'sex worker' are not mutually exclusive. Certainly feminists ?like many other women in the community ?have worked and do work in the sex industry. To varying degrees, however, most feminists disapprove of the pornography and prostitution industries, at least as they are presently organised. But this is a view that would be shared by a large percentage of the Australian population as well as a large proportion of sex workers.

Feminists also disapprove of rape and domestic violence, child sexual abuse, sex discrimination, the lack of value assigned to most women's work (including housework) and the damage being done to the ozone layer by pollution. Of course, these are things that many ordinary people, including sex workers and Christian fundamentalists, would also disapprove of. So what features are characteristic of feminist approaches to the sex industry and, perhaps more importantly, of what practical use are feminist analyses? In this chapter attention will be directed primarily at the prostitution trade rather than at prostitution and pornography. This is not because the pornography trade is a less important aspect of the sex industry or less significant in terms of a feminist approach. It is because the author's geographical location is in Queensland where the processes of law reform are presently being directed at the prostitution industry.

This chapter will also focus on Australian feminism which, since the mid-1970s, has developed a rather unique and practical engagement with sex industry issues. Thus, Australian feminist approaches to the sex industry have, to a significant degree, been different from the approaches adopted by feminists in other countries. This is partly the effect of a specifically Australian history and political culture. This chapter will begin with a historical perspective and show how feminists have engaged with some sex industry issues in the recent past. From this analysis some of the main features of feminist approaches to the sex industry will be drawn out and some practical uses for these suggested.

The prostitution industry arrived in Australia with the First Fleet. Many of Australia's 'founding mothers' ?the convict women who were transported to the colony of New South

Wales between 1788 and 1840 ?were probably working prostitutes in the home country. Clearly, many of Australia's 'founding fathers' were also participants in the sex industry although, as clients, they were members of a historically invisible group. These historical facts were explicitly linked to a feminist political analysis in 1975 with the publication of Anne Summers' Damned Whores And God's Police.

This text, along with Germaine Greer's The Female Eunuch (1971), became one of the most widely read feminist texts in Australia during the 1970s. Summers developed an analysis of contemporary Australian society that was premised upon its historical roots in the sex industry. She argued that, in the early days of Australian settlement, all women ?free settlers, Aboriginal and convict women ?were subject to an 'enforced whoredom'; that is, they were forced to trade sex in exchange for food, clothing and shelter. Summers (1975) suggested that in contemporary society Australian women were still largely in this position. However, after the early days of convict settlement, women were increasingly separated into 'good' or 'bad', that is into 'damned whores' or 'God's police'.

It was, Summers argued, the assigned social role of 'good' women (a category that included married women, celibate spinsters and the early feminists) to both discipline and divert 'bad' women from their evil ways. However, the overall effect of this process was to divide and classify women as 'either maternal figures who are not sexual or as whores who are exclusively sexual'. Summers argued that these stereotypes in fact functioned to discipline all women for they ignored or actively repressed 'good' women's sexual needs ('good' women were represented as asexual) while all 'bad', sexually active, women were represented as prostitutes. Summers argued that it was in the interests of all women for these stereotypes of appropriate sexual behaviour to be broken down.

She thought that one way this might be achieved was for 'good' women to refuse their traditional 'policing' functions and for feminists to publicly identify themselves with those who were designated as 'bad' women a category that clearly included sex workers. Strong links were forged between feminists and prostitute rights groups in the mid-1970s in Australia and, as a result, some real advances were made in the area of prostitution law reform. Summers (1975) text was particularly important in this process. The 'damned whores and God's police' dichotomy was widely cited by Australian feminists as 'a form of social control of female sexuality' which 'makes the support of prostitutes by other women a matter of self-interest rather than moral imperative'.

The laws controlling prostitution were described as property laws over women's bodies which simply aimed to prohibit women from selling something that men regarded as their property. Like Summers, many Australian feminists in the 1970s drew out the connections, rather than the traditional distinctions, between marriage and sex work. Marriage was described, in many cases, as a poorly paid form of prostitution in which women were more vulnerable to violence (from their husbands) and had less control over their daily lives than sex workers. Thus, support for sex workers was combined with a critique of traditional social and sexual arrangements such as marriage. Feminists also used socialist concepts to marshal support for prostitutes as workers.

A major problem for prostitutes is that they are often disregarded as workers and are said to be involved in the sex industry only out of a desire to avoid 'real' work. In the 1970s feminists began to argue that sex work was a form of women's work (although sex work was not seen to be confined to the sex industry). They contended that the decriminalisation of prostitution and (for some authors) the unionisation of the prostitute workforce was a necessary pre-condition for immediate improvements in the working conditions of prostitutes who were simply workers who worked in the sex industry. The focus within Australian feminism on the prostitute as worker has been both theoretically and strategically productive.

Shifting the central concern from issues of sexuality and ethics to industrial issues such as wages and working conditions facilitated a feminist support for sex workers at a time when the prostitution trade ?and sex workers in particular were becoming subject to a range of new cultural prohibitions and legal sanctions around Australia. It is perhaps ironic that one of the side effects of the 'sexual revolution' has been a renewed emphasis upon the importance of mutuality (if not monogamy) in 'normal' sexual relations. In this process, prostitution (as well as other forms of non-reciprocal sexual behaviour) have attracted a new stigma.

While the prostitute has long been regarded as a deviant and unnatural woman within governmental and legal discourse, a similar classification of male clients did not occur until the post-war period. While the prostitution trade has become subject to increased legal surveillance and regulation over the last forty years, the evidence shows that it is female sex workers ?and not to any great extent their male clients ?who have borne the main legal burden of this process.

The focus within Australian feminism on the prostitute as a worker has also facilitated an examination of the prostitution industry from an industrial perspective. Various feminist historians have produced research which emphasised the role of anti-prostitution laws, health and policing practices in the organisation of the industry. This approach made visible hitherto unexplored aspects of the structural conditions within which sex work occurred. Judith Allen (1984), for example, has explored the changes which occurred in the organisation of the prostitution industry in New South Wales after the passage of the Police Offences Act 1908 which outlawed street soliciting for the first time.

Her work contains some important lessons for contemporary law reformers as she shows that legal measures designed to suppress prostitution usually produce a restructuring of the industry in ways that are both conducive to the growth of organised crime and police corruption and detrimental to the interests of sex workers. Some feminists, however, have argued that there are potential disadvantages and unintended consequences of adopting a theoretical/ political focus on prostitution as work. Socialist feminists, for example, have argued that prostitutes do not form an homogeneous group in class terms and 'can vary from the most extreme case of exploited and disadvantaged workers to women who own and manage the brothel or parlour in which they work'.

Giving everyone who works in the sex industry the title 'sex worker' prevents a focus on class differences and on the struggle which we might expect to be waged within the industry between 'sex workers' and 'sex capitalists'. Another disadvantage of addressing prostitution as work is that the primary object of analysis remains the sex worker and as in traditional analyses of prostitution ?the client is rendered invisible. Thus, the sexual desires and aspirations of clients and the ways that these reflect broader cultural practices and patterns of masculinity remain both unprioritised and assigned to the realm of natural male sexual needs. Feminists (and others) argue that the visibility of prostitutes and the invisibility of clients is an important political issue and one that needs to be addressed by future research on the sex industry.

Despite the problems just discussed, the analysis of prostitution as work (and as simply a particular form of women's work) was widely adopted within Australian feminism in the mid- to late-1970s. It was an analysis that was compatible with both the 'labourist' orientation of the Australian Labor Party (ALP) and the feminism of the Women's Electoral Lobby (WEL). In 1974 the national conference of the WEL adopted a resolution which advocated the decriminalisation of all prostitution-related activities in Australia. Many members of WEL were also supporters or members of the Australian Labor Party (ALP).

By the late 1970s, Labor Party feminists in both New South Wales and Victoria were lobbying within and outside the ALP for the decriminalisation of prostitution. In New South Wales, for example, the Labor Women's Committee passed a resolution in 1976 which characterised prostitution as a private sexual matter and argued for the removal of all prostitution-related laws. The advent of a Labor government in New South Wales in 1976 and continuing feminist pressure both from within the party and from the WEL eventually led to a focus by government on the 'sex discrimination' faced by sex workers.

Prostitution laws were identified as 'discriminatory' because only female prostitutes were charged and not their male clients. Moreover, the particular discrimination faced by street workers (who were more prone to arrest and imprisonment than those who worked in parlours) was raised in terms of a class discrimination. Feminists argued then, that the decriminalisation of street soliciting was an urgent priority. The Prostitution Act 1979 decriminalised loitering and soliciting for the purposes of prostitution in New South Wales. It was the outcome of an effective campaign waged by feminists and prostitutes' rights groups.

This success, however, was contingent upon feminists and sex workers being prepared to work within and alongside the established political parties in a way that related their concerns to existing areas of party policy. In New South Wales, for example, civil liberties groups and sections of the ALP had long been advocating the decriminalisation of 'victimless crime' (which included prostitution). In addition, and partly as a result of libertarian campaigns around pornography in the 1970s, all expressions of sexuality including the transaction between prostitute and client were increasingly being regarded as 'private' sexual behaviour and not, therefore, a proper concern of government.

As mentioned previously, the representation of prostitution as sex work meant that effective links could be forged with the labourist orientation of the ALP. For many reasons then, the Labor Party in New South Wales in 1979 was pre-disposed to accept feminist and sex worker arguments about the need to decriminalise prostitution. It was, however, the more public manifestations of prostitution soliciting and loitering in a public place for the purposes of prostitution that were decriminalised rather than 'private', off-street, prostitution.

This was consistent with the demands elaborated by feminists and sex workers that decriminalisation should not merely render prostitution invisible (and thus, simply reinforce the deviant status and oppression of prostitute women) (Johnson 1984) and should address the particular legal 'discrimination' faced by street prostitutes. In the long run, however, this did not prove to be a viable political strategy for the ALP. In 1983, after a substantial and politically damaging campaign waged by inner-city resident groups, soliciting for the purposes of prostitution was recriminalised by the Labor government. The legal sanctions against street prostitution were again increased in 1988.

Perhaps the most characteristic feature of feminist approaches to the sex industry is their focus on gender and on the connections between sex and power. Feminist analyses identify as significant the different structural locations which men and women tend to have in the sex industry (women as workers, men as clients). But they also connect this difference to an argument about power and to a wider theory of oppression which locates all women, whether they are sex workers or not, to a social system of male dominance and control. Feminists advocate the establishment of non-oppressive work structures in the sex industry which empower workers in their interactions with clients and owners.

They also argue for an end to the legal harassment of sex workers. Feminists argue for the importance of an ongoing dialogue and support between feminists and sex workers. Feminists argue that the nature of client demand in the sex industry is a cultural construct (that is, client demand is not simply the expression of natural male needs) which has varied both across history and between cultures. As such, it is open to changes which may or may not be in the best interests of women and sex workers in particular.

While feminists are supportive of sex workers they are critical of many aspects of the sex industry, particularly as it is presently organised. Some feminists would look to the long-term abolition of the sex industry whereas others would say that it might be possible to create a less oppressive prostitution (where, for example, sex workers had the same rights and privileges as other Australian workers and were not subject to harsh criminal sanctions) or pornography which addresses women's erotic interests and does not only represent women as sex objects.

The emphasis which feminists place on a gendered analysis of the sex industry makes visible some of the power mechanisms which operate both within and on the sex industry. Feminist approaches can, therefore, be used to identify and address some of the power structures that sex workers are subject to and to explain why these are unjust. In Australian political parties and parliaments there is usually some concern to address the issue of sex discrimination and gender based injustices. Feminist analyses can then be used to assist in the process of drawing such issues to public attention. As an example of this it can be suggested that the Information and Issues Paper that was issued by the Criminal Justice Commission (1991) in Queensland is seriously flawed by its lack of attention to the gendered structures of the sex industry.

The following is part of a submission which has been made by the author to the Criminal Justice Commission on this matter: While prostitution is usually defined in gender-neutral terms, as the sale of sexual services for money or material gain, this is an approach that specifically disavows the gendered nature of the prostitution industry. The vast majority of 'sex workers' are women while the consumers of prostitution services are almost wholly men. The present configuration of prostitution-related laws in Queensland penalises those who sell prostitution services (that is, largely women) but not those who purchase such services (that is, men). All prostitution-related laws in Queensland are couched in gender-neutral language. Thus, they are said to not directly discriminate on the basis of gender and 'whether homosexual or heterosexual activities are involved are of little consequence'.

However, the law is in effect discriminatory for the vast majority of those prosecuted for prostitution-related offences are women. This is an issue which has not been addressed at all by the Criminal Justice Commission so far. The fact that 'solicitation for the purpose of prostitution provides the only charge which can be levelled at the clients of sex workers' (Criminal Justice Commission 1991) (if considered in conjunction with the fact that most clients are male) is an indication that the present configuration of prostitution-related laws in Queensland institutionalises discrimination against women. A gendered analysis on the prostitution industry appears in the Discussion Paper. The argument is made that a disproportionate number of males (as compared to females) receive prison sentences for prostitution-related offences.

No indication is given as to whether this, in fact, indicates differential treatment. Are men and women imprisoned at different rates for the same offences or is it that men are more likely to commit more serious offences? If it is the case that male sex workers are more heavily penalised in the Queensland criminal justice system than female sex workers then this would indicate that, in practice, the system does discriminate on the basis of a perceived hetero or homosexuality; in general, male sex workers are servicing a male clientele and engaging in homosexual acts. But the fact that a disproportionate number of men go to prison for prostitution-related offences also indicates that a disproportionate number of women (*vis-a-vis* men) are being arrested for these types of offences. Even if most women arrested for prostitution-related offences do not end up going to prison, their liability to arrest and financial penalties together with their (male) clients relative immunity from prosecution constitutes further evidence in support of the argument that the present configuration of prostitution- related laws in Queensland discriminates against women.

The argument that the present configuration of prostitution-related laws in Queensland constitutes sex discrimination was not used to argue that the laws needed to be extended to be more inclusive of men and clients. The sex discrimination claim was used to argue for a more equitable means of regulating the prostitution industry. The present method of wide-ranging criminal sanctions against prostitution-related offences and selective policing has proved susceptible to organised corruption; but it is also a system in which women have suffered particularly harsh and discriminatory penalties. (It is not suggested that male sex workers do not also suffer significant disadvantage in this system. Male sex workers are clearly punished for being prostitutes and for being men who service other men sexually.)

Feminist approaches to the sex industry are also useful in establishing a broad base of political support for prostitution law reform. Sex worker organisations already mobilise some feminist support; this could, however, be extended to encompass feminist networks in the ALP, the Liberal Party and the Australian Democrats, in the union movement, in state and federal bureaucracies and in the universities. As the experience in New South Wales in 1979 showed, the political support for prostitutes rights and for prostitution law reform can be broadened by feminist support. This could be an important factor in the process of law reform presently being undertaken in Queensland.

4

The Politics of Oppression and Action

Global industrialisation and demographic and economic restructuring in the U.S. compel us to challenge existing paradigms and search for new visions to promote interethnic coalitions. During the past two decades, a large influx of immigrants of color has dramatically changed the country's composition. Income polarization and status differences within and across various racial communities have created lines of division that further complicate race relations. Notwithstanding this fragmentation, the diverse composition of the present-day metropolis underlines the necessity of mobilizing the various ethnic groups around urgent projects and issues that stem from common life chances. Furthermore, structures of inequality and ideological differences inevitably lead to conflict and destruction as demonstrated by the Los Angeles Civil Unrest of 1992. With these and other considerations in mind, scholars must develop new strategies for bringing together such diverse constituencies.

Recent changes in the racial composition of American society have been accompanied by increased conflict among various racial and ethnic groups, including Blacks, Asians, and Latinos. Building coalitions of color in contemporary society is much more formidable than it was in the 1960s as a result of contextual shifts and new complexities in the internal organizational structure and, hence, in the objective interests of different racial groups.

Traditionally, both internalized oppression and internalized domination have been viewed almost exclusively as internal, deep, unchanging, psychological qualities or characteristics of the oppressed, on the one hand, and the privileged, on the other. There are, however, serious limitations to such an overemphasis on the personal, individual, psychological dimensions of both these phenomena. For one, it obscures the role that systemic, structural, institutionalized forces play in producing and reproducing both privilege and oppression. In addition, the "internalized" image suggests that oppression and domination become deep, internal psychological qualities, characteristics, or "marks" that are extremely difficult (if not impossible) to resist, interrupt, or abandon once they are in place.

This perpetuates a static and ultimately pessimistic view of both oppression and privilege that is at odds with any kind of educational or developmental effort to challenge the status quo. In the end, therefore, any solution to the problems of privilege and oppression must focus as much on structural/systemic change as it does on personal transformation. This is where the socio-cultural concept of mediated action can be most useful. The goal of socio-cultural inquiry, in contrast to strictly psychological inquiry, is to understand the relationship between the individual and the social, cultural, historical, and institutional contexts in which the individual lives.

To accomplish this goal, we must be careful not to limit our focus to individual mental functioning, on the one hand, or to the social/cultural/historical setting, on the other. Rather, we must find a way to focus on both the personal and the systemic, and thus to avoid the tension between the individual and society, and the perils of both individualistic and social reductionism, that have plagued us for generations. The concept of mediated action, as articulated by James Wertsch, offers one way to undertake such a sociocultural analysis of any form of human action. Mediated action entails two central elements: an "agent," the person who is doing the acting, on the one hand, and "cultural tools" or "mediational means," the tools, means, or "instruments," appropriated from the culture, and used by the agent to accomplish a given action, on the other.

This concept is heavily influenced by Lev Vygotsky's work on the role that tools play in facilitating human development, and by Mikhail Bakhtin's exploration of the process of appropriation, whereby persons achieve both "mastery" and "ownership" of specific forms of discourse that initially "belong" to others. Both "internalized" oppression and "internalized" domination can also be understood as forms of mediated action. This conceptual re-interpretation allows us to salvage the central descriptive features of the classical view of both "internalized oppression" and "internalized domination" (and a corresponding understanding of the very real personal and experiential consequences of both), while at the same time moving away from the "internal/interior/introjected" remnants of the psychodynamic language first used to explain them - language that implies that these are exclusively psychological, rather than sociocultural, phenomena.

We should, therefore, replace the term "internalized oppression" with the term appropriated oppression. As such, appropriated oppression results from the mastery and ownership of cultural tools that transmit oppressive ideologies, messages, and scripts. Similarly, we should replace the term "internalized domination" with the term appropriated domination/privilege. As such, appropriated domination results from the mastery and ownership of cultural tools that transmit dominating/privileging ideologies, messages and scripts. These tools, both oppressive and privileging, come from a variety of sources, including parents, teachers, friends, the media, etc. They take a variety of forms, from words, phrases, jokes, books, pictures, images, television shows, films, etc. And they are mastered and owned via cultural participation, guided participation, and participatory appropriation.

No matter the source or the form, these tools are marked by a set of white-supremacist, male-supremacist, classist, heterosexist, etc., ideologies that are promulgated in and by the dominant culture, and then appropriated by the both the oppressed and the privileged. The classic documentary A Class

Divided provides a clear example of both appropriated oppression and appropriated domination at work in an elementary school classroom. This film reports on the work of Jane Elliot, a third-grade teacher in the nearly all-white, all-Christian farming community of Riceville, Iowa, who, in 1970, devised an experience for her students to explore the nature of prejudice and discrimination. During "Brotherhood Week" she divided her class into two groups, blue-eyed children (the dominant group) and brown-eyed children (the subordinate group).

The film provides clear examples of the various forms that appropriated oppression and appropriated domination take in the subsequent experience of the children in Jane Elliot's class. It also illustrates well the types of cultural tools/ mediational means that the children appropriate and use to mediate their action as either subordinates or dominants. Most importantly, the film provides clear evidence that appropriated oppression does not require years and years of "internalizing" and "intrapsychic processing." It can, and does, occur almost instantaneously, in a few hours on a Tuesday morning: just as one picks up a tool and begins to use it, one's "physical and mental functioning"--one's thoughts, feelings, and actions--begins to change, as one appropriates, in the case of the brown-eyed children, oppressive cultural tools.

The same thing goes for members of the dominant group--they very quickly assume the role of the privileged group (a role, of course, that they already inhabit, as white members of our society). Imagine, therefore, the power that these cultural tools amass, over the course of many years and many generations, as folks experience repeated opportunities to appropriate and use either oppressive or dominating cultural tools/mediational means. Imagine, also, the challenge that this poses to critical educators seeking to change both oppression and domination. This chapter concludes with a consideration of the implications of this view of appropriated oppression and appropriated domination for the practice of critical pedagogy and anti-oppressive education. In the end, a move away from the language of "internalization" moves us away from an image of the oppressed as "victims" and the privileged as "villains" - operating out of set and static mind-sets that cannot be changed.

A conception of appropriated oppression and appropriated privilege, in contrast, gives rise to a measure of hope, and a sense that these dynamics, both at the individual level and at the structural/systemic level, can be changed, can be made different. A move toward a conception of both oppression and privilege as mediated action also entails the understanding that both oppression and privilege typically emerge from the same social-cultural-historical-institutional-structural-systemic context. As such, it enables us to see both the oppressed and the privileged as full and equal participants in a common history and an ongoing dialogue that, while it may not be easy (and may, in fact, at times seem impossible), is, in fact, our only hope for both personal and social transformation.

The Psychological to the Socio-cultural

Toward the end of the classic documentary A Class Divided, Jane Elliot, the third grade teacher from Riceville, Iowa, who gave her students a lesson in prejudice, discrimination, and oppression by privileging the blue-eyed students in her class one day, and the brown-eyed students the next, conducts a phonics flash-card exercise with the brown-eyed students. This is the second day of the exercise, and the brown-eyed students, who had been in the subordinate position in the class the previous day (and wearing cloth collars to designate their status), were in the dominant position today. On the first day they had done very poorly on the card pack. Today, however, it was a different story:

- After the brown-eyed children had sped through the phonic card pack that second day, Jane congratulated them. "You went faster than I have ever seen anyone go through the card pack," she said, smiling at their excitement and pleasure. "Why couldn't you get them yesterday?"
- "We had those collars on," Donna Reddel said. The others agreed.

- "Oh," Jane said. "You think the collars kept you
- "We couldn't think with those collars on," Roy Wilson said excitedly. "My eyes just kept going around and around."
- "Oh," Jane said again, "and you couldn't think as well with the collars on."

I will return to this video, and the example it offers, later in this chapter. For now I simply want to note Jane Elliot's own description of the phenomenon represented here: "[I]n everything...they did on those two days, it was clear that the children that had been labeled inferior were, in fact, behaving as though they were inferior, while the 'superior' children performed in a consistently superior manner" (Peters, 1987, p. 86).

Main goal of this chapter is to take a new look at the twin concepts that typically might be invoked to interpret such a phenomenon: "internalized oppression" and "internalized domination." Internalized oppression is a concept widely used these days across a variety of disciplines and critical projects, including contemporary critical pedagogy, to describe and explain the experience of those who are members of subordinated, marginalized, or minority groups (like the "inferior" children in Jane Elliot's class), those who are powerless and (often) victimized (both intentionally and unintentionally) by members of dominant groups, those who have "adopted the [dominant] group's ideology and accept their subordinate status as deserved, natural, and inevitable" Griffin, 1997, p. 76).

Internalized domination, on the other hand, describes and explains the experience and attitudes of those who are members of dominant, privileged, or powerful identity groups (like the blue-eyed children in Jane Elliot's classroom). It derives, at least in part, from the groundbreaking work of Jean Baker-Miller (1976) on the dialectic between domination and subordination that characterize all relations marked by differences in power and privilege, primarily in male-female relationships. The concept of internalized domination, as it is now more widely used, captures the phenomenon whereby "members of the [dominant] group accept their group's socially superior status as normal and deserved".

Traditionally, both internalized oppression and internalized domination have been viewed almost exclusively as internal, deep, unchanging, psychological qualities or characteristics of the oppressed, on the one hand, and the privileged, on the other. I believe, however, that there are serious limitations to such an overemphasis on the personal, individual, psychological dimensions of both these phenomena. Eduardo Bonilla-Silva (2003) argues that "whereas for most whites racism is prejudice, for most people of color, racism is systemic or institutionalized". The same holds true, I think, for internalized oppression and internalized domination, in general. It is easy, particularly from a dominant point of view, to see the oppressed as "victims," and to see their reaction to oppression as reflecting a set of "psychological problems"--thereby obscuring the role that systemic, structural, and institutionalized forces play in the production and reproduction of oppression.

Similarly, it is very easy, from a dominant point of view, to see racism, sexism, homophobia, etc., as personal, psychological shortcomings that are too easily interpreted, and thus dismissed or minimized, as the result of prejudice, bias, ignorance, etc. ("I'm not a racist!" or "I didn't mean anything by that remark"). This view, moreover, leads to a solution to prejudice and bias that stresses the need for individual attitude change, via education, training, therapy, etc. (interventions at the individual level), and nothing more. But privilege and oppression are the result of forces and mechanisms that go far beyond the individual, psychological level.

Consequently, the social, cultural, institutional, and historical forces, that lead racism, sexism, homophobia, etc. to become systematically embedded in the structure of our social lives must be acknowledged in any attempt to challenge the status quo. In the end, any solution to the problems of privilege and oppression must focus as much on structural/ systemic change as it does on personal transformation. This is where the sociocultural concept of mediated action can be most useful. Mediated action entails two central elements: an "agent," the person who is doing the acting, on the one hand, and "cultural tools" or "mediational means," the tools, means, or "instruments," appropriated from the culture, and used by the agent to accomplish a given action, on the other.

In this essay I will argue, therefore, that that both "internalized" oppression and "internalized" domination are better understood as forms of mediated action - are better understood, in other words, as sociocultural phenomena, rather than simply as psychological phenomena. Such a reinterpretation, among other things, helps to hold both the individual and the structural/systemic levels together at one and the same time. In constructing this argument, I will first sketch a general description of the classical conceptions of internalized oppression and internalized domination. I will then sketch a similarly general description of the concept of mediated action.

Then I will bring these two descriptions together, and, in so doing, I will present my re-interpretation of internalized oppression and internalized domination as mediated action. I will then return to A Class Divided, to illustrate these concepts more fully, before turning to a necessarily incomplete consideration of the implications of this analysis for the practice of critical pedagogy, in general, and what has come to be called "anti-oppressive education" (Kumashiro, 2000, 2002), in particular.

INTERNALISED OPPRESSION AND INTERNALIZED DOMINATION

The phenomenon of internalized oppression has been extensively explored in the work of the Martiniquean psychiatrist Frantz Fanon (1963, 1967), the Tunisian Jewish writer Albert Memmi (1967), and the Brazilian educator Paulo Freire (1970). However, as Dan Foster (1993) suggests, the notion of a psychological "mark of oppression" (a term first coined by two American psychiatrists, Kardiner & Ovesey [1951]), a notion which focuses on the consequences and implications of living under various forms of oppression (particularly colonization and racial oppression) is one of a whole host of labels, drawn primarily from the human and social sciences, that have been used to describe this phenomenon over the past 50 years or so.

Whatever the label, all of these notions carry a common referent: "the idea of internalized psychological consequences [e.g., a sense of inferiority, low self-esteem, and aggression] due to social systems of prejudice, discrimination and oppression".

Paulo Freire (1970) provides a well-known and useful summary of these consequences. He begins by arguing that the goal of the oppressed is to liberate themselves and their oppressors. The difficulty of achieving this goal, says Freire, comes about because in the initial stage of their struggle against oppression, the oppressed, instead of striving for liberation, tend to become oppressors themselves (or "sub-oppressors"). This is because while their ideal is to be fully human, their model of "full humanity" has been the oppressor.

This is what Freire calls "identification with the oppressor" - at a certain moment of their existential experience the oppressed have adopted an attitude of "adhesion" to the oppressor, they "find in the oppressor their model of 'manhood", and they may even "feel an irresistible attraction towards the oppressor and his way of life". They have "internalized the image of the oppressor and adopted his guidelines" for action and interaction in the world.

Freire offers two other insights about this "duality" under which the oppressed live. The first is to call attention to the phenomenon of "self-deprecation" - a sense of shame, humiliation, self-hatred, and low self-esteem that is characteristic of the oppressed (cf. the brown-eyed children's performance on the phonics flash-cards). This attitude derives, he says, from the oppressed's adoption of the opinion that the oppressors hold of them. "So often do [the oppressed] hear that they are good for nothing, know nothing, and are incapable of learning anything - that they are sick, lazy, and unproductive - that in the end they become convinced of their own unfitness".

Here Freire clearly echoes Memmi's (1967) analysis of the experience of colonization, in which the "mythical portrait" created by the colonizer profoundly shapes the view that the colonized hold of themselves:

> Constantly confronted with this image of [themselves], set forth and imposed on all institutions and in every human contact, how could the colonized help reacting to [their] portrait? It cannot leave [them] indifferent and remain a veneer which, like an insult, blows with the wind. [They] end up recognizing it as one would a detested nickname which has become a familiar description. The accusation disturbs [them] and worries [them] even more because they admire and fear their powerful accuser. "Are not they partially right?," [they] mutter. "Are we not a little guilty after all? Lazy, because we have so many idlers? Timid, because we let ourselves be oppressed?" Willfully created and spread by the colonizer, this mythical and degrading portrait ends up being accepted and lived with to a certain extent by the colonized.

Freire also introduces the notion of "horizontal violence" - in which members the oppressed group engage in violence against their own comrades. "Because the oppressor exists within their oppressed comrades," Freire says, when they attack those comrades [the oppressed] are indirectly attacking the oppressor as well". To support his analysis, Freire quotes Fanon's (1967) analysis of causes of the aggressiveness and violence that the oppressed/colonized "natives" direct toward each other, often for the pettiest of reasons:

> The colonized man will first manifest this aggressiveness which has been deposited in his bones against his own people. This is the period where the niggers beat each other up, and the police and the magistrates do not know which way to turn. While the settler or the policeman has the right the livelong day to strike the native, to insult him and to make him crawl to them, you will see the native reaching for his knife at the slightest hostile or aggressive glance cast on him by another native; for the last resort of the native is to defend his personality vis-à-vis his brother.

While there is much more that can and should be said about Freire's conception of the dynamics of oppression and domination, suffice it to say that the strictly individual, psychological understanding of internalized oppression to which Freire's description seems to point has been widely adopted in the contemporary literature on oppression. Gail Pheterson (1990) provides a classic summary of this perspective:

> Internalized oppression is the incorporation and acceptance by individuals within an oppressed group of the prejudices against them within the dominant society. Internalized oppression is likely to consist of self-hatred, self-concealment, fear of violence and feelings of inferiority, resignation, isolation, powerlessness, and gratefulness for being allowed to survive. Internalized oppression is the mechanism within an oppressive system for perpetuating domination not only by external control but also by building subservience into the minds of the oppressed groups.

Note, in this description, the primary emphasis on feelings and emotional responses, and the use of internal, interior images ("into the minds") to characterize this phenomenon. Let me turn now to a brief consideration of what I call the "classical" conception of internalized domination. While the concept of internalized domination has not been as widely used as the concept of internalized oppression, and its sources are less clear, it nevertheless has become, in recent years, a familiar concept to many.

Pheterson (1990), once again, provides a useful summary of how this phenomenon is typically conceptualized:

> Internalized domination is the incorporation and acceptance by individuals within a dominant group of prejudices against others. Internalized domination is likely to consist of feelings of superiority, normalcy, and self righteousness, together with guilt, fear, projection, denial of reality, and alienation from one's body and from nature. Internalized domination perpetuates oppression of others and alienation from oneself by either denying or degrading all but a narrow range of human possibilities. One's own humanity is thus internally restricted and one's qualities of empathy, trust, love, and openness to others and to life-enhancing work become rigid and repressed.

Rita Hardiman and Bailey Jackson (1997) expand on this definition, offering some specific examples:

> Internalized domination refers to the behaviors, thoughts, and feelings of agents [dominant group members] who through their socialization as members of the dominant group, learn to think and act in ways that express internalized notions of entitlement and privilege. Examples of internalized domination include men talking over and interrupting women in conversation, while simultaneously labeling women as chatty. There is an absence of feeling that one has to prove oneself, or that one's status, talent, and qualifications would be questioned in any situation.

Jeff Hitchcock (2002), in his book, Lifting the white veil, discusses what he calls internalized dominance, informed by work of both Pheterson and Maureen Walker:

> Internalized dominance is a belief system grounded in miseducation and in the politics of social inequality. This belief system is the result of an advantaged relationship to privilege, power, and cultural affirmation. The premise of white superiority under girds the various attitudinal and behavioral expression of internalized dominance.

Hitchcock explores the way internalized dominance influences whites' relationship with themselves (leading, for example, to shame, guilt, and defensiveness), whites' relationships to other white people (leading, for example, to the assumption that other whites are racist, or to competition with other whites to be the "best ally" to folks of color), whites' relationships with people of color (leading, for example, to fear people of color, to feel superior to people of color, to take on the role of "savior" of people of color), and whites' relationship to the racial structure of United States culture (leading, for example, to marginalizing talk and feelings about racial structure, or experiencing uncertainty or paralysis in mixed race settings). He also argues that "our internalized dominance affects us every bit as much as internalized oppression affects people of color".

Finally, Hitchcock presents his version of the argument that internalized dominance, like internalized oppression, becomes a part of the psyche, both consciously and unconsciously:

> The ready-made imagery of our society is so prevalent and interwoven with everything else that it becomes a part of our inner psychological makeup. We incorporate this imagery even before we can think clearly. By the time we are adults it has become part of our psychological framework. While we might be aware of it, and thus work to reduce its effect upon us, we can never completely remove or expunge its effects from our conscious and, more importantly, subconscious minds.

In sum, while the classical conceptions of both internalized oppression and internalized domination are undeniably powerful and compelling, it is important to note, once again, the pervasiveness of "internal" and "internalizing" language and images in both conceptions. This language has clearly been influenced by the psychodynamic, psychiatric, psychological discourse that, since Freud, has become so much a part of the language we use for self-understanding. But there are limitations, I would argue, in the use of this kind of language, and these kinds of images.

For one, as I have suggested above, it obscures the role that systemic, structural, institutionalized forces play in producing and reproducing both privilege and oppression. In addition, the "internalized" image suggests that oppression and domination become deep, internal psychological qualities, characteristics, or "marks" that are extremely difficult (if not impossible) to resist, interrupt, or abandon once they are in place. This, to me, perpetuates a static and ultimately pessimistic view of both oppression and privilege that is at odds with any kind of educational or developmental effort to challenge the status quo.

Mediated Action

The concept of mediated action has been explored and articulated most fully by James Wertsch. Wertsch (1998) argues that the goal of sociocultural inquiry, in contrast to strictly psychological inquiry, is to understand the relationship between the individual and the social, cultural, historical, and institutional contexts in which the individual lives. To accomplish this goal, he suggests, we must be careful not to limit our focus to individual mental functioning, on the one hand, or to the social/cultural/historical setting, on the other. Rather, we must find a way to "live in the middle," to focus on both the personal and the systemic, and thus to avoid the tension between the individual and society, and the perils of both individualistic and social reductionism, that have plagued us for generations.

Wertsch proposes that the notion of mediated action provides the most useful way to "live in the middle." Mediated action, as I have indicated above, entails two central elements: an "agent" and specific "cultural tools" or "mediational means". Understanding that virtually all human action is mediated action therefore involves focusing on both agent and agency, on both "what person or kind of person performed the act" in question, and "what means or instruments she used". The concept of mediated action is heavily influenced by the work of Lev Vygotsky and his colleagues and contemporaries writing in Russia in the early decades of the Soviet era.

Key to Vygotsky's theoretical perspective is his claim that in order to understand the mind and its development we must understand the "tools" that mediate and shape its functioning. Beginning with an idea borrowed from Marx and Engels, that all genuinely human activity is necessarily mediated by tools, Vygotsky considered the role of both physical or "technical tools" and "psychological tools," or "signs," in human life. The concept of mediation by psychological tools became so important to Vygotsky that by 1933, one year before his death, he wrote that "the central fact about our psychology is the fact of mediation".

Wertsch (1998) provides a number of examples to illustrate mediated action and its properties. One is the track and field event of pole-vaulting. The modern event of pole vaulting involves a vaulter running down a 125-foot runway with a fiberglass pole in her hands, planting the pole in a vaulting box at the end of the runway, and using the pole and her momentum to carry herself off the ground and over a bar that can be as much as 20 feet above the ground. Even though vaulting over a bar 20 feet in the air may appear, at first glance, to be an individual achievement, when it is considered as a form of mediated action it illustrates the impossibility of separating the individual agent (the vaulter) and her cultural tool (the pole):

> On the one hand, the pole by itself does not magically propel vaulters over a cross bar; it must be skillfully used by the vaulter. On the other hand, a vaulter without a pole or with an inappropriate pole is incapable of participating in the event, or at best can participate at less than an optimal level of performance.

But there is more to this example, as there is to all forms of mediated action. That is, the mediational means employed by a pole vaulter when she successfully vaults over a bar 20 feet in the air are not limited to the physical tool of the pole. Rather, there are a host of other cultural tools - primarily linguistic or semiotic tools - that a vaulter employs.

These include information from books and videos about how to pole-vault, guidance and direction from coaches about style and technique, etc. This guidance and direction, moreover, may even be experienced as a specific voice or voices that the vaulter "hears" in her mind, perhaps without even being fully conscious of it, while she is vaulting ("Hold your hands this way, take this many steps, don't look at the bar, etc."). In any case, the point here is that a vaulter employs a variety of mediational means, both physical and linguistic, when engaged in her sport. Thus one should not assume that any given form of mediated action employs only one kind of cultural tool; in fact, mediated action typically entails multiple mediational means, of various kinds.

This brings me to a central question - one that is essentially a developmental question: how are mediational means/ cultural tools acquired? The term that most helpfully describes this process, I would argue, is "appropriation." I use the term "appropriation," rather the more commonly used term, "internalization", to ensure that the process by which individuals acquire cultural tools is not viewed as one in which something static is taken across a boundary from the external world to the internal psyche, but rather to foreground a process by which persons actively participate in the ongoing process of gaining proficiency and expertise in using specific mediational means, whether they are physical tools or linguistic tools.

There are two dimensions or characteristics of the process of appropriation that I want briefly to highlight here. The first is mastery. This entails "knowing how" to use a given cultural tool with a relatively high degree of skill or facility. Acquiring mastery in the use of particular cultural tools typically takes some time, and, in many cases, complete "know-how" is never fully achieved.

A second dimension or characteristic of the process of appropriation is ownership. This entails, following Bakhtin (1981), understanding how an agent takes a given cultural tool, something, quite commonly, "that belongs to others," and "make[s] it one's own". Moreover, as Bakhtin (1981) notes, medational means often "resist" the process of appropriation, and agents do not always easily come to a sense of ownership of the cultural tools they use:

> [N]ot all words for just anyone submit equally easily to this appropriation, to this seizure and transformation into private property: many words stubbornly resist, others remain alien, sound foreign in the mouth of the one who appropriated them and who now speaks them; they cannot be assimilated into his context and fall out of it; it is as if they put themselves into quotation marks against the will of the speaker.

So, a pole vaulter, as she learns how to pole vault, gradually appropriates the mediational means associated with her sport. She works to master the use of the relevant physical tools (e.g., the pole, the track, the equipment she uses and wears), and linguistic tools (e.g., the guidance about form, style, and technique she receives from her coach). She also seeks to "own" those tools, to make them her own as much as possible, to use them in her own way, to make them part of herself in a fundamental sense - -all of which are hallmarks of expertise in her sport.

But how, precisely, do individuals, like this pole vaulter, acquire such expertise in the use of new mediational means to perform new types of mediated action? This is a question that Barbara Rogoff (1995) attempts to answer, in analyzing what she calls "sociocultural activity" on three inter-related planes or dimensions, focusing on three inter-related processes that contribute to the mastery and ownership- i.e., the appropriation- of mediational means. The first plane is the social, cultural, institutional, plane. Here the process of cultural participation (Rogoff calls this apprenticeship) provides the means for analyzing the development of mediated action as it emerges in a communal context.

> [The concept of cultural participation] provides a model in the plane of community activity, involving active individuals participating with others (experts) in culturally organized activity that has as part of its purpose the development of mature participation in the activity by the less experienced people. This [concept] extends the idea of craft apprenticeship to include participation in any other culturally organized activity, such as other kinds of work, schooling, and family relations. This idea of apprenticeship necessarily focuses attention on the specific nature of the activity involved, as well as on its relation to practices and institutions of the community in which it occurs- economic, political; spiritual, and material.

Hence the model of cultural participation/apprenticeship is one of active learners engaged in a community of people who support, challenge, and guide novices as they increasingly participate in skilled, valued, and valuable forms of mediated action. The second plane is the interpersonal plane. Here the concept of guided participation provides the means for analyzing the development of mediated action as it emerges in the context of interpersonal relationships.

> The concept of guided participation refers to the processes and systems of involvement between people as they

communicate and coordinate efforts while participating in culturally valued activity [forms of mediated action]. This includes not only face-to-face interaction...but also the side-by-sided joint participation that is frequent in everyday life.... The "guidance" refereed to in guided participation involves the directions offered by cultural and social values, as well a social partners; the "participation" in guided participation refers to observation, as well as hands-on involvement in an activity.

The third and final plane is the personal plane. Here the concept of participatory appropriation provides the means for analyzing the development of mediated action as it emerges as a result of persons' active participation in sociocultural activities:

The concept of participatory appropriation refers to how individuals change (how mediated action develops) through their involvement in one or another activity, in the process of becoming prepared for subsequent involvement in related activities. With guided participation as the interpersonal process through which people are involved in sociocultural activity, participatory appropriation is the personal process by which, through engagement in an activity, individuals change and handle a later situation in ways prepared by their own participation in the previous situation. This is a process of becoming, rather than acquisition.

So, returning once again to the pole vaulting example, we can see how developing expertise as a pole vaulter involves three inter-related processes: participatory appropriation, guided participation, cultural participation. The vaulter ultimately both masters and owns the mediational means necessary to be an effective pole vaulter, and thus undergoes change, transformation, and development on the individual plane. But to acquire or appropriate these tools she must participate in at least one, if not more, interpersonal relationships with others (i.e., coaches and teammates), through which she gains facility in using these tools. And, finally, she must participate in a sociocultural context which provides these tools in the first place. In short, all three planes are necessary if the process of appropriation is to occur, and each one contributes uniquely to the development of pole vaulting as a form of mediated action.

Internalised Oppression and Domination as Mediated Action

With this brief description of mediated action in hand, let me now turn to my claim that the phenomena that have been called "internalized oppression" and "internalized domination" should be understood, like all human action, as forms of mediated action. This conceptual re-interpretation allows us to salvage the central descriptive features of the classical view of both "internalized oppression" and "internalized domination" (and a corresponding understanding of the very real personal and experiential consequences of both), while at the same time moving away from the "internal/interior/introjected" remnants of the psychodynamic language first used to explain them- language that implies that these are exclusively psychological, rather than sociocultural, phenomena.

Therefore, that we should replace the term "internalized oppression" with the term appropriated oppression. As such, appropriated oppression results from the mastery and ownership of cultural tools that transmit oppressive ideologies, messages, and scripts. Similarly, we should replace the term "internalized domination" with the term appropriated domination/privilege. As such, appropriated domination results from the mastery and ownership of cultural tools that transmit dominating/privileging ideologies, messages and scripts. These tools, both oppressive and privileging, come from a variety of sources, including parents, teachers, friends, the media, etc. They take a variety of forms, from words, phrases, jokes, books, pictures, images, television shows, films, etc.

And they are mastered and owned via cultural participation, guided participation, and participatory appropriation. No matter the source or the form, these tools are marked by a set of white-supremacist, male-supremacist, classist, heterosexist, etc., ideologies that are promulgated in and by the dominant culture, and then appropriated by the both the oppressed and the privileged. When we make this move from "internalized" oppression and domination to "appropriated" oppression and domination, a move that makes clear that both oppression and domination are fundamentally sociocultural phenomenon, not simply psychological phenomenon, we enrich and expand Freire's (1970) original conception of these dynamics.

Freire certainly offers a neo-Marxist conception of the social, in which forms of subjectivity (like "internalized oppression," "false consciousness," and the forms of discourse that mediate them) arise from particular forms of social interaction and social structure (i.e., forms of material life). Yet I would argue that when oppression is seen as a form of mediated action, it also becomes possible to understand the effect that mediational means, cultural tools, and other artifacts of consciousness (e.g., forms of discourse) have on material life. Once again, my intent here is to suggest a bi-directional view of causality-and thereby to complicate the strictly psychological conception of both oppression and domination that holds sway over our collective understanding of these experiences.

As an example of what such a re-interpretation offers, consider Suzanne Lipsky's (1987) discussion of what she calls "internalized stereotypes:"

> Patterns of internalized racism have caused us [as Blacks] to accept many of the stereotypes of Blacks created by the oppressive majority society. We have been taught to be angry at, ashamed of, anything that differs too much from a mythical idea of the middle-class of the majority culture--skin that is "too dark," hair that is "too kinky," dress, talk, and music that is "too loud."

From a mediated action point of view, such appropriated racial stereotypes are not internal psychological categories, or structures. Rather, they are material, commodifiable, cultural products - cultural tools - that are used, transmitted, and thus reified in order to reinforce and perpetuate appropriated oppression among black folks.

Another example of the way such cultural tools operate to reproduce privilege comes from the work of Eduardo Bonilla-Silva. Bonilla-Silva describes the phenomenon of what he calls "color-blind racism" - whereby racism, racial oppression, and racial inequality are perpetuated in the US, in the absence of explicitly racist practices, policies, or laws, by specific ideological constructions and discursive practices (i.e., forms of "mediated action"). He argues, instead, that "racism without racists" is produced and reproduced by a set of white-supremacist ideologies (i.e., particular discursive frames, rhetorical styles and strategies, and common storylines), all of which promote a racist world-view, and which can be identified in the everyday talk of whites. These discursive frames, strategies, and storylines, I would argue, are precisely the kinds of mediational means/cultural tools that continue to promote and encourage appropriated domination/privilege among white folks.

A Class Divided

To illustrate these phenomena, both mediated oppression and mediated domination, let me return the documentary A Class Divided. As I have indicated above, this film reports on the work of Jane Elliot, a third-grade teacher in the nearly all-white, all-Christian farming community of Riceville, Iowa, who, in 1970, devised an experience for her students to explore the nature of prejudice and discrimination. During "Brotherhood Week" she divided her class into two groups, blue-eyed children and brown-eyed children.

"It might be interesting to judge people today by the color of their eyes," [Jane Elliot] said speculatively. Three children began bouncing up and down in their seats with excitement.

"Would you like to try this?" "Yeah!" The answer was almost a shout as the entire class was caught up in enthusiasm for the idea. It sounds like fun, doesn't it?" Jane asked. "Yeah!" the whole class shouted again. Jane began by explaining that blue-eyed children are more intelligent, better behaved, quicker to learn, and in every way superior to brown eyed-children:

"All right. Since I'm the teacher, and I have blue eyes, I think maybe the blue-eyed people should be on top the first day."

Roy Wilson, a serious-looking boy with brown eyes, close-cropped hair, and a long, oval face, frowned with puzzlement. "You mean . . ." He stopped, unsure what she could mean.

"I mean," Jane said with finality, "the blue-eyed people are the better people in this room." "Uh-uh!" It was Brian Saltou, his blue eyes flashing. "Oh, yes, they are," Jane said, turning to face him. "Blue-eyed people are smarter than brown-eyed people . . ." "What color eyes did George Washington have?" Jane asked.

Sandra Dohlman and Julie Smith, both brown-eyed, seated alongside each other, turned at this to stare at each other's eyes. "Blue?" Sandra asked, blinking, clearly hoping she was wrong. Brian's head was up again. "Blue," he said disgustedly, "or else brown." "Blue," Jane said. "Blue." She paused. "This is a fact. Blue-eyed people are better than brown-eyed people."

Moreover, to call attention to the "inferior" brown-eyed children, she asked the blue-eyed children to place a collar round the neck of each brown-eyed child. As the day proceeded, the domination/privilege of the blue-eyed children, and the subordination/oppression of the brown-eyed children, played out in a myriad of both overt and covert ways:

After the blue-eyed children had been given seats in the front of the room and the job of row leader in each row had been reassigned to a blue-eyed student, Jane told them to get out their English workbooks. "Turn to page 127," she said, writing the number on the blackboard.

"Is everyone ready?" she asked finally, glancing around the room. "Everyone but Laurie," she said, watching brown-eyed little Laurie Mayer squirm as she paged rapidly through her workbook. "Ready, Laurie?" she asked when Laurie had found the page. Laurie nodded, looking up unhappily through her harlequin glasses.

"She's a brown-eye!" someone jeered.

"She's a brown-eye," Jane confirmed. "You'll begin to notice today that we spend a great deal of time waiting for brown-eyed people." Laurie pursed her lips unhappily, and Donna, sitting near her, flashed a brown-eyed, resentful look at Jane.

That was the way it went all morning. Whenever a brown-eyed child was slow, whenever one made a mistake, Jane made a point of picking it up. Blue-eyed children could seemingly do no wrong. As the brown-eyed children became tense and unhappy, the blue-eyed children relaxed and all but blossomed under the approving eye of their teacher....

At morning recess, the blue-eyed children were excused five minutes early, and they left the room in a bustle of enthusiasm. The brown-eyed children remained behind, working gloomily at their desks. When it was time for them to go out, they pinned their collars to their coats and trudged morosely out to the snowy playground, sullen, disgruntled, angry children. Three brown-eyed girls marched fiercely across the playground, avoiding the crowded swings, slides, and jungle gym, giving a wide berth to clusters of playing children. Their heads together, they talked furiously as they stomped briskly the length of the frozen yard.

Two brown-eyed boys slipped around a corner of the building and seated themselves, alone, on a step against the brick wall. By the time recess was over, all of the brown-eyed children had found each other and were huddled in little groups along that wall. Two girls consoled a third, who was close to tears.

Much more happened the first day, including a fight between two boys, after the blue-eyed boy called the brown-eyed boy a "brown eye." Then, the next day Jane Elliot reversed things, and the brown-eyed kids were on top, and the blue-eyed kids were on the bottom. The same dynamics emerged.

First, let me highlight the ways in which both appropriated oppression and appropriated domination/privilege manifest themselves in this documentary:

Appropriated oppression manifests itself as:

- Brown-eyed children became tense and unhappy; sullen, disgruntled, angry.
- "You feel like you can't do anything," says Julie Smith.
- "I feel mean," says Donna Reddel.
- "It's like you don't have any friends anymore," says Vera Buls.
- Brown-eyed children become violent (John punches Russell because he called him "brown-eye".
- Brown-eyed children do poorly on the phonics flash-cards timed test.

Appropriated domination/privilege manifests itself as:

- Blue-eyed children became relaxed and all but blossom under the approving eye of their teacher.
- Blue-eyed children look for ways to surveil and oppress the brown-eyed children (suggesting that Jane keep a yardstick handy in case the brown-eyed children "get out of hand", and reminding Jane to tell the lunch monitor not to allow the brown-eyed children to go back for seconds.
- Blue-eyed children tease and taunt the brown-eyed children (Russell calls John a "brown-eye".
- Blue-eyed children do very well on the phonics flash cards timed test .

Next, let me highlight the cultural tools/mediational means that the children appropriate to mediate their oppression and domination/privilege, respectively.

Examples of the cultural tools/mediational means, appropriated by the brown-eyed group, that give rise to *appropriated oppression* include:

- Jane Elliot's words/messages about their subordinate status: "Do you think a blue-eyed father would kick his son?"; "brown-eyed people don't get to use the drinking fountain because we might catch something from you"; "brown-eyed people are not to play with the blue-eyed people on the playground, because you are not as good as blue-eyed people"; "you'll begin to notice today that we spend a great deal of time waiting from brown-eyed people"; etc.

- Cultural scripts for oppression, prejudice, name-calling (re. Native Americans, Blacks, etc.) that they already have appropriated.
- Collars worn by themselves to identify them as subordinate.

Examples of the cultural tools/mediational means, appropriated by the blue-eyed group, that give rise to *appropriated domination/privilege* include:

- Jane's words/messages about their dominant status (this is where she starts): "the blue-eyed people are the better people in this room"; "blue-eyed people are smarter than brown-eyed people"; "my dad's blue-eyed and he's never kicked me"; what color eyes did George Washington have? Blue"; "blue-eyed people get five extra minutes of recess; "blue-eyed people can go back for seconds at lunch"; etc.
- Cultural scripts for oppression, prejudice, name-calling (re. Native Americans, Blacks, etc.) that they already have appropriated.
- Collars worn by the "others" to identify them as subordinate.

There is obviously much more that can and should be said about this example. For my purposes here, however, I simply want to highlight, as I have done, the ways in which it illustrates both appropriated oppression-as-mediated action and appropriated domination-as-mediated-action, by focusing, specifically, on the cultural tools/mediational means provided in Jane Elliot's classroom, appropriated by the children, and used to mediate their action as either subordinates or dominants. In addition, it is critical to note, I think, that the emergence of appropriated oppression, in particular, occurs very quickly, in the course of several hours on a Tuesday morning.

This provides evidence, I would suggest, for the re-interpretation of the classical conceptions of internalized oppression and internalized domination for which I have been arguing. Appropriated oppression does not require years and years of "internalizing" and "intrapsychic processing." It can, and does, occur almost instantaneously: just as one picks up a tool and begins to use it, one's "physical and mental functioning"—one's thoughts, feelings, and actions—begins to change, as one appropriates, in the case of the brown-eyed children, oppressive cultural tools, via the inter-related processes of cultural participation, guided participation, and participatory appropriation.

The same thing goes for members of the dominant group—they very quickly assume the role of the privileged group (a role, of course, that they already inhabit, as white members of our society). Imagine, therefore, the power that these cultural tools amass, over the course of many years and many generations, as folks experience repeated opportunities to appropriate and use either oppressive or dominating cultural tools/mediational means. Imagine, also, the challenge that this poses to critical educators seeking to change both oppression and domination.

IMPLICATIONS FOR CRITICAL PEDAGOGY AND ANTI-OPPRESSIVE EDUCATION

Let me offer, if I may, a few brief ideas about the implications of this analysis for the practice of critical pedagogy or, what Kevin Kumashiro (2000, 2002) calls "anti-oppressive education." First, let me consider what this perspective offers the classical Freirean (1970) conception of critical pedagogy, designed to promote *concientizacao* or "critical consciousness raising." If one's response to oppression is not internalized, but is mediated action that results from the appropriation of oppressive cultural tools and resources (like the response of the brown-eyed children in "A Class Divided"), then it can be changed, through the same process that gives rise to mediated action in the first place. This is precisely what Freire (1970, p. 40) and others suggest is necessary for attaining freedom/liberation:

1. Unveiling the world of oppression.
2. Expelling the myths and images created and promulgated by the old order - rejecting the oppressive images of one's

own culture (i.e., rejecting oppressive cultural tools and resources, voices, ideologies, etc.).

3. Replacing old myths and images with new images, stories, ideologies that are more liberating (i.e., appropriating liberating cultural tools and resources, voices, ideologies, etc.).

This is also what might be called the appropriation of "critical capital" - i.e., cultural tools and resources that enable the oppressed to challenge the status quo, critique the dominant paradigm, and move toward true freedom/liberation ("appropriated liberation"). As such, this process resonates with a number of current accounts of how identity develops among those who have been oppressed or subordinated. I have in mind, in particular, the development of black racial identity, from the "pre-encounter" stage to the "commitment" stage; the development of ethnic identity, from the "unexamined" stage to the "achieved" stage; and the development of gay and lesbian sexual identity, from "first awareness" to "identity integration"— all of which entail the gradual emergence of a "liberated" and "committed" sense of identity from an original position of subordination and/or oppression. I would argue that the same three-step process of *concientizacao* and re-appropriation must also occur for members of dominant/privileged groups. Such a process might look something like this:

1. Unveiling the world of privilege.
2. Expelling the myths and images created and promulgated by the old order - rejecting the privileging images associated with one's dominant culture (i.e., rejecting privileging cultural tools and resources, voices, ideologies, etc.).
3. Replacing old myths and images with new images, stories, ideologies that are more liberating for all people (i.e., appropriating liberating cultural tools and resources, voices, ideologies, etc.).

The "critical capital" involved in this process is intended to offset and counterbalance, at least somewhat, the privileging power of unexamined cultural capital to which members of dominant groups tend to have such easy access. This is not something that has been talked about extensively in the literature on critical pedagogy, but, on principal, I would argue, this is what lies behind efforts of Peggy McIntosh (1988), Michelle Fine (1997), Adam Howard (forthcoming), Alan Johnson (2001), Michael Kimmel and Abby Ferber (2003), Paula Rothenberg (2002), John Stoltenberg (1989), and others to foreground the issue of white privilege, male privilege, upper class privilege, compulsory heterosexuality, and other ideologies associated with what I have called appropriated domination/privilege.

And it parallels the description, provided by Janet Helms, of the six-stage process of white racial identity development, which entails both the gradual abandonment of racism (contact, distentegration, reintegration), and the formation of a positive, nonracist white identity (pseudo-independence, immersion/emersion, autonomy). Both of these descriptions also resonate, I would argue, with Kevin Kumashiro's recent discussion of "anti-oppressive education." Kumashiro (2000) presents a typology of four different approaches to anti-oppressive education: (1) Education for the Other; (2) Education about the Other; (3) Education that is Critical of Privileging and Othering; and (4) Education that Changes Students and Society.

Let me say something, briefly, about the last two types. I would argue that the conception of appropriated oppression and appropriated domination/privilege that I have presented in this chapter helps to address one of the primary critiques that Kumashiro (2000) offers of "Education that is Critical of Privileging and Othering." While the strength of this approach, he says, is that it not only teaches about oppression but also seeks to change society, by understanding the interrelationship between oppression and privileging, the notion that both oppression and privileging are fundamentally, and exclusively structural implies that oppression has the same effect on all people:

This critique does not deny that members of any particular group share common experiences with oppression, or that certain groups have historically be subject to the same general form of oppression. However, because all individuals have multiple identities, not all members of the same group necessarily have the same or even similar experiences with oppression. Structural explanations cannot account for this diversity and particularity. For example, in her research on nursery classrooms, Walkerdine (1990) argues that females who at one moment were able to exert power over males, at another were rendered powerless by them, because in each situation a different discourse was being recreated or "cited."

Structural explanations of oppression and privileging may not be able to account for the diversity of experiences of subordination and domination, but a sociocultural explanation can. This is because a conception of appropriated/mediated oppression, as I have argued above, does not assume that the experience of oppression leaves a set of universal, internal, deep, psychological "marks" or characteristics. Rather, it assumes that oppression is mediated by a wide variety of possible cultural tools/mediational means, and that those tools lead to various and varied forms of mediated action ("agents-acting-with-mediational-means"), depending, as in the case of the Walkerdine (1990) example, on the discourse being appropriated and used in a given situation. As such, I would argue, a mediated action approach to understanding oppression and privileging serves to address, in helpful ways, the limitations of this otherwise very valuable approach to anti-oppressive education.

Let me turn now to Kumashiro's (2000) fourth and final type of anti-oppressive education, "Education that Changes Students and Society." This approach employs post-structural insights to formulate a conception of oppression that focuses on discourse and the process of "citation." Referring once again to Walkerdine's (1990) work, Kumashiro argues that:

> Her analysis suggests that oppression and harm originate in (or are produced by) not merely the actions and intentions of individuals or in the imperatives of social structures or ideologies. Rather, oppression originates in discourse, and, in particular, in the citing of particular discourses, which frame how people think, feel, act, and interact. In other words, oppression is the citing of harmful discourses and the repetition of harmful histories.

Kumashiro (2000) illustrates this notion of citation by considering the "model minority" stereotype that is so often associated with Asian American students (i.e., that they are all smart, hardworking, successful students). While the traditional view of the harm that such stereotypes inflict focuses either on the inherent power of the stereotype (used like a "weapon"), or on the role that such stereotypes play in reinforcing existing social structures and ideologies, Kumashiro offers a different reading. He suggests, instead, that every time a stereotype is used it invokes past "iterations" of that stereotype:

In other words, the power of a stereotype to harm derives from a particular history of how that stereotype has been used and a particular community of people who have used that stereotype and who constitute that history. If someone was to tell me that I should be a better student because I am Asian American, I would likely conclude that the speaker is making racist assumptions about me because I have heard other people talk about and generalize about Asian Americans in similar ways before. The speakers words would have racist meaning to me because would read them as constituting part of the history of how the model-minority stereotype has been and is being used. Furthermore, if I believed that the speaker was judging me based on this stereotype and I valued the speaker's judgment, the speaker's words would likely produce in me feelings of failure or abnormality.

Kumashiro (2000) has much more to say about the details and the implications of this poststructurally-inspired approach to anti-oppressive education; details and implications to which I can not possibly do justice in this chapter. As such, let me just briefly suggest that I think that an approach to understanding oppression-as-mediated action is quite compatible with a perspective that employs notions of discourse and citation to conceptualize the same phenomena. The forms of discourse that frame how people think, feel, act, and interact, to which Kumashiro (2000) refers are precisely those cultural tools/ mediational means that are employed in any given example of mediated action—as the case of the brown-eyed children in Jane Elliot's classroom makes crystal clear.

Moreover, this perspective clarifies precisely *why* the dynamics of domination and subordination were established in that classroom so quickly. The messages and the stereotypes about the superiority of the blue-eyed children, and the inferiority of the brown-eyed children, that Jane Elliot offered, and the children appropriated, were not powerful simply because they reinforced individual prejudice and discrimination, or a particular social structure. Rather, they gained their power because they reiterated messages and stereotypes with which they were quite familiar (different in form, perhaps, but not in kind) - messages and stereotypes about African Americans and Native Americans in particular. For this is precisely the way that Jane Elliot introduced the eye-color exercise:

Jane glanced at the calendar on the front wall and said, "This is a special week. Does anybody know what it is?

'National Brotherhood Week," several children responded....

Jane took a few steps toward the door and then turned to ask, "Is there anyone in the United States that we do not treat as our brothers?"

"Yeah," several children answered.

"Who?"

Raymond Hansen answered instantly. "Black people."

"The black people," Jane said. "Who else?"

"Indians?" asked Sandra.

"Absolutely, the Indians," Jane said. "And when many people see a black person or a yellow person or a red person, what do they think? What do they sometimes say?"

Sandra made a disgusted face. "Ew, look at the dumb people," she said.

"Look at the dumb people," Jane said flatly. "What else do they think sometimes? What kinds of things do they say about black people?"

Greg Johans...frowned and said, "They call them 'Negroos,' 'niggers,' things like that."

Simply put, the action and interaction that followed from

this introduction by Jane Eliot, exemplifying both mediated oppression and mediated domination, clearly had its start in this initial exchange, as the children built on their knowledge of "harmful discourses" and "harmful histories", citing those discourses and repeating those histories (i.e., those cultural tools and resources) as they constructed their own system of domination and subordination right in the middle of their classroom.

In this chapter, I have sought to sketch an alternative to what I have called the "classical" conception of both "internalized oppression" and "internalized domination" as internal, deep, psychological qualities or characteristics. Employing the sociocultural notion of "mediated action" (an agent acting with mediational means/cultural tools), I have argued for a conception of "appropriated oppression" - and its mirror image, "appropriated domination/privilege" - as more helpful theoretical formulations of these phenomena. And I have briefly explored the implications of this re-framing for the practice of critical pedagogy and anti-oppressive education.

Let me stress, again, that this move from what I have called a psychological interpretation of oppression and privilege to a sociocultural interpretation does not, in any way, deny the real and very powerful personal and experiential, consequences of oppression. Rather, it is intended allow us to "live in the middle," to recall Wertsch's (1998) image, and thus to call our attention, as well, to the pervasive and insidious role that systemic forces, in the form of cultural tools and resources (ideologies, images, stereotypes, scripts, etc.) play in promoting and promulgating both oppression and privilege - -tools and resources that, depending on when and how they are appropriated (both "mastered" and "owned"), have profound and long-lasting psychological ramifications.

A move toward a mediated action perspective on both oppression and privilege, in other words, challenges both an exclusively individualistic view and an exclusively systemic/structural view. Both of these views meet, I would argue, in the concept of mediated action. Furthermore, I would argue that a move away from the language of "internalization" moves us away from an image of the oppressed as "victims" and the privileged as "villains" - operating out of set and static mind-sets that can not be changed.

A conception of appropriated oppression and appropriated privilege, in contrast, gives rise to a measure of hope, and a sense that these dynamics, both at the individual level and at the systemic level, can be changed, can be made different. A move toward a conception of both oppression and privilege as mediated action also entails the understanding that both oppression and privilege typically emerge from the same social-cultural-historical-institutional-structural-systemic context. As such, it enables us to see both the oppressed and the privileged as full and equal participants in a common history and an ongoing dialogue that, while it may not be easy (and may, in fact, at times seem impossible), is, in fact, our only hope for both personal and social transformation.

At the moment, let me be the first to admit, this conception of both oppression and privilege as mediated action raises more questions than it answers. These include questions about the processes by which mediational means/cultural tools are appropriated (both mastered and owned) in different contexts and social locations, and at different ages. Questions also remain about why some people move from positions of oppression, or positions of privilege, to positions of liberation, while others do not. And the pedagogical implications of all of this remain to be spelled out in much more depth and detail than I have been able to do in this context.

Ultimately, however, I remain hopeful that such a sociocultural perspective on the dynamics of privilege and oppression will contribute in a useful way to the ongoing dialogue about these processes, and how they can be resisted. For, as Freire (1970) says, in this well known passage:

Education as the practice of freedom—as opposed to education as the practice of domination—denies that [humans are] abstract, isolated, independent, and unattached to the world; it also denies that the world exists as a reality apart from [humans]. Authentic reflection considers neither abstract [humans] nor the world without [humans], but [humans] in their relations with the world. In these relations consciousness and world are simultaneous; consciousness neither preceded the world nor follows it.

This, in effect, is the sociocultural perspective on mediated action in a nutshell-"humans in their relations with the world" are "agents-acting-with-mediational-means". And, as Freire suggests, in the end this perspective is not simply a means to understand the world, it is also a means to change it—to make it a more just, more compassionate, and more liberating place for all people.

5

Education for the 21st Century

When one gives serious consideration to the process for restructuring education on the basis of the new paradigm of inclusiveness, the question that arises is, how? It is important in answering this question that the process used be consistent with the ends of inclusion and compassion one is seeking to achieve. We are all acquainted by experience with processes that are dehumanizing in an endeavor to accomplish goals of humanization. In order to effect change, the focus must not be just on individual change, but also on institutional change. Change will never come about if the unit of change on which one focuses is the individual rather than on the institution as an organization. What is being sought is not a mere cosmetic change but a change of basic orientation. Stephen Covey brings this out in a clear manner in *The 7 Habits of Highly Effective People*, when he states:

> If we want to make relatively minor changes in our lives [and institutions], we can focus on our attitudes and behaviors [our prejudices and discriminations]. But if we want to make significant, quantum change, we need to work on our basic paradigms.

To try to change our attitudes and behaviors does very little good in the long run if we fail to examine the basic paradigms from which these attitudes and behaviors flow.

This is not possible without a complete change of orientation. Human service organizations like churches and schools often tend to have an orientation toward the past, toward a "we-have-always-done-it-this-way" type of approach. This is a past-orientation. To confront the future with a past-orientation is much like driving using only the rearview mirror-the focus is on where one has been and not on where one is going. An occasional rearview focus is essential so that one may know what is coming up from behind. But for the most part the focus must be on what lies ahead. Is the educational system headed into the 21st century with a rearview focus, oriented toward the past? Or is it[1]s focus oriented toward the future, toward change?

THE NEED FOR VISION

This calls for a need of vision, because as a wise man reminded us long ago, "without vision a people perish". But what is vision? Vision is the bifocal ability to see what lies ahead (farsightedness), as well as the various impediments in the present (nearsightedness), and how to avoid them in order to arrive at the future. Seldom are both types of vision found in the same individual. Yet that is precisely what organizations need, a leadership and a staff that are bifocal. More often than not, much of the conflict that arises within systems comes when the farsighted and the nearsighted are not able to see the other's perspective. Yet both are needed for the one helps to put the other into perspective. But most people err on the side of nearsightedness because of their concentration on their daily, individual tasks. Therefore the need for a futures-orientation entails a new paradigm, a new way of seeing.

The first action in the direction of effecting change is a need for perspective-grasping a vision, a sense of direction, a new paradigm of where education is headed. This entails having an understanding of where society is headed, how the world of work is changing, and the demographic shifts in the neighborhoods. Here is where the school needs vision, values and mission statements. In order for a school to operate effectively in a rapidly changing society, it needs to process Vision, Values and Mission Statements. What is the difference?

A Vision Statement answers the "Where?" question. It addresses where an organization is headed-its direction, perspective and paradigms in view of the changes taking place in our nation and in the world today. A Values Statement addresses the "What? question. It is concerned with what the school is becoming-the effective end/goal behaviors it needs to model in the present. A Mission Statement, on the other hand, answers the "Why?" question. It addresses the reason(s) why an organization exists in view of the direction taken and the needs of its target population. At every step of the process certain key questions have to be answered:

The Four Crucial Questions:

- The Where Question: addresses Vision: "Where are we headed?
- The What Question: addresses Values: "What are we becoming?"
- The Why Question: addresses Mission: "Why do we exist?"
- The How Question: addresses Goals: "How do we get there?"

The key dynamic here is vision, for "without vision a people perish" (Proverbs 29:18). Vision is the most essential dynamic an organization needs to have, for from it proceed its values, mission and goals. These three elements without vision will find themselves being formulated in a social vacuum, divorced from social reality. An organization, such as a school, can have a good internal climate: clear goals, well shaped programs, and skilled teachers and staff who relate and communicate well, and still cease to function properly if it has not taken into account its external climate, the ways in which it is being influenced by the larger society of which it is a part, and the other environmentally impacting systems within it.

This is the role of vision. If a school is not aware nor has an understanding of the social forces impacting change, such as the political climate, economic conditions, demographic changes, and the social environment, it can quickly become a historical and social anachronism. The following graphic lays out the process for effecting change. Once these four questions are answered than appropriate training, giving people the right knowledge and skills to implement programs can be undertaken. The process for developing a Vision Statement and Values Statement differs from the one used for a Mission Statement. Developing the Vision Statement is the responsibility of the Administrator/Principal, with the assistance of the School Board.

On the other hand, the Values Statement and Mission Statement are developed by the entire school staff with a number of representative students working together in small groups. The importance of the three is that the first is where the principal gives the school a sense of the direction the school needs to go in view of changes in the society. With this vision in mind, the school faculty, staff and students, under the leadership of the principal, go on to develop a Statement of Values that helps all-faculty, administrative staff, and students-model behaviors reflective of inclusiveness and a Statement of Mission that depicts the school's purpose for existence, both of which they can take ownership.

Why does a school need all three statements, addressing vision, values and mission? Lewis Coser gives the rationale for this. Coser declares: "The greater the structural or cultural diversity of those who unite in a coalition, the more their interests other than in the immediate purpose are likely to be divergent if not antagonistic." The value of this statement will be seen immediately by anyone who has been involved in a multicultural environment. Groups differ in their interests. When the differences are due cultural/racial diversity, the greater will be the potential for antagonism within the group. A homogeneous group, in terms of race and class, is a potentially less conflictual group than a heterogeneous one.

Coser tells us where the solution is be found. "Such a coalition, if it is not to fall apart, must attempt to keep close to the purposes for which it was formed." The only way to keep a culturally diverse group from focusing exclusively on its differences, is by enabling it "to keep close to the purposes for which it was formed." If there is any group that must know up front why it exists, it is a racially/ethnically diverse group. Without this purpose for existence clear in everyone's mind, differences will creep in which will divide and deviate the group. Thus, the need for a clear Mission Statement, based on a singular Vision and inclusive Values. It is virtually impossible to maintain, over an extended period of time a multicultural institution, without a precise Statement of Mission based on a clear vision and a set of operational inclusive Values.

A school without Vision, Values and Mission Statements is like a ship without a rudder, with no destination port in mind, tossed here and there by the social forces in our changing society. A multicultural school will find itself in potentially more turbulent waters due to its ethnic makeup, and the influence which a socially divided society will have on the members within. This is the reason for a different set of operational values, which continually place before the school the question: "What are we becoming?" Without a Vision Statement, a Values Statement and a Mission Statement-the first gives the school direction, the second gives it character, the third keeps it on course-the possibility of shipwreck and self-destruction is an ever-present reality. Thus, the Vision, Values and Mission Statements need to regarded as dynamic working documents and not museum pieces merely to be displayed. This has much to do with paradigms.

Paradigms

The word paradigm comes from the Greek paradeigma, para = "to place along side"; deigma = "to show." It means to show by placing along side, as in an Example, Pattern or Model. Thus a paradigm is a mental construct, or conceptual model, influenced by our socialization, which defines and delimits the way we perceive reality and is the basis of our worldview. It is a particular way of seeing. For education this particular way of seeing has been one oriented toward the past. To change toward a futures-orientation requires a paradigm shift. A paradigm shift is a movement away from old explanations and structures that no longer explain reality, resulting in a redefinition of taken for granted boundaries due to the emergence of a new model or paradigm, which returns everyone back to zero.

The concept of paradigms and paradigm shifts is nothing new. It is the old problem of new wine and old wineskins that Jesus spoke about in Luke 5:37,38 when He said. "No one puts new wine into old wineskins; otherwise the new wine will burst the skins and will be spilled, and the skins will be destroyed. But new wine must be put into fresh wineskins." As long as one is dealing with the old wine, then the old wineskins will do. But the moment one shifts to new wine, the fermenting creative process will create an expansionism that will burst the old wineskins already stretched to their limit. For this reason, "new wine must be put into fresh wineskins." Mikhail Gorbachev learned he could not place the new wine of democracy into the old wineskins structures of communism.

The result was spillage, as in the failed coup and August Revolution of 1991 which brought about the demise of the Soviet Union. South Africa is also drinking the new wine of multiculturalism and diversity, thus the need for new wineskins to accommodate change. Where does change come from? Change comes from the outsiders, the young, those new to a reality (age is not a factor), as well as from those who are at the periphery, the marginal; all of whom have little investment in the prevailing paradigm, and thus have nothing to lose. Those most open to change are those who are not benefiting from the way things are presently structured. Those most resistant to change are those who are benefiting from the present system, and who therefore stand to lose if things were to change.

CRISIS OR FORESIGHT MANAGEMENT

The choice before us is either to be proactive or reactive. A reactive person is one who is overwhelmed and threatened by the challenge of diversity and change, and reacts with a defensive posture. The proactive person, on the other hand, anticipates change by putting into play behaviors which turn problems into challenges. Let me propose a new model of management, "Foresight Management," for bringing about change. We all go through experiences in life. The word "experience" is a good term since it is value neutral, as opposed to the word "problem" that is negative, or "challenge" that is positive. As Aldous Huxley once declared, "Experience is not what happens to a man; it is what a man does with what happens to him." In Chinese, for example, the word for "crisis" Wei-Ji is composed of two picture-characters, the one meaning "danger" and the other meaning "opportunity."

How one responds to life[1]s experiences or crises makes a big difference in the final outcome, for the same experience can be seen either as a problem or as a challenge. Whether one views the experience as a problem or a challenge, is to a large extent determined by the action one takes towards the experience, whether a reactive (negative) posture based on Crisis Management or a proactive (positive) process, based Foresight Management. Crisis Management in this context is a style of management that takes a reactive posture towards unexpected change, by using short term interventions in order to return operations to normal-the way they were before the crisis. Thus if the experience is perceived to be a problem, then the approach that is automatically taken is that of Problem Solving, in which the principal question is: "Who owns the problem?" Such an approach leads to the process of finding whom to blame. Why? Because the goal in this approach is to solve the problem as quickly as possible in order to get back to normal operation.

This is because the orientation is to the past, to a "we-have-always-done-it-this way" mindset. Such an approach is not open to that which is new, but is steeped in tradition and its preservation, whether corporate or domestic. But the result of such a past-oriented, blaming process is that it creates division, for people often want to distance themselves from the one who has been identified as the problem. It also creates division in spirit and a climate of distrust. Am I next? Who[1]s watching? Who can I trust? Will I be found out? By immediately looking for blame because of the desire to quickly get back to business as usual, the result may be an overlooking of the possibility that the problem may reside elsewhere, such as in the system, the structure or corporate culture. In which case, nothing is resolved, except cosmetic changes.

In time the same problem or a similar one will reemerge, only to be temporarily suppressed. In the end, one is left with a lose-lose situation. The result of such reactive posture is institutional crisis and systemic bog-down, because the focus is on immediacy instead of long-term change. The opposite methodology is to view our experiences as challenges, based on Foresight Management as the style of leadership. Foresight Management is a proactive style of management that anticipates change by critically analyzing trends, on the assumption that nothing is constant, by putting into operation processes that turn potential problems into challenging opportunities.

The focus is thus on a Change-Anticipating approach. There are reasons why things don¹t always work out the way we desire. Some are easily grasped, others may elude us. Nevertheless, the concern of the proactive process is not, "Who is to blame?", but, "What can we learn?" With learning comes change, whether minor or major. One of the learnings is that things cannot continue as they are. This approach builds on the maxim of Max DePree, "We cannot become what we need to be by remaining what we are." Thus the approach is a change-anticipating one; what needs to be different? Such an approach immediately forces one to realize that this is not the concern of anyone person exclusively. Therefore, the process that emerges is one of ownership by everyone who is affected by this experience or situation.

Focusing on ownership instead of blame, enables people to bring to the process several qualities:

1. Commitment-this is my concern also;
2. Community-since it is everyone¹s concern, we are all in this together;
3. Creativity-because it affects me, let me give it my best effort;

4. Cooperation-since we are all involved it can only be resolved through group effort;
5. Compassion-in taking the role of the other, I act in order to bring change that may relieve pain.

What is the difference between sympathy, empathy and compassion? These three concepts tend to be confused in the minds of many as similar or even the same, but they are not. They are vastly different and elicit from the respondent three different types of behavior. These three behaviors can best be illustrated with the following graphics.

1. In Sympathy there is sorrow for the other in need. But with sorrow there is also a sense of distance, separation from the other, an "I'm not like you" type of response. Even though there is an emotional response, the "bridge of identification" with the other has not been crossed.
2. In Empathy there is not only sorrow, but also an identification with the other in need. Here the person crosses the "bridge of identification" and enters into the emotional sphere of the other and identifies with the pain. The other senses and knows that identification has taken place.
3. In Compassion there is not only sorrow and identification with the other in need, but also an involvement in action to meet the need.

Here the response does not stop at identification, but goes one step further to take the necessary steps of action to alleviate suffering. The two-way arrow symbolizes that the action takes into consideration the wishes and, if possible, the involvement of the other in a reciprocal process to bring about change. Much of what passes for compassion is often an imposition from the outside, without regard for what might be best for the other nor for their input. There is nothing wrong with sympathy, per se, however. There are many times when the only action a person can take is limited at a sympathetic response. There are other times when one can go further and express empathy. And there will be times when the opportunity will be there to express compassion. The problem comes when one has the ability to demonstrate compassion, but for reasons of one[1]s own choosing, decides to limit the action only to sympathy or at best empathy.

The Goal of this process is Change!-things cannot continue as they presently are. This is because the orientation of the process is toward the future, toward a concern with how improvement can be made. The end result of this proactive process is unity-everyone working together for the common good in a win-win manner where everyone benefits. This model not only provides a method for conflict resolution, but also reflects different philosophical approaches towards leadership, as well as a new style of management. The first is patriarchal, focused on the individual, independence and power; the other tends to be egalitarian, concerned with the group, interconnectedness and team-building. In essence both represent two methods for dealing with change, one static, the other dynamic.

This model also exposes two different styles of leadership: the old style of Problem Solver-Crisis Management-a reactive posture which dominated management in the 1960's, 70s and 80s, versus the new style of leadership for the 21st century, that of Change Anticipator-Foresight Management-a proactive process. The model is simple, yet useful, whether one is dealing with domestic/family difficulties or corporate/institutional concerns. The choice between reactive and proactive responses can best be illustrated by hurricane Andrew. On August 24 and 25, 1992, hurricane Andrew struck a most devastating blow to the southern portions of the states of Florida and Louisiana. Two important lessons on how to deal with change can be learned from hurricane Andrew. The first is: Failure to anticipate impending change with a proactive process, will result in great loss, due to a come-from-behind reactive response.

All the meteorological reports from the National Hurricane Center in Dade County, Florida said the same thing-Andrew is rushing towards land at a speed of 180 mph. But none of the appropriate persons and agencies quickly mobilized into action. President Bush continued campaigning and at first did little. Four days later FEMA was still trying to get organized, the National Guard had not moved into action, and the American Red Cross was struggling with the immensity of the damage. All were paralyzed by the failure to act proactively, resulting in a lot of finger pointing. But there is a second lesson from Andrew: Be careful how you build, for the storm will show what sort of work has been done.

The vast devastation was in large measure due to the faulty housing construction of the building boom during the 1980s. Yet some houses experienced minimal damage, primarily those built by Habitat for Humanity, the agency with whom former president Jimmy Carter is affiliated. How we build during periods of great change, determines what lasts and what doesn't. Interestingly, the Great Mississippi Flood of 1993 found FEMA prepared. The point of this illustration is that in the years ahead we are going to be experiencing a whirlwind of changes. From a distance they will all look like problems, and the temptation will be to unfurl the "danger" flag and take a reactive, defensive posture. However, such an approach will leave one hurried, hassled and harassed because the changes are happening so quick one will not have the time nor the energy to solve all the problems, many of which are self-perpetuating.

The better approach is a proactive process which views the changes as challenges, thereby turning potential problems into "opportunities" for growth and change. Thus, a negative is turned into a positive, where everyone wins. This is Foresight Management, and what managing diversity is all about. It addresses the question of how do people respond to the need for change? This is a question raised by Thomas S. Kuhn in his book The Structure of Scientific Revolutions. Writing primarily to the scientific community, Kuhn asks: "How do scientists [and I would add preachers, professors, politicians or people in general] proceed when aware only that something has gone fundamentally wrong at a level with which their training has not equipped them to deal?"

Kuhn suggests there are four responses to the stage of crisis:

1. An immediate change to the new paradigm.
2. A "wait-and-see" attitude.
3. A seeing of "new discoveries" upon examining anomalies.

4. A refusal to accept change-the new.

Thus the type of response one takes depends on how much one has invested in the old paradigm.

THE STRUCTURE MUST CHANGE

If schools are to undergo a paradigm shift toward equity, then the prevailing structures must be broken up, to be replaced by more egalitarian, inclusive ones. Our present exclusive structures, with a majority of ethnically diverse student body, but a homogeneous administration, faculty, and staff do not reflect the needs of a changing society nor the multicultural world economic market for which school are seeking to prepare students. Let me make it very clear: As long as our present semi-exclusive academic structures continue to persist, there will always be racial/ethnic conflict in our schools at all levels from K-to graduate. But, is this the way for education to go into the 21st century? Absolutely not! A new age demands new methods-a new paradigm. Thus the need for structural change.

There are three methods of implementing change that schools can take, each one more inclusive than the next:

1. The introduction of diversity modules into an existing structure. [Normative-old paradigm left intact]
2. The addition of diversity as a total dimension of existing structures and processes. [Reformative-the old paradigm with new attitudes]
3. The reconceptualisation of the total culture/structure of an organization according to the modus operandi of diversity. [Transformative-the new paradigm of inclusion]

THREE METHODS OF IMPLEMENTING CHANGE

These three methods are not procedural, meaning that you do the first, then the second and finally the third. They are either or methods. One simply decides which one to implement, and goes with it. The first method is one where diversity is accommodated within the present structure. No effort is made to change the structure since it is regarded as "normative," the "traditional" way things have always been done. The only difference now is that one makes concessions to "accommodate" dissenting and disgruntled groups, by introducing diversity modules.

It tends to be paternalistic, and gives people a sense of, "Hey, be happy with what you got." The inclusion of students of color in schools and courses that are inclusive is an example of the first method. The approach here is to put new wrapping paper on the box. But its the same old box with a new covering. The old paradigm of exclusion is left in tact, since the concern is with maintaining as normative the traditional way of doing things, though the door of opportunity has been made available.

The second method is slightly better but not by much. It looks at the overall structure and recommends making diversity an integral part of the total dimension of what presently exists. In this sense it is reformative, in that it is an improvement that on the surface looks good, since it appears that diversity is now part and parcel of the whole structure. The current concern with diversity and with women issues is an example of the second method. Here, the approach to remove the lid of the box and change the contents within the box, along with a new wrapping, but to leave the box itself unchanged. Thus the basic structure of the organization has not essentially changed, it is still the same old paradigm-the same old box with new wrappings and new contents.

It has merely been added to, it has been reformed, with a new attitude about diversity and inclusiveness. The vast majority of the efforts of organizations to work with diversity today fit here. Both of these methods merely place new wine in old wineskins. The fact that spillage results should not surprise anyone, but because of a short-sighted vision and a wrong set of values it usually does. The third method is an effort to step back take a good look at where society is headed (vision statement) and then look at the organization and ask, "What values does our behavior reflect?" (values statement), "Where do we fit in all of this?" (mission statement). For schools it means looking at change seriously in terms of its demands.

It means looking at the box, cracked and warped because of the contents, and asking oneself: "How can we completely redesign this thing to be consistent with the challenges faced?" "If we were to start fresh from the ground up to reconstruct schools today for the 21st century, in what way would our they be different from what they presently are, in order to meet the new demands of change?" With this information in hand, the third method necessitates examining the total structure, curriculum and culture of education, and then transform them in harmony with the new paradigm of inclusion. It means creating a structural and cultural paradigm shift, which will give rise to a new way of doing administration and instruction consistent with the times and needs of a changing society. Yet as Paulo Freire so forcefully reminds us in all his writings, "the transformation of education cannot take place before the transformation of society."

What the times demand is thus the third approach. Anything short of this is merely a reworking of the old paradigm of exclusion. What education needs is a restructuring according to the Principle of Inclusiveness-new wineskins to handle the new wine of diversity. In the end this may only be possible through technology. Michael Crichton, in Disclosure, brings out this possibility, when he suggests that, technological firms today are "selling" what both religion and revolution have promised but have not been able to deliver-freedom!-freedom from the body, freedom from race, gender, country and nationality. Religion has been a force that, while proclaiming the oneness of the human creation, has been the most pervasive factor in society in creating and maintaining exclusion. Revolutions have been no better, proclaiming the need for change, but often ending up as the biggest opponents of change. Technology will move education "from print to digital displays to virtual environments." Thus, computer technology may very well be the means by which to bring about a restructuring of society, with a level playing field for all.

Change is upon us; this is a given. Our present academic structures, from K-graduate, modeled on the basis of the needs of an industrial society, are not longer functional nor adaptable to the needs of the 21st century. Merely seeking to reform them will not do. Radical surgery is needed, not just band-aid efforts. Corporations are already making it clear that school simply have to change. This is why so many of them are investing in schools to help with the process. What is needed is an academic leadership that is proactive, that operates on the basis of Foresight Management, anticipating rather merely responding.

Such a focus will turn what may appear to many to be a potentially dangerous situation, and turn it into a challenging opportunity. What is at issue here is not just sensitivity to other cultures and racial/ethnic groups that are marginal to the dominant culture, but an entire paradigm shift -a different mindset-which gives rise to a whole new way of seeing the world, as inclusive; and brings a change in institutional and societal structures, so as to create an environment (local, national and global) which is inclusive of all groups, is safe for differences and where everyone benefits. May we have the courage to proceed . . . with caution.

AN EMPLOYMENT IMPERATIVE

The United Nations has continuously emphasized the role of productive employment in reducing poverty and promoting social development ever since the 1995 World summit for social development. Every two years the United Nations issues a Report on the World Social Situation. The key findings from the latest report in this series relate to the millennium development Goals in the context of globalization. The report has a specific emphasis on promoting social development and achieving poverty reduction through policies for productive employment of labor. In the current phase of globalization, labor markets have been evolving in the direction of greater economic insecurity and greater levels of inequality, adversely affecting the opportunity of people to achieve satisfactory employment in a decent work environment.

Many of the world's young persons live in poverty; an estimated total of 130 million young persons are illiterate. Indigenous peoples are among the poorest members of the global population. In most countries, unemployment rates among indigenous peoples are significantly higher than the national average. Governments and employers around the world, in their desire to become economically competitive, have taken numerous steps to increase flexibility in labor markets, thereby producing greater insecurity among workers. Globally, there has been a spread of informal employment and short-term contracts, giving workers fewer entitlements and very little actual security in their employment.

Deregulation and privatisation of social services are powerful forces that have led to reductions in employment and income security as well as loss of representation for workers providing these services. Standard collective contracts are giving way to contracts based on terms of employment established at an individual level between employers and workers, resulting in a shift in the balance of power and control in favor of the employers. Labor security is being eroded by the globalization of industry and financial markets and the emergence of global labor supply. Statutory regulation is being replaced by self-regulation as part of the liberalization that has accompanied globalization, engendering greater work insecurity.

The principle of social insurance, a component of social protection systems, is weaker in economies dominated by informal economic activities and employment in the informal economic sector. According to the United Nations report, policies and strategies devised to promote employment should also address issues of income and socio-political inequalities. The design of policies to promote employment also needs to reflect demographic and social changes in society. Political reforms and legal provisions for achieving greater equality among ethnic groups, cultures, genders and age groups, as well as protecting immigrants' workplace rights and civil rights are also essential.

With more and more workers in employment situations that are casual, informal and outside of standard collective contracts, either by choice or by necessity, the universality of social protection coverage becomes even more important. Decent work opportunities, balanced with economic growth and job creation, should be placed at the center of economic and social policymaking. Global demographic forces have had a significant impact on the employment and unemployment situations. The aging populations and declining birth rates in developed countries contrast with the younger populations and relatively higher fertility rates in developing countries. In 2006, about 84 per cent of the global labor force was located in developing countries, with Asia and the Pacific region accounting for about 60 per cent of world employment.

It is estimated that in 2006, about 1.4 billion of workers did not earn enough to lift themselves and their families above the $2-a-day poverty level. The proportion of the $2-a-day working poor in total employment decreased from around 60 per cent over the previous ten years to around 48 per cent. Nevertheless, the number of people surviving on less than $2-a-day actually increased in sub-Sahara Africa over the same period. Deindustrialization has been a characteristic of developed countries since the 1980s; it has been occurring in many developing countries as well, where a net transfer of jobs from agriculture to the service sector has taken place.

The world is rapidly becoming an economic system dominated by the service sector in which many jobs are low-paying and not covered by formal arrangements for social protection. The issue of long-term unemployment is of particular concern since it results in impoverishment, loss of networks of support, individual dignity, energy and willpower. Concern about the extent and seriousness of long-term unemployment is pervasive; given the lack of long-term unemployment benefits in many countries, many of the unemployed drift into informal activities and underemployment.

The world of work is being profoundly transformed. Sectoral shifts are themselves making the concept of full-time single-occupation employment almost an anachronism. Above all, the sense of insecurity accompanying the different types of informal economic activity, and the lack of employment security, pose major challenges for policymakers that make the employment imperative one of the highest economic priorities in today's world. Unemployment and underemployment lies at the core of poverty.

For the poor, labour is often the only asset they can use to improve their well-being. Hence the creation of productive employment opportunities is essential for achieving poverty reduction and sustainable economic and social development. It is crucial to provide decent jobs that both secure income and empowerment for the poor, especially women and younger people. Rapid economic growth can potentially bring a high rate of expansion of productive and remunerative employment, which can lead to a reduction in poverty. Nevertheless, the contribution of the growth process to poverty reduction does not depend only on the rate of economic growth, but also on the ability of the poor to respond to the increasing demand for labour in the more productive categories of employment.

Given the importance of employment for poverty reduction, job-creation should occupy a central place in national poverty reduction strategies. Many employment strategies are often related to agricultural and rural development and include using labour-intensive agricultural technologies; developing small and medium-size enterprises, and promoting micro projects in rural areas. Many strategies promote self-employment, non-farm employment in rural areas, targeted employment interventions, microfinance and credit as means of employment generation, skill formation and training.

Such strategies, however, often address the quantity of employment while the qualitative dimensions, such as equity, security, dignity and freedom are often absent or minimal. In general, national poverty reduction strategies including Poverty Reduction Strategies do not comment on employment programmes, social protection or rights at work. Neither do they offer in-depth analysis of the effects of policies on poverty reduction. A social perspective on development emphasizes the view that the best route to socio-economic development, poverty eradication and personal wellbeing is through decent work. Productive employment opportunities will contribute substantially to achieving the internationally agreed development goals, especially the Millennium Development Goal of halving extreme poverty by 2015.

There should be a focus on creating better and more productive jobs, particularly those that can absorb the high concentrations of working poor. Among the necessary elements for creating such jobs are investing in labour-intensive industries, especially agriculture, encouraging a shift in the structure of employment to higher productivity occupations and sectors, and upgrading job quality in the informal economy. In addition, there should also be a focus on providing poor people with the necessary skills and assets that will enable them to take full advantage of any expansion in employment potential.

6

Rural Women, Mental Health, and Economic Development

Although women constitute 52% of the rural population (30% of all women in the United States), their representation in professional psychological literature is almost nonexistent. There is a dearth of research concerning the behavioral health needs of this substantial, but frequently unnoticed population. The research which has been done is usually specific to very limited geographic regions which are not necessarily representative of other rural communities or, when larger samples are employed, demographic information including age, ethnicity, and cultural background are often not provided, further limiting the generalizability of findings.

Moreover, many studies have compared rural with urban samples and drawn conclusions even though the operational definitions of rural and urban often differ widely. Rural women are not a homogenous group. They reside in rural areas that are diverse in their geography, economic base, demographics, and development. The Midwestern farmlands, western frontier areas, Alaskan villages, West Virginian mountains, Deep South countryside, Island villages, so called "boom towns," and "bust towns" all comprise rural America.

While several definitions of rural exist, there are common elements throughout rural life: low population density; geographical distance from large metropolitan areas; isolation; dense social networks; a culture of self-sufficiency; and fewer economic and manpower resources. How these characteristics affect the manifestation, prevention, and treatment of the behavioral health care needs of rural women will be explored. This report attempts to direct attention to this underrepresented group and presents a review of the literature related to the behavioral health care needs of rural women. With this knowledge, psychologists and other health professionals will be able to more effectively plan and deliver services to this population.

Additional goals for this report include identifying those questions, which still remain unanswered, and providing recommendations for future research, action, and advocacy related to addressing the needs of this underserved population. The literature review was confined to the United States rural population, concentrating on research published after 1975. Because so little research has focused exclusively on rural women, it was necessary to look at the secondary analyses reported in studies and the reader is again cautioned to remember that many studies will have only limited generalizability. This report concentrates on the broad area of behavioral health care needs including, but not limited to, the domain of mental health needs, for several reasons. First, by focusing on behavioral health care needs, a vast array of lifestyle and psychological factors can be addressed.

These factors contribute to health and well being as well as to susceptibility to illness and outcome of treatment. As the role of psychologist evolves, these lifestyle factors become increasingly important points for intervention. Second, the broad sociocultural and lifestyle factors that typify rural life will likely affect physical and mental health in similar ways. For example, geographic barriers, distance, lack of transportation, and inadequate funding affect access to both medical and mental health services. Third, because of the lack of resources in most rural areas, a generalist approach toward intervention is often the most effective. Lastly, the public heath model for combating physical and mental health problems in rural areas has had a long history of acceptance.

The incidence and prevalence rates of most behavioral

health disorders are at least as high in rural areas as in urban communities. The Epidemiological Catchment Area Study, which compared rural and urban prevalence rates for a large variety of psychiatric disorders, the urban lifetime prevalence rate was 34%, which was only slightly higher than the 32% rate in rural areas. In a study of rural Tennessee households, women reported higher levels of anxiety and depression than their urban counterparts, coupled with poorer physical, mental, and general health.

However, rural America lacks political influence and, as a consequence, rural mental health services do not figure prominently in mental health policy. Stressful life events that are unique to rural environments have been linked to feelings of depression and worthlessness in many rural communities. High levels of stress may be the result of limited access to the resources required to meet both personal and interpersonal needs. According to the Surgeon General of the United States, rapid social change and widely experienced catastrophes such as the farm crisis of the 1980s which unleashed a period of severe economic hardship in many areas already beset by poverty, adversely affected the mental health of the population.

Between 1981 and 1985, 500,000 jobs were lost in rural areas, adding tremendously to unemployment. Many, though not all, rural economies continue to decline and pastoral America is no longer a stable or homogeneous environment. Fifty-three percent of the nation's poor reside in the rural southeast and a disproportionate percentage of the nation's poor live in rural regions across the United States. More than 800 rural counties have high poverty rates and the majority of impoverished United States counties are located in nonmetropolitan areas.

Sixty-seven percent of the nation's substandard housing is in rural areas. According to the United States Department of Agriculture (1998), the most current information related to poverty consistently shows higher levels of poverty are in nonmetropolitan communities than in more urban locations. The poverty rate in nonmetropolitan America stood at 15.9% in 1996 (essentially the same as the figure for 1995), which was significantly higher than the poverty rate of 13.2% in metropolitan areas. Moreover, the rate of poverty in nonmetropolitan regions has been quite stable over the last 8 years, only varying within a range of 1.6%.

The non metropolitan-to-metropolitan poverty gap, currently at 2.7 percentage points, has continued to widen (United States Department of Agriculture, 1998). Non metropolitan poverty rates continued to be higher than those in metropolitan regions across many demographic groups (United States Department of Agriculture, 1998). Families headed by women experienced the highest poverty rates of all family types, (over 40% in non metropolitan areas compared to urban rates of 34.4%), and a high proportion of non metropolitan women living alone were also poor (30.4%). More than one-fifth of rural children lived in poor families.

Over half of the non metropolitan poor (52%) live in the South, a disproportionate concentration compared with the South's 44% of the total non metropolitan population. Poverty rates among rural minorities are much higher than those of rural Caucasians and substantially higher than those of minorities residing in urban centers (United States Department of Agriculture, 1998). The poverty rate was highest for non metropolitan Blacks (35.2%), followed by non metropolitan Native Americans (33.7%) and non metropolitan Hispanics (33.4%). Almost two-thirds of the rural poor were non-Hispanic Caucasians, a factor largely due to the large Caucasian majority in the rural population (United States Department of Agriculture, 1998).

Nearly all states have distinct rural populations and more than 60% of rural areas have been designated as federal Mental Health Professional Shortage Areas. Rural residents are less likely than their urban counterparts to have access to inpatient mental health services; in many isolated rural counties, inpatient psychiatric services are almost nonexistent. The public mental health system is often the only provider in rural areas and primarily serves persons with serious mental illnesses. Therefore, isolated rural residents who seek mental health services will most likely have to travel long distances for services and will probably see a mental health provider with less advanced training than their urban peers.

Both psychologists and psychiatrists tend to be concentrated in urban areas. Rural areas have serious shortages of doctoral trained mental health professionals. This shortage of doctoral level mental health professionals often means that rural residents must receive psychological services from primary care physicians who may be poorly prepared to recognize and treat mental illness and behavioral disorders. Moreover, as noted by Geller and Muus (1999), in the absence of trained mental health providers, rural individuals often are forced to seek mental health services from the "de facto mental health system", including ministers, self-help groups, and family or friends.

While these services may be important components of total care, they are unlikely to be comprehensive, thorough or adequate. Numerous community surveys and treatment studies have consistently reported that women exhibit higher levels of psychological distress, particularly depressive symptomatology, than do men. Although the factors responsible for this gender difference have not been clearly identified, it is suggested that they may include socio-demographic variables and the nature and extent of multiple roles often assumed by women.

For rural women, in particular, certain variables do appear to increase the risk for depression. These include age, race, motherhood, poverty, and single parenting. Rural women who reside in the South may be particularly "at risk" with respect to the development of an emotional or mental health disorder as a result of factors such as poverty, isolation, and limited opportunities. Delworth, Veach, and Grohe (1988) and Gallagher and Delworth (1993) discussed two primary stressors of rural farm women: role overload (i.e., concurrently working on the farm, in the household, and as an employee or student outside the home); and "invisibility" or lack of recognition for the work that they do on the farm.

Scholl (1983) found little difference between non employed and employed farm women in their participation in farm work, providing evidence for overload. Gallagher and Delworth (1993) describe this role overload in terms of the "third shift" experienced by many farm women. As a result of financial need, one-third to one-half of all rural women are employed either part-time or full-time outside of the farm. Thus, many farm women are participating in a "first work shift" of off-farm employment and then work the "second shift" of housework and child care, often with little participation from their husband and with few community options for child care.

The "third shift" is the farm work, which these women continue to do even while employed off-farm. These duties include keeping farm financial records, paying taxes and bills, fieldwork and farm chores. This demanding schedule of responsibilities and roles leaves rural women little time to attend to their own needs or to seek out social support. This decreased opportunity to visit friends or participate in social and religious functions is related to increased feelings of anxiety and depression and feelings of loneliness and isolation are common experiences for many rural women.

Other common stressors faced by rural farm women include declining farm productivity; managing conflict as family members work in close proximity with each other; unpredictable and irregular income; and weather problems. The farm crisis of the 1980s contributed significantly to the already-existing stress that many rural farm women experienced. The job of caring for aging parents and ailing relatives often falls on the shoulders of rural women. Large extended families are more common in rural areas and family members often live in close proximity.

Bushy stated that ruralites tend to resist having people they do not know well take care of them, as the rural cultural norms reinforce "taking care of your own." These care giving chores then become another responsibility of the rural woman. Additionally, the caregivers for the severely mentally ill in rural areas are generally mothers who are expected to fill the caregiver role at the expense of their own physical and emotional well-being. The stress of caring for others is made even more difficult because of the lack of available services that can be used to support home care, the distances that often must be traveled to obtain services, and financial difficulties. Therefore it is not surprising to find that rural residents with chronic mental and health illnesses employ crisis services more frequently.

Although depression is quite prevalent in rural areas, and psychological complaints account for more than 40% of all patient visits to rural family practitioners, rural family practice physicians detect 50% less depression in their patients than do their urban counterparts. Unfortunately, even when mental health professionals were available near physicians' offices, only 5% of the depressed patients received any form of mental health care and it is not uncommon for more than two thirds of the unidentified depression cases initially seen by family practitioners in rural primary care settings to meet the criteria for major depression five months later.

These findings may be the result of the physicians' failure to detect psychological problems and to refer for mental health treatment, or to the stigma still attached to receiving mental health care, and the financial difficulties associated with care. Rural residents often do not associate somatic symptoms with psychiatric or psychological concerns or stressors, and do not want to receive treatment that is obviously psychiatric in nature. Rather, they often favor a perspective which integrates social, mental and physical health and refer to problems and concerns which can be acceptably defined as "problems in living," suggesting that appropriate and culturally sensitive mental health services integrated into rural primary care settings are likely to be more effective and to reach a larger number of patients than outside referrals to mental health providers.

Van Hook (1996) has noted that rural women in particular are unlikely to discuss the symptoms of depression with their primary care providers, and frequently present in primary care settings with psychosomatic symptoms such as headaches, backaches, insomnia, fatigue, and abdominal pain. Other Chronic Illnesses Rural women are beset with a number of health concerns, often to a greater extent than rural men and urban residents in general. When compared to urbanites, ruralites suffer from higher incidences of chronic illness and experience more disability and morbidity related to diabetes, cancer, hypertension, heart disease, stroke, and lung disease.

This may partially be due to ruralites lack of knowledge about early detection and prevention measures. Duelberg (1992) reported that rural women had PAP smears less often than urban women did. Therefore many health problems are in advanced stages by the time rural women seek out medical care, resulting in poorer prognoses. Moreover, rural women who are diagnosed with breast cancer are less likely to be offered breast conserving treatment options (including reconstruction) and significantly more likely to undergo radical mastectomy than urban women, despite the medical availability of other, less disfiguring procedures.

Discharge data from the Hospital Cost and Utilization Project (1981-1987) show that women treated in urban hospitals are nearly twice as likely to have a breast-conserving procedure and 40% less likely to have a radical mastectomy than rural patients. Rural women surveyed in this study cited transportation as a major factor in this decision process, noting that they anticipate problems traveling on icy rural roads to complete radiation treatments associated with lumpectomy and similar procedures.

This study suggested that these rural residents have remained unconvinced of the validity of publicized information on the comparability of therapeutic outcomes of lumpectomy and mastectomy. Maternal health problems are particularly acute for rural women. Fetal, infant, and maternal mortality are disproportionately high in rural areas. Over half a million rural residents live in counties that are without a physician trained to deliver obstetric care. The lack of medical specialists means that rural women are more likely to receive obstetric care from family practitioners than from obstetricians.

Even family practitioners are often reluctant to provide obstetric care because of the high cost of malpractice insurance, fear of lawsuits, and the lack of time off from work. Rural women suffer from the hazards of employment specific to rural environments. In a study of the cancer risks related to agriculture exposure among female farmers, McDuffie (1994) found excesses of non-Hodgkin's lymphoma, leukemia, multiple myeloma, and cancers of the breast, ovary, lung, bladder, and cervix. Secondary exposure to agricultural chemicals by laundering the clothing of agriculture workers also poses considerable risk to women. Rural women are susceptible to injury as a result of accidents.

Traumatic injuries are more common in rural areas, and residents face worse outcomes and higher risks of death than urban patients, partly because of transportation problems and lack of advanced life support training for emergency medical personnel. Identifying these factors may help shape solutions. Rural women are also less likely to engage in healthy lifestyle activities such as regular physical exercise and activity. They are more likely to be obese and think less favorably about their weight than urban women.

ACQUIRED IMMUNE DEFICIENCY SYNDROME

Although most of the women with HIV/AIDS reside in metropolitan areas, 6% reside in rural regions. Women are most at risk as the result of heterosexual intimacy which is the most common cause of HIV infection in rural areas, and the infection of the female by the male during heterosexual contact is far more likely than the reverse. In rural eastern North Carolina, people with HIV are more likely to be female, heterosexual, non-Caucasian, and younger. In many rural areas, heterosexual contact accounts for the most HIV transmission. In rural Monroe County, LA, women accounted for 33.3% of all new HIV infections and adolescents 9.7%.

In addition, having a sexually transmitted disease (STD) such as syphilis and gonorrhea may increase the likelihood of HIV transmission. Monroe also has one of the highest syphilis rates in the nation. In addition, the rate of increase in incidence of HIV/AIDS is higher in non metropolitan than metropolitan areas. From 1991 through 1992, there was a 9.4% rate of increase in incidence in non metropolitan areas in comparison to the 3.1% to 3.3% rate of increase in urban areas (National

Rural Health Association, 1997) and from 1992-1995 there was a 30% increase in AIDS cases in rural areas, especially among women, blacks, and adolescents, in comparison to 25.8% in the largest urban centers.

The most rapid escalation is occurring in southern states. Between 1988 and October, 1995, southern states reported both the largest increase in actual numbers and in proportion of population diagnosed with HIV/AIDS (National Rural Health Association, 1997). Ellerbrock, et. al., (1992) found the proportion of women with AIDS in smaller cities and rural areas to have increased from 22% in 1986 to 28% in 1990. Slightly more than half of these AIDS cases were found in intravenous (IV) drug users. However, even after controlling for IV drug use, infection rates for rural African American women are 20 times higher than for their Caucasian counterparts. Injection drug use and non-injection drug use, especially crack cocaine use, puts many rural residents at risk for HIV. Drug use is closely linked to prostitution, especially among women and teens.

The combination of crack cocaine use and a flourishing sex industry have caused Belle Glade, FL, an agricultural community near West Palm Beach, to have the highest cumulative per capita incidence of AIDS in the US. Empirical examinations of the knowledge, attitudes, and behavior of ruralites with respect to HIV/AIDS have yielded mixed results, with some populations showing better than average knowledge while other populations show large gaps in information and negative attitudes about various AIDS related issues. These authors found that 29% of rural women living in the southeastern United States who received an anonymous questionnaire believed AIDS could be contracted when donating blood.

Rozmus & Edgil (1993) also found that women residing in rural areas tend to view AIDS as a problem found only in large cities. Worse, rural residents are likely to be diagnosed in later stages of illness because local health professionals often do not consider them to be at risk, shortening the duration of treatment but increasing the need for more aggressive medical and mental health interventions. Also contributing to the incidence of HIV/AIDS are the high risk sexual or drug using behavior that rural residents may engage in when they travel to urban centers.

Rural men who engage in sexual activities with other males, either in their home communities or in larger urban centers, usually remain secretive about their behaviors. Rural communities can be wellsprings of strong condemnation at times, and traditional moral values, conformity to community norms and intolerance of diversity, homophobia, racism, sexism, stigmatization of people with AIDS, homosexuals, minorities and drug users may make effective HIV prevention nearly impossible (National Commission on AIDS, 1992). Confidentiality can be hard to maintain in rural areas.

Testing for HIV, discussing sexual practices with clinicians, obtaining drug treatment, or buying condoms in local stores are preventive mechanisms which may be less likely to occur in rural communities where a lack of confidentiality and anonymity are perceived. The accuracy of reported rates of HIV/AIDS in rural areas may be detrimentally influenced by several factors, resulting in serious misrepresentations of the need for resources in non metropolitan communities. The CDC did not begin to report AIDS incidences by non metropolitan area until 1991, and those published are typically cumulative totals.

The allocation of resources related to HIV/AIDS is based on where cases are diagnosed and on reported residence at the time of the diagnosis. Rural residents are more likely to underestimate their personal risk and less likely to seek testing for HIV/AIDS than urbanites. Those who do seek services commonly travel to metropolitan areas for testing, diagnosis and treatment, citing concerns about confidentiality, competence of local health providers, and the availability of newer technological interventions.

Further, many rural residents with HIV/AIDS have migrated to non metropolitan areas only after becoming infected and/or having been diagnosed in metropolitan centers, and the migration of people from urban to rural areas is cited as one possible contributor to the increasing AIDS rates in rural areas. A study conducted by the CDC (1995) which followed 49,621 injecting drug users supports this migration theory in a population previously thought to be sedentary. While most of the study participants were recruited in high HIV-prevalence areas, two-thirds of them later migrated to areas that were considered to be low-prevalence communities.

Migration patterns of racial and ethnic groups may vary significantly. For example, research suggests that Hispanics and Caucasians with AIDS migrate to other major metropolitan areas as often as to rural communities. African Americans with AIDS were generally less likely to migrate than other racial and ethnic groups. However, when they did leave the large metropolitan areas, African Americans were twice as likely to migrate to the south.

VIOLENCE AND RURAL WOMEN

Violence committed by women and against women, poverty, and homelessness are complex and interrelated social phenomena which are no less prevalent and problematic in rural areas than in urban and metropolitan settings. The incidence of spousal abuse does not differ significantly across these residential conditions. Although metropolitan rates for attempted rapes per 1,000 women are approximately twice as high as that reported for rural residents, the incidence of completed rape does not differ between settings.

Greater financial and economic dependence on men by women has been associated with increased rates of domestic violence. Approximately half of the homeless women in the United States are without shelter because they are fleeing from spousal abuse. Single women and women-heads of household with total incomes that fall below the poverty line are five times more likely to be victims of violence.

Forty-five to 60% of women headed households in the United States have incomes which fall below the poverty line, and as many as 80% of households headed by African-American women have incomes below the poverty level. More than half of these impoverished families are rural (National Low Income Housing Commission, 1998). Women in major metropolitan areas have the highest risk of being victims of violent assault perpetrated by strangers. However, the majority of violent and homicidal assaults against women are perpetrated by persons known to their assailant.

Rural women who are victimized are significantly more likely to report that they knew the perpetrator than their urban counterparts. Overall suicide rates are highest in rural areas of the western states, with young women in this region committing suicide three times more than those living in metropolitan settings. Both homicides and suicides occur disproportionately among young Native Americans living in rural areas. Homicide is the third leading cause of death for Native American females 15 to 34 years of age.

Rural residents of both genders are more likely to use firearms in homicides and suicides than urban residents. High levels of rurality, frequently in conjunction with poverty, have been associated with higher rates of homicide throughout the United States. The rural environment has a unique impact on the manifestation, reporting, and outcome measurement of violence against and by women. For example, suicide rates for rural women may be underreported because, to protect the immediate family or avoid religious or ideological implications, rural coroners may be reticent to identify suicide as the cause of death.

In small, close knit rural communities, victims and perpetrators of sexual assault or spouse abuse are often involved in family or other relationships with the local emergency personnel who would be responding to any call for help. These multiple relationships and the general lack of anonymity common to small communities can virtually eliminate such needed safeguards as confidentiality and responder objectivity. Rural communities are isolated from larger metropolitan areas and individual homes may be separated by long distances. Geographic barriers and inclement weather conditions may enhance this isolation.

Not only do such circumstances lessen the likelihood that the actions of the perpetrator will be identified or witnessed by others, but the rural violent offender often uses this isolation to great advantage. Many families do not have telephones and telephone access is easily controlled by simply removing the equipment that may be available. Public transportation is almost never available in rural areas and access to any available vehicles can be easily denied.

Rural women who seek escape from a violent situation face difficulties that are not encountered by victims in more metropolitan settings. Farm women are often an integral component in the labor and finances of the farm and leaving the home may entail losses that can never be recouped. Rural women, and rural residents in general, may be very attached to the land itself and without continued care, precious livestock may be endangered. Shelters, when available, may be so far from the woman's work location that escape would require the abandonment of a job or child care placement in an area where these resources are extremely scarce.

Escape may also require the rural woman to separate herself from the primary sources of support she has depended on throughout her lifetime or to violate local customs in a manner that results in alienation and censure of the victim. Victims who do report violent assaults are likely to discover that services are substandard or entirely unavailable. Few rural hospital emergency rooms have rape kits or personnel who are trained to examine and interview rape victims. Shelters are scarce and may be difficult to access. The objectivity and confidentiality of local services and local service providers may be limited by the existence of multiple relationships and shared cultural biases.

SPECIAL POPULATIONS

Elderly Rural Women The elderly within rural communities are a population of special concern. The United States Bureau of the Census (1991) reported that one out of four older Americans live in rural areas, comprising 15% of the total rural population as compared to 11% of metropolitan regions. The proportion of elderly in the rural South is significantly higher than in other regions. Women have a greater representation among the rural elderly than males, with women outnumbering men three to two at age 65 and five to two at age 85.

These women often outlive their husbands by as much as 20 years. Data on elderly rural women includes few cross-classifications by minority status. The Centers for Disease Control (1993) found that 92% of the nonmetropolitan elderly and 88% of the metropolitan elderly were Caucasian. A phenomenological article by Carlton-LaNey (1992) of 10 elderly rural African-Americans revealed risk areas that include economic security, health, care giving responsibilities, social isolation, and dependency upon others. Dorfman and Moffett (1987) completed an eight-year epidemiological study on 91 married and 77 widowed retired women age 65 and older in rural Iowa counties.

They found that aid received from others by widowed women negatively affected satisfaction with retirement, perhaps symbolizing the loss of independence. The authors postulated that needing help from others may serve as a reminder that their spouse is deceased and reinforce their sense of loneliness. Schwenk (1994) stated rural elderly women experience high levels of stress associated with their inability to provide care for themselves and loved ones. Volunteer work was related to satisfaction with retirement for both groups of women. It appears that the more active these women are within their community, the greater sense of self and connectedness they feel. Self-perceived health was related to retirement satisfaction for both groups. Incomes of rural elderly women are considerably less than their urban counterparts.

The average income was $8,209, although the urban population received $11,869. Nonmetropolitan elders have significantly higher rates of poverty than their metropolitan counterparts. They compose 20.3% of those in poverty compared with 13.5% in metro areas. Economic status was found to be strongly affected by marital status. Glasgow, Holden, McLaughlin & Rowles (1993) found that 8% of elderly rural couples were poor, while more than 33% of single or widowed women were below the poverty level. Rural elderly are more likely to be disabled than their urban counterparts, to have chronic health and physical impairments, and to consider themselves in fair or poor health.

The most common disorders afflicting rural elderly women are arthritis, hypertension, and cardiovascular problems. However, older rural adults are less likely than their urban counterparts to use non institutional service providers to deal with their health issues and concerns. Rural residents and their health care providers are more dependent on receiving Medicare for services than urban residents. Seccombe's study (1995) that consisted of 1,425 low-income elders found that those individuals living in rural areas were nearly twice as likely to receive Medicaid and rely on this service as a supplement to Medicare than those elderly living in urban areas. However, only one-fourth of the rural poor qualify for Medicaid, compared to 43% of the poor in urban areas.

Adolescents comprise another rural population deserving of serious attention. Pregnancy rates for 18 and 19 year old rural girls are 30 to 40% higher than their urban counterparts. However, pregnancies are equal in numbers for urban and rural girls under the age of 17. Abortions are half the rate for rural teenagers as they are for urban adolescents and the rural teenagers are more likely to give birth (77.4 per 1,000 births compared with 66.3 urban). Rural African-American teenagers between the ages of 10 to 14 years have an infant mortality rate of 28.5 per 1,000 births, more than twice the rate for African-American urban adolescents.

Alcohol abuse is higher in rural than urban areas, with 43% of rural adolescents and 40% of urban adolescents abusing alcohol. Rural adolescents in the eighth grade are 29% more likely to drink alcohol than their urban counterparts and they are also 70% more likely to get "drunk". Rural youths are more likely to drive an automobile under the influence of alcohol than their urban counterparts. Eighty percent of rural youth report that their parents approve of their alcohol consumption versus 63% for the urban youth. Rural eighth grade adolescents are 83% more likely to use crack cocaine, 50% more likely to use cocaine, 34% more likely to use marijuana, and 104% more likely to use amphetamines (including methamphetamine) than their urban counterparts.

They are twice as likely to smoke cigarettes and nearly 5 times more likely to use smokeless tobacco than urban teens. Among 10th grade youth, aged 15 to 16 years, rural adolescents are more likely to use almost all illegal drugs, with the exception of MDMA (known as "ecstasy" on the street) and marijuana. Similar results hold true for rural versus urban youth in the 12th grade (ages 17 to 18 years) (Center on Addiction and Substance Abuse, 2000). Unmarried Mothers Thirty-one percent of rural births are to unwed mothers, compared to 33% urban. Of these births, 73% were to African-American women which are slightly higher than the 70% reported for their urban counterparts.

One out of nine infants born in rural areas is to an unmarried teenage mother compared with one out of ten in urban areas. Teenagers represent a higher proportion of births out of marriage in rural areas. Although rural women were more likely to be married than urban women, the marital birth rate was lower in rural areas for 1994. Rural Lesbians Lesbians are shunned from rural society because of the traditional values and strong conservative ideas found within these communities. This population is perhaps the most invisible of all rural women. D'Augelli and Hart (1987) suggested that the anonymity often found in large cities is non existent in the rural areas. There can be few opportunities for social connection and a lack of a helping community, as these women are not all publicly open about their homosexuality.

This can lead to low self-esteem and depression. It is difficult to find common places to meet for socialization where others will not chastise them. This sense of cultural heterosexism is common among rural residents. If someone engages in homosexual behavior or is identified as such, society shuns them. However, rural lesbians are increasingly, and successfully, using the internet to improve their social contacts and to provide mutual assistance.

Rural Women with Disabilities

Women with disabilities constitute approximately 8% of the total U.S. population and approximately 26% of all women with disabilities are living in rural areas. Disabled rural women tend to be poorer, in worse health, less-educated and more dependent on government social service programs than others. They face limited access to employment and economic opportunities, limited transportation options, scarce or unaffordable housing, and lack of access to health care providers who are knowledgeable about disabilities.

Rural women with disabilities are approximately three times less likely to be employed (27%) than rural women without disabilities. In comparison, rural men with disabilities are approximately two times less likely to be employed (38%) than men without disabilities. Rural women with disabilities are the "poorest of the poor"- 80.51% make less than $10,000 a year. Elderly women with disabilities living in rural areas experience the most severe poverty. These stressors are likely to be exacerbated in rural areas due to lower levels of education, limited opportunities, and isolation.

Women with disabilities are more likely to report urinary tract infections, depression, osteoporosis, restrictive lung disease, inflammatory bowel disease, heart disease, seizure disorders, and kidney disease than able bodied women; those with mobility impairments experience an average of 14 secondary conditions per year (rural and urban did not differ). Rural women with physical disabilities who are victims of domestic violence typically experience abuse of longer duration and have fewer options than urban women, or even non disabled rural women, for escaping the abusive situation.

BARRIERS TO TREATMENT

Many residents of remote rural areas who suffer from mental illnesses do not seek care. Various factors affect the utilization of health care services within the rural community. As in urban areas, people do not seek care in part because of the stigma associated with mental illness, lack of understanding about mental illnesses and their treatments, lack of information about where to go for treatment, and the inability to pay for care. Cultural Barriers: Mistrust, Stigma and Loss of Independence The Surgeon General of the United States has recently cited the importance of providing culturally competent services to diverse groups, including rural residents.

Policies and programs designed for urban mental health services often are not appropriate for rural mental health services. Some barriers to "help-seeking" are "cultural," insofar as rural America reflects a range of cultures and life styles that are distinct from urban life. Urban culture and its approach to delivering mental health services dominate mental health services. Cultural attitudes commonly observed in rural communities include a distrust of others they do not know on a personal level. A high value is placed on self-reliance, and rural residents may fear that community members will find out that they required assistance for emotional difficulties which would directly conflict with that value.

The stigma that mental illnesses have in rural areas has been cited throughout the literature as have fears about confidentiality in rural settings that tend to lack anonymity. Finally, the health care workers in rural settings may contribute to the barriers perceived by the people they are serving. Therapists are often trained according to urban standards, which do not mesh in rural communities. Strickland & Strickland (1996) reported that physicians interact differently with lower socioeconomic and minority status clientele, giving less medical information and shorter consultations than with other patients of non minority status. Lack of Awareness of Services/ Lack of Perceived Value Mohatt & Kirwan (1995) found that rural residents lacked an awareness of the need for mental health care. Strickland & Strickland (1996) reported that preventive services were perceived as unnecessary, as evidenced by one-fifth of the rural women they studied not receiving gynecological care due to personal preference.

Fewer preventive services in rural versus urban areas, coupled with community values that discourage their use, and perceived prejudice and discrimination throughout the health care system may account for much of the under utilization. Lack of Services Should a rural woman decides to seek outreach services, she will find that professional psychologists are not evenly distributed and can not effectively meet the needs of isolated persons. Similarly, the lack of quality inpatient care for severely mentally ill people is another serious problem in rural areas. These patients must often obtain care in hospitals that are located far from family and friends or be hospitalized in general medical settings where no psychiatric consultation is available.

Once discharged back into the community, there are limited psychosocial rehabilitation services available and thus patients are often re-hospitalized at a very high cost compared to outpatient care. Rural residents may not be aware of the various entitlement programs available to them. Because of the high levels of poverty in rural areas, there is a limited tax base to fund these services, causing under funding and understaffing of health care centers which further exacerbates the problem. Cost The cost of services is a major barrier. Cost is consistently cited as the main deterrent to using mental health services. Beck et al. (1996) reported that out of 75 rural residents who did not receive health care because of the high cost, 68% were women.

Strickland & Strickland (1996) completed a study on 281 rural minority households and found that more than half reported the inability to pay as the main reason for not seeking the help of a physician. This is understandable, as poverty is far more prevalent for rural women than their male counterparts. Beck, Jijon & Edwards (1996) and Rowland & Lyons (1989) stated that a lack of health insurance is a significant barrier to treatment and rural areas have disproportionate populations of uninsured and underinsured. As a result of a large percentage of rural persons being employed in small business or self-employed, they are more likely to be uninsured or have only "catastrophic" insurance coverage, which lacks behavioral health benefits.

Only one-fourth of the rural poor qualify for Medicaid, compared to 43% of the poor in urban areas. Muller (1990) found that rural women were less likely to have health insurance than males due to the lack of employment opportunities and poverty. Of those people who have medical insurance, many lack insurance coverage for psychotherapy even if they can find a therapist in their area. Many of the newer psychoactive medications are very expensive so that treatment combining medication and psychotherapy is usually not an option for people in rural areas.

Access, Transportation, and Communication Barriers

Because large distances may separate patient and provider, transportation difficulties have been cited in the literature as another barrier to access of treatment. Rural residents may not own individual automobiles; some may not have driver's licenses and there is rarely any form of public transportation in rural and frontier regions. Strickland & Strickland (1996) found that some rural residents listed not having a telephone as a barrier to obtaining transportation to centers. Weather can also be detrimental to transportation needs and lack of ancillary services like child care can limit access to services.

Catchment Areas and Policy Catchment areas, established by a now lapsed act of Congress in 1963, still endure and can also complicate access to services for rural residents. Under this system, the delivery of public mental health is tied to county and state policy and revenues streams, often having to do with the reality of how persons seek services. Rural residents who routinely enact business in one area may be required to use services provided in another as a result of the funding mechanism in place. Longer travel is often mandated where the population density is low and frequently the travel has little to do with the rural resident's normal trade and commerce.

7

Equality, the Family and the Law

Family denotes a group of people or animals (many species form the equivalent of a human family wherein the adults care for the young) affiliated by a consanguinity, affinity or co-residence. Although the concept of consanguinity originally referred to relations by "blood," anthropologists have argued that one must understand the idea of "blood" metaphorically, and that many societies understand 'family' through other concepts rather than through genetic distance. One of the primary functions of the family is to produce and reproduce persons, biologically and socially.. Thus, one's experience of one's family shifts over time. From the perspective of children, the family is a family of orientation: the family serves to locate children socially, and plays a major role in their enculturation and socialization.

From the point of view of the parent(s), the family is a family of procreation the goal of which is to produce and enculturate and socialize children. However, producing children is not the only function of the family; in societies with a sexual division of labor, marriage, and the resulting relationship between two people, is necessary for the formation of an economically productive household. A conjugal family includes only the husband, the wife, and unmarried children who are not of age. The most common form of this family is regularly referred to as a nuclear family.

A consanguineal family consists of a parent and his or her children, and other people. This kind of family is common where mothers do not have the resources to rear their children on their own, and especially where property is inherited. When important property is owned by men, consanguineal families commonly consist of a husband and wife, their children and other members of the husband's family. A matrifocal family consists of a mother and her children. Generally, these children are her biological offspring, although adoption of children is a practice in nearly every society. This kind of family is common where women have the resources to rear their children by themselves, or where men are more mobile than women.

ECONOMIC FUNCTIONS

Anthropologists have often supposed that the family in a traditional society forms the primary economic unit. This economic role has gradually diminished in modern times, and in societies like the United States it has become much smaller - except in certain sectors such as agriculture and in a few upper class families. In China the family as an economic unit still plays a strong role in the countryside. However, the relations between the economic role of the family, its socio-economic mode of production and cultural values remain highly complex.

POLITICAL FUNCTIONS

On the other hand family structures or its internal relationships may affect both state and religious institutions. J.F. del Giorgio in *The Oldest Europeans* points out that the high status of women among the descendants of the post-glacial Paleolithic European population was coherent with the fierce love of freedom of pre-Indo-European tribes. He believes that the extraordinary respect for women in those families meant that children raised in such atmospheres tended to distrust strong, authoritarian leaders. According to del Giorgio, European democracies have their roots in those ancient ancestors.

KINSHIP TERMINOLOGY

Archaeologist Lewis Henry Morgan (1818–1881) performed the first survey of kinship terminologies in use around the world. Though much of his work is now considered dated, he argued that kinship terminologies reflect different sets of distinctions. For example, most kinship terminologies distinguish between sexes (the difference between a brother and a sister) and between generations (the difference between a child and a parent). Moreover, he argued, kinship terminologies distinguish between relatives by blood and marriage (although recently some anthropologists have argued that many societies define kinship in terms other than "blood").

Morgan made a distinction between kinship systems that use classificatory terminology and those that use descriptive terminology. Morgan's distinction is widely misunderstood, even by contemporary anthropologists. Classificatory systems are generally and erroneously understood to be those that "class together" with a single term relatives who actually do not have the same type of relationship to ego. (What defines "same type of relationship" under such definitions seems to be genealogical relationship. This is more than a bit problematic given that any genealogical description, no matter how standardized, employs words originating in a folk understanding of kinship.)

What Morgan's terminology actually differentiates are those (classificatory) kinship systems that do not distinguish lineal and collateral relationships and those (descriptive) kinship systems which do. Morgan, a lawyer, came to make this distinction in an effort to understand Seneca inheritance practices. A Seneca man's effects were inherited by his sisters' children rather than by his own children.

Morgan identified six basic patterns of kinship terminologies:

- Hawaiian: only distinguishes relatives based upon sex and generation.
- Sudanese: no two relatives share the same term.
- Eskimo: in addition to distinguishing relatives based upon sex and generation, also distinguishes between lineal relatives and collateral relatives.
- Iroquois: in addition to sex and generation, also

distinguishes between siblings of opposite sexes in the parental generation.

- Crow: a matrilineal system with some features of an Iroquois system, but with a "skewing" feature in which generation is "frozen" for some relatives.
- Omaha: like a Crow system but patrilineal.

Western kinship

Most Western societies employ Eskimo kinship terminology. This kinship terminology commonly occurs in societies based on conjugal (or nuclear) families, where nuclear families have a degree of relatively mobility.

Members of the nuclear family (or immediate family) use descriptive kinship terms:

- Mother: a female parent
- Father: a male parent
- Son: a male child of the parent(s)
- Daughter: a female child of the parent(s)
- Brother: a male child of the same parent(s)
- Sister: a female child of the same parent(s)
- Grandfather: father of a father or mother
- Grandmother: mother of a father or mother

Such systems generally assume that the mother's husband has also served as the biological father. In some families, a woman may have children with more than one man or a man may have children with more than one woman. The system refers to a child who shares only one parent with another child as a "half-brother" or "half-sister". For children who do not share biological or adoptive parents in common, English-speakers use the term "stepbrother" or "stepsister" to refer to their new relationship with each other when one of their biological parents marries one of the other child's biological parents.

Any person (other than the biological parent of a child) who marries the parent of that child becomes the "stepparent" of the child, either the "stepmother" or "stepfather". The same terms generally apply to children adopted into a family as to children born into the family. Typically, societies with conjugal families also favor neolocal residence; thus upon marriage a person separates from the nuclear family of their childhood (family of orientation) and forms a new nuclear family (family of procreation). However, in the western society the single parent family has been growing more accepted and has begun to truly make an impact on culture.

The majority of single parent families are more commonly single mother families than single father. These families face many difficult issues besides the fact that they have to raise their children on their own, but also have to deal with issues related to low income. Many single parents struggle with low incomes and find it hard to cope with other issues that they face including rent, child care, and other necessities required in maintaining a healthy and safe home.

Members of the nuclear families of members of one's own (former) nuclear family may class as lineal or as collateral. Kin who regard them as lineal refer to them in terms that build on the terms used within the nuclear family:

- Grandparent
    - Grandfather: a parent's father
    - Grandmother: a parent's mother
- Grandson: a child's son
- Granddaughter: a child's daughter

For collateral relatives, more classificatory terms come into play, terms that do not build on the terms used within the nuclear family:

- Uncle: father's brother, mother's brother, father's/mother's sister's husband
- Aunt: father's sister, mother's sister, father's/mother's brother's wife
- Nephew: sister's son, brother's son, wife's brother's son, wife's sister's son, husband's brother's son, husband's sister's son
- Niece: sister's daughter, brother's daughter, wife's brother's daughter, wife's sister's daughter, husband's brother's daughter, husband's sister's daughter

When additional generations intervene (in other words, when one's collateral relatives belong to the same generation as one's grandparents or grandchildren), the prefix "grand" modifies these terms. (Although in casual usage in the USA a "grand aunt" is often referred to as a "great aunt", for instance.) And as with grandparents and grandchildren, as more generations intervene the prefix becomes "great grand", adding an additional "great" for each additional generation.

Most collateral relatives have never had membership of the nuclear family of the members of one's own nuclear family.

- Cousin: the most classificatory term; the children of aunts or uncles. One can further distinguish cousins by degrees of collaterality and by generation. Two persons of the same generation who share a grandparent count as "first cousins" (one degree of collaterality); if they share a great-grandparent they count as "second cousins" (two degrees of collaterality) and so on. If two persons share an ancestor, one as a grandchild and the other as a great-grandchild of that individual, then the two descendants class as "first cousins once removed" (removed by one generation); if the shared ancestor figures as the grandparent of one individual and the great-great-grandparent of the other, the individuals class as "first cousins twice removed" (removed by two generations), and so on. Similarly, if the shared ancestor figures as the great-grandparent of one person and the great-great-grandparent of the other, the individuals class as "second cousins once removed". Hence the phrase "third cousin once removed upwards".

Cousins of an older generation (in other words, one's parents' first cousins), though technically first cousins once removed, often get classified with "aunts" and "uncles". Similarly, a person may refer to close friends of one's parents as "aunt" or "uncle", or may refer to close friends as "brother" or "sister", using the practice of fictive kinship. English-speakers mark relationships by marriage (except for wife/husband) with the tag "-in-law".

The mother and father of one's spouse become one's mother-in-law and father-in-law; the female spouse of one's child becomes one's daughter-in-law and the male spouse of one's child becomes one's son-in-law. The term "Sister-in-law" refers to three essentially different relationships, either the wife of one's sibling, or the sister of one's spouse, or the wife of one's spouse's sibling. "Brother-in-law" expresses a similar ambiguity. No special terms exist for the rest of one's spouse's family. The terms "half-brother" and "half-sister" indicate siblings who share only one biological or adoptive parent.

FAMILY IN THE WEST

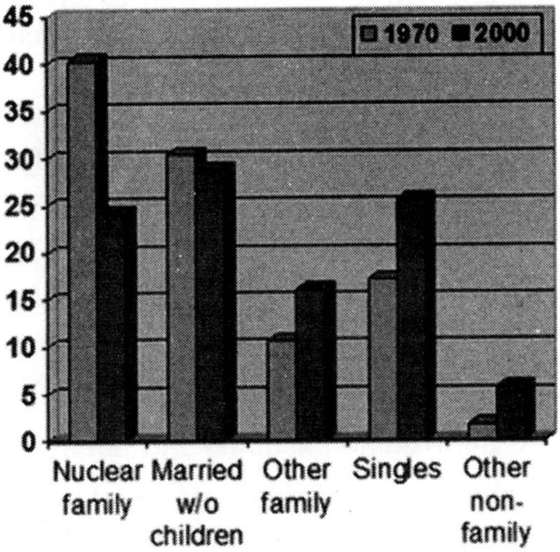

Family arrangements in the United States have become more diverse with no particular household arrangement representing half of the United States population.

The diverse data coming from ethnography, history, law and social statistics, establish that the human family is an institution and not a biological fact founded on the natural relationship of consanguinity. The different types of families occur in a wide variety of settings, and their specific functions and meanings depend largely on their relationship to other social institutions. Sociologists have a special interest in the function and status of these forms in stratified (especially capitalist) societies.

The term "nuclear family" is commonly used, especially in the United States and Europe, to refer to conjugal families. Sociologists distinguish between conjugal families (relatively independent of the kindreds of the parents and of other families in general) and nuclear families (which maintain relatively close ties with their kindreds). The term "extended family" is also common, especially in the United States and Europe. This term has two distinct meanings. First, it serves as a synonym of "consanguinal family". Second, in societies dominated by the conjugal family, it refers to kindred (an egocentric network of relatives that extends beyond the domestic group) who do not belong to the conjugal family.

These types refer to ideal or normative structures found in particular societies. Any society will exhibit some variation in the actual composition and conception of families. Much sociological, historical and anthropological research dedicates itself to the understanding of this variation, and of changes in the family form over time. Thus, some speak of the bourgeois family, a family structure arising out of 16th-century and 17th-century European households, in which the family centers on a marriage between a man and woman, with strictly-defined gender-roles. The man typically has responsibility for income and support, the woman for home and family matters.

Philosophers and psychiatrists like Deleuze, Guattari, Laing, Reich, explained that the patriarchal-family conceived in the West tradition (husband-wife-children isolated from the outside) serves the purpose of perpetuating a propertarian and authoritarian society. The child grows according to the Oedipal model, which is typical of the structure of capitalist societies, and he becomes in turn owner of submissive children and protector of the woman. Some argue the family institution conflicts with human nature, and that one of its core functions is performing a suppression of instincts, a repression of desire commencing with the earliest age of the child.

This psychic repression is such that social repression becomes desired, forming docile subjects for society. Michel Foucault, in his systematic study of sexuality, argued that desire, other than being repressed, is shaped and used as a tool, to control the individual and alter interpersonal relationships. He believed organized religion, through moral prohibitions, and economic powers, through advertising, make use of unconscious sex drives. Dominating desire, they dominate individuals.

According to the analysis of Michel Foucault, in the west:

> the [conjugal] family organization, precisely to the extent that it was insular and heteromorphous with respect to the other power mechanisms, was used to support the great "maneuvers" employed for the Malthusian control of the birthrate, for the populationist incitements, for the medicalization of sex and the psychiatrization of its nongenital forms.

According to the work of scholars Max Weber, Alan Macfarlane, Steven Ozment, Jack Goody and Peter Laslett, the huge transformation that led to modern marriage in Western democracies was "fueled by the religio-cultural value system provided by elements of Judaism, early Christianity, Roman Catholic canon law and the Protestant Reformation".

In contemporary Europe and the United States, people in academic, political and civil sectors have called attention to single-father-headed households, and families headed by same-sex couples, although academics point out that these forms exist in other societies. Also the term blended family or stepfamily describes families with mixed parents: one or both parents remarried, bringing children of the former family into the new family.

CONTEMPORARY VIEWS OF THE FAMILY

Contemporary society generally views family as a haven from the world, supplying absolute fulfilllment. The family is considered to encourage "intimacy, love and trust where individuals may escape the competition of dehumanizing forces in modern society from the rough and tumble industrialized world, and as a place where warmth, tenderness and understanding can be expected from a loving mother, and protection from the world can be expected from the father. However, the idea of protection is declining as civil society faces less internal conflict combined with increased civil rights and protection from the state. To many, the ideal of personal or family fulfilllment has replaced protection as the major role of the family. The family now supplies what is "vitally needed but missing from other social arrangements".

Social conservatives often express concern over a purported decay of the family and see this as a sign of the crumbling of contemporary society. They feel that the family structures of the past were superior to those today and believe that families were more stable and happier at a time when they did not have to contend with problems such as illegitimate children and divorce. Others dispute this theory, claiming "there is no golden age of the family gleaming at us in the far back historical past". The Family Equality Council envisions a future where all families, regardless of creation or composition, will be able to live in communities that recognize, respect, protect, and celebrate them.

The organization envisions a world that celebrates a diversity of family constellations and respects individuals for supporting one another and sustaining loving families. A study performed by scientists from Iceland found that mating with a relative can significantly increase the number of children in a family. A lot of societies consider inbreeding unacceptable. Scientists warn that inbreeding may raise the chances of a child getting two copies of disease-causing recessive genes and in such a way it may lead to genetic disorders and higher infant mortality.

Scientists found that couples formed of relatives had more children and grandchildren than unrelated couples. The study revealed that when a husband and wife were third cousins, they had an average of 4.0 children and 9.2 grandchildren. If a woman was in relationship with her eight cousin, then the number of children declined, showing an average of 3,3 children and 7,3 grandchildren.

SIZE

Natalism is the belief that human reproduction is the basis for individual existence, and therefore promotes having large families. Many religions, e.g., Judaism, encourage their followers to procreate and have many children. In recent times, there has been an increasing amount of family planning and a following decrease in total fertility rate in many parts of the world, in part due to concerns of overpopulation. Many countries with population decline offer incentives for people to have large families as a means of national efforts to reverse declining populations.

Family law is an area of the law that deals with family-related issues and domestic relations including, but not limited to:

- The nature of marriage, civil unions, and domestic partnerships;
- Issues arising during marriage, including spousal abuse, legitimacy, adoption, surrogacy, child abuse, and child abduction
- The termination of the relationship and ancillary matters including divorce, annulment, property settlements, alimony, and parental responsibility orders (in the United States, child custody and visitation, child support awards).

This list is by no means dispositive of the potential issues that come through the family court system. In many jurisdictions in the United States, the family courts see the most crowded dockets. Litigants representative of all social and economic classes are parties within the system.

CRITICISM OF FAMILY LAW

Members of the fathers' rights movement criticize the "win or lose" nature of family law in determining issues of divorce and child custody in many Western countries. Cross-national parties dealing with legal systems in different countries simultaneously grapple with substantive and procedural issues regarding child abduction, child custody and visitation. International human rights treaties and the Hague Convention agreements seek to address such concerns. Same-sex couples have made significant progress towards legal equality with different-sex couples through Charter litigation.

There have been a number of Charter challenges alleging discrimination on the basis of sexual orientation that have proceeded through the courts both in and apart from the family law context. Same-sex couples have used the Charter to gain rights and obligations similar to those available to different-sex couples. Same-sex couples built on the work of different-sex unmarried couples who sought, and sometimes obtained, the rights and obligations that the state made available to married couples. The history of the extension of rights and benefits to different-sex unmarried couples is intimately linked to the history of the extension of benefits to same-sex couples, and ultimately to the decision to allow same-sex couples to marry in Canada.

SEXUAL ORIENTATION AND MARITAL STATUS AS ANALOGOUS GROUNDS

The Charter does not explicitly protect people from discrimination on the basis of sexual orientation. Sexual orientation is not an "enumerated ground." That is, it is not a ground that is listed in s.15(1) of the Charter. Neither is marital status. It was critical for both unmarried different-sex couples and same-sex couples that the courts acknowledge that marital status and sexual orientation were "analogous grounds." That is, that marital status and sexual orientation were like the enumerated grounds set out in s.15(1), and the courts should protect people from discrimination on the basis of these grounds.

In Miron v. Trudel, [1995] 2 S.C.R. 418, one of these battles was won. In this case, the Supreme Court of Canada recognized marital status as an analogous ground of discrimination. The court in this case held that different-sex cohabiting couples were functionally similar to married couples and should not be denied benefits simply because they were not married. This provided different-sex couples with a powerful tool to challenge discriminatory laws that treated them differently than married couples. Similarly, gaining recognition of sexual orientation as a recognized analogous ground of discrimination was a vital first step for same-sex couples, which laid the foundation for the path toward equality in family law.

The Supreme Court held unanimously in Egan and Nesbit v. Canada, [1995] 2 S.C.R. 513 that sexual orientation was an analogous ground of discrimination for the purposes of s.15 of the Charter. While this was an important victory for same-sex couples, the case itself was ultimately lost. A 5-4 majority of the court found that a different-sex definition of spouse in the Old Age Security Act was discriminatory, but also that the discrimination was justifiable under s.1 of the Charter. The narrow majority in Egan found that there were characteristics, such as economic interdependence, present in married relationships and in different-sex common law relationships that did not necessarily exist in same-sex relationships.

TRYING TO CHANGE THE DEFINITION OF SPOUSE

The decision in Egan was short lived. Only four years later an 8-1 majority of the Supreme Court rejected the Egan approach to same-sex relationships in M. v. H., [1999] 2 S.C.R. 3. That case dealt with the support provisions of Ontario's Family Law Act (FLA), which allowed spouses who had been married or who had lived common law with someone of a different sex to sue for spousal support. People who had been part of a same-sex couple were not included in the legislation and therefore could not sue for spousal support.

The majority of the court found that the failure to provide same-sex partners with spousal support was discriminatory and could not be justified under s.1 of the Charter. The majority demanded that same-sex relationships be accorded equal dignity and respect under the law. In response, the Ontario government passed An Act to Amend Certain Statutes Because of the Supreme Court of Canada Decision in M. v. H, which amended provincial statutes to extend rights to same-sex couples. This included the right to seek spousal support. Interestingly, although the challenge in M. v. H. was to the different-sex requirement in the definition of "spouse" in the FLA, that definition remained intact. The Ontario government created a new "same-sex partner" category, rather than changing the definition of spouse.

Next Steps: After M. v. H.

Despite the widespread reforms enacted by governments across Canada in response to M. v. H., disparities still existed between different-sex and same-sex couples, not the least of which was that same-sex couples could not legally marry. Despite the Supreme Court's decision in M. v. H. that same-sex relationships were to be accorded equality and dignity under the law, no Canada-wide legislative scheme existed to regulate same-sex relationships. Rights parallel, or nearly parallel, to those granted to different-sex couples were conferred on same-sex couples in the areas of spousal support, adoption, health care decision making powers, pension benefits, custody and access, marital status discrimination, and insurance benefits. This list is not exhaustive, but it does demonstrate the dramatic changes in the law that occurred in a relatively short time.

Because of Canada's federal structure, not all of these rights were available to same-sex couples across Canada. Same-sex couples were entitled to a patchwork of rights depending on the province they lived in.

DIFFERENT-SEX COUPLES HIT A WALL

Prior to the introduction of the Charter, different-sex couples secured some rights without arguing that they had been discriminated against. In a series of important cases, women who had lived in different-sex cohabiting relationships were compensated for work they did to increase their partner's worth. Many of these cases involved women who worked on farms that were in their partner's name. Because they were not married, they could not seek a division of property after they separated and anything that was in one partner's name, remained his after separation. Women argued that they should be compensated for the work they had done and the courts agreed. Using trust principles, courts compensated women for work they had done that increased the value of their former partner's homes and businesses in cases like Pettkus v. Becker, 1980 CanLII 22.

Despite this progress, the law continues to distinguish between married couples and unmarried couples when it comes to the division of property. After martial status was determined to be an analogous ground, many believed that it was only a matter of time before laws preventing common law couples from claiming a division of property would be found to be unconstitutional. However, notwithstanding decisions like Pettkus, which have questioned and ultimately blurred the legal line between married and common law couples, the case of Nova Scotia (Attorney General) v. Walsh, 2002 SCC 83 unequivocally held that some distinctions between the two groups are constitutionally sound.

In Walsh, the Supreme Court of Canada considered a challenge to s.2(g) of Nova Scotia's Matrimonial Property Act. Section 2(g) of the Act, which applied only to married, rather than to common law spouses (be they different- or same-sex partners), created a presumption of equal division of marital property upon marriage breakdown. Ms. Walsh, had cohabitated with her common law spouse for 10 years and she challenged the exclusion of common law couples from this presumption, claiming that the denial of the presumption constituted the denial of a benefit of the law on the basis of marital status, and was discriminatory.

The majority of the Supreme Court found that s.2(g) of the Act drew a distinction between married and unmarried cohabitating couples, but did not discriminate against unmarried cohabitants. Eight of the nine justices found that the distinction did not affect the dignity of unmarried cohabitants and did not deny them access to a benefit available to married persons. It was, therefore, not discriminatory within the meaning of s.15(1) of the Charter. The court's reasoning focused on the perceived need to allow people to consciously choose, or not choose, the rights and obligations of marriage.

This decision brought a rather abrupt end to a line of appellate decisions that had consistently struck down distinctions between married and unmarried cohabitating different-sex couples. While this decision was arguably a failure to protect the substantive equality rights of unmarried different-sex couples, and in particular women, it was an important precursor to the same-sex marriage cases that followed. By establishing that there were concrete and material differences between marriage and cohabitation, the court set the stage for a constitutional challenge to the different-sex requirement for marriage.

One of the principle arguments put forward in opposition to same-sex marriage was that "marriage" was merely a name and that same-sex couples could have access to all the same rights and benefits of marriage without having access to the label "marriage." By maintaining a distinction between marriage and cohabitation, the court made this argument more difficult. At the time, same-sex couples in many provinces could not "opt-in" to the benefits of marriage. The availability of this choice was a primary consideration in Walsh. It was because (different-sex) couples had the choice to marry that the court decided it was not discrimination to provide married couples with a regime of property division not available to unmarried cohabitants.

SAME-SEX MARRIAGE: THE CASES

Constitutional challenges to the requirement that partners be of different sexes in order to get married were brought in several provinces. The first cases were heard in British Columbia, Ontario and Quebec. In 2001, the British Columbia trial court decided that the different-sex requirement was not unconstitutional. In other words, restricting marriage to different-sex couples was fine. While the court held that s.15(1) had been violated, it held that the violation was saved under s.1. The court emphasized that marriage was the means to promote procreation and the biological "reality" that only different-sex couples could procreate naturally. While this was an inauspicious start, this decision was rejected by lower courts in Ontario (July 2002) and Quebec (September 2002).

In 2003, the Court of Appeal for British Columbia, relying on decisions from the lower courts in Ontario and Quebec, overturned the 2001 decision and held that same-sex couples in that province could marry. On June 10, 2003, the Court of Appeal for Ontario upheld the lower court decision finding the different-sex requirement unconstitutional. The Court of Appeal held (at Para. 10) that "Marriage is, without dispute, one of the most significant forms of personal relationships... Through the institution of marriage, individuals can publicly express their love and commitment to each other. Through this institution, society publicly recognizes expressions of love and commitment between individuals, granting them respect and legitimacy as a couple..."

Importantly, the Court of Appeal for Ontario decided that since the different-sex requirement was a judge-made law, judges could change it. In other jurisdictions, courts had declared the different-sex requirement unconstitutional, but had suspended their judgments to give the legislature a chance to respond. In other words, although it was held that the different-sex marriage requirement was unconstitutional in both British Columbia and Quebec, couples could not immediately marry.

In Ontario, the Court of Appeal decided that couples did not have to wait. Immediately upon the release of the decision, same-sex couples in Ontario could marry, and a few did so that very day. This incredible achievement was followed quickly by a decision from the Yukon court extending equal marriage to same-sex couples. Manitoba and Nova Scotia were quick to follow, as was a decision from the Quebec Court of Appeal.

LEGISLATION TO LEGALIZE SAME-SEX MARRIAGE IS PASSED

On June 17, 2003, Prime Minister Chretien and Justice Minister Cauchon announced that the federal government was going to introduce legislation legalizing same-sex marriage across the country. The government submitted four questions to the Supreme Court of Canada, asking the court to provide an opinion on them. This is called a reference and it is within the court's jurisdiction to answer questions of this sort posed by the government. The Supreme Court assured the government that it was capable of legalising same-sex marriage. A law was introduced in 2005 and was passed on June 28. The law was proclaimed into force when it received Royal Assent on July 20, 2005.

INEQUALITY AND DEVELOPMENT

For a pursuer, his pursued quantity does not increase monotonously. Pursued quantity difference between pursuers is called inequality of pursued quantity. Theorem of inequality:

Inequality of pursued quantity in unit time will grow with system expansion.

In order to develop, inequality is necessary. Equality, pursuers having the same pursued quantity, will sacrifice expansion speed. If all pursuers have the same pursued quantity everywhere, there is no acceleration and so no expansion. Inequality of pursued quantity is an inevitable property for a pursuit system.

In the universe, pursuer's energy increases slowly, about 10 years to double, while its state changes very fast, about 10^{-} second. In economy, personal happiness usually changes much smaller than his state changes. In universe, each particle pursues correctly, but the average result is zero (when expected pursued quantity of field is not considered): increase and decrease of Lagrangian is nearly symmetrical. Similarly in economy, for a market full of intelligent pursuers, pursuers have average results in a long time. So, theorem of equality:

For identical pursuers in a perfect pursuit system, there is equality for their pursued quantity in a long term.

With a perfect methodology, pursuers' average pursued quantity in unit time will increase, because of the expected influence of field. The increase is statistical in a small area, but is inevitable in a large scale. If success is defined as pursuer's pursued quantity larger than a given value. Probability for the success of a pursuer grows with time. Theorem of success:

In a perfect pursuit system, probability of success increases with time.

Growth of pursuer's pursued quantity is not a uniformly divergent process - it is possible to find a pursuer that its pursued quantity is smaller than now after any given time. For example, in strong attractive field, correction for pursued quantity will be strong enough. Maybe this is a little disappointing for a perfect pursuit system, but risk always accompanies with single pursuer.

On the other hand, systematical expansion is 100% safe, because feedback always increases total pursued quantity in whole system. So a perfect pursuit system expands monotonously. A bonded charge's negative action is larger than a free charge now, while a free charge has larger feedback statistically, and will have larger negative action after enough long time. So both bonded charges and free charges have their advantage and disadvantage for pursuit: the former feels better now; the latter develops faster. Always pursuing present benefit is not the perfect pursuit behavior.

In the universe, a proton in cosmic ray can be billions of times of a static proton's energy. So the problem for human beings is that inequality is not enough. The reason is discrimination to pursuers with high income. If pursuers can live healthy, it is unnecessary to protect those below average pursued quantity. If happiness reward (not monetary reward) is proportional to contribution, inequality of pursued quantity will be as large as contribution difference. In the following, I explain three principles about equality: occupying equality for pursuers, possible contract equality for exchange and possible state equality for market.

OCCUPYING EQUALITY IN PERFECT PURSUIT SYSTEM

Desire freedom between different pursuers and different time is part of desire equality. For a perfect pursuer, desires at different time have equal rights to choose contracts by themselves. Present desires do not have the right to choose for future desires. Present behaviors ought to choose for present desires, no earlier and no later. Of course, desire of one pursuer does not have the right to decide pursuit behaviors for other pursuers. Possible contract is propagated to search pursuers. In space, field searches region with high density of pursuers the same as region with no pursuer. In society, there is serious discrimination between realized desires and unrealized desires. This will reduce the probability for possible desires to be realized. Unrealized desires have their right to be treated as realized desires.

In society, there is a long way to go for desire freedom - to treat every unrealized desire the same as realized desire. So desire freedom can also be called equality for realized and unrealized desires. Generally, equality is a more broad condition than freedom. Similar to law equality in society, there is method of methodology equality:

In universe, all pursuers follow the same laws about motion; field from all pursuers follows the same laws about propagation. In society, big companies have privileges in field distribution. Methodology equality is also result of desire equality.

PERFECT METHODS FOR THE DISTRIBUTION OF FIELD

Field is similar to possible contract because field has the following property, method of possible contract:

When a pursuer receives field, it has the corresponding potential energy; when it does not receive field, it will not have the potential energy.

In society, a pursuer normally exchanges with familiar pursuers. This will reduce other pursuers' probability to exchange with him, so he will pay more because of fewer choices. Exchanging with familiar pursuers is reasonable in an imperfect system, but in a perfect pursuit system, you can trust everyone. In universe, there is method of exchange:

Exchange between two pursuers includes three independent steps: one pursuer output field to open market, field propagating in market, and another pursuer input field from market.

So a contract between two pursuers can be reached when both agree. Any relation between two pursuers is a kind of contract. For two pursuers without contract exchange, distance is infinitely large. Contract agreed by one and disagreed by the other is forbidden in a perfect pursuit system, but happens in society everyday.

Method of propagating widely:

Possible contracts from any pursuer are propagated to all the other pursuers.

So, in society, information about goods and services ought to be spread the widest. In universe, an electron in an atom can be excited by photons, so a contract can be terminated at any time. In a perfect pursuit system, contract is similar to an intensity contract, which regulate the intensity of the contract only. Method of renting:

A pursuer can change the intensity of any possible contract at any time.

Renting is a way to replace ownership exchange by intensity ownership exchange. In universe, pursuer's field is propagated from near to far. In perfect society, possible contracts from a pursuer ought to be propagated from the largest profit ratio to the smallest profit ratio. Method of order:

Possible contract is propagated from near to far.

So motion order and field propagation order is identical.

Method of searching equality:

Electromagnetic field is propagated with constant velocity.

Method of independence:

If a pursuer connecting with all the other pursuers by exchanging possible contracts, it is an independent pursuer who decides his motion by himself.

In society, few pursuers have enough independence, because public opinions influence personal decisions strongly.

PERFECT METHODS ABOUT MARKET

With the unification of Europe, people have realized the advantage of unified market to some extent. In universe there is method of unified market:

There is only one space-time in universe.

In society, there are too many trade barriers. In a perfect market, trade between any two pursuers is free of charge.

In society, immigration and emigration is not free. In universe, there is method of free migration:

In universe, every pursuer can move to any place (in order to get largest feedback negative action, there is upper limit for velocity).

Method of instant reaction:

A pursuer changes its state at once when field arrives.

It is obviously a good method for personal pursuit. Human beings cannot follow it well because their bodies are not good enough: they need rest. Human beings can discover causality in universe easily because of the method. Suppose that particles reacting to interaction after a randomly chosen time (like people do in society), causal law cannot be discovered easily in universe.

In society, personal behavior is not just influenced by his feelings because he plays games with others' feelings. Method of honesty:

For a pursuer in the same field, his behaviors, including motion and field output, are irrelevant with other pursuers' behaviors (decisions).

8

Women at Risk, Women in Action

Marriage may be putting Sub-Saharan Africa's women in a risky situation when it comes to HIV/AIDS, challenging perceptions about what is sacred, what is "safe" and what should be constituting prevention methods. What makes marriage dangerous for these women? Among other things: more sex, less condom use and a virtually non-existent ability to abstain. Being faithful as a means to prevent HIV only works if both partners are HIV negative when they begin the relationship, and both partners in the relationship do not have sex outside of it.

The bond of marriage is not the protection against HIV infection that many assume it to be. Many of the same risk factors continue to apply. Marriage - whether in Lusaka or Pretoria - may then not be as safe, or as sacred, as once thought. This is especially true for younger married women. According to research done in recent years, married adolescent girls in both Kenya and Zambia demonstrate higher rates of HIV infection than their stereotypically more "at-risk" single, sexually active female counterparts. The same studies also point out these young girls' often have much older husbands who are about three times as likely to be HIV-positive than the boyfriends of single girls.

A 2003 study found that married adolescent girls in Southern and Eastern Africa had much more unprotected sex than single girls their age. There are obvious reasons for this. In some instances, married persons may not feel the need to use a condom

- convinced of a partner's fidelity and status, or with the goal of having children. In other cases, women lack the negotiating power in a relationship to insist on condom use, even when they know that their partner is unfaithful. All over the continent, multiple sexual partners for men is often viewed as a testament to one's masculinity.

However, certain prevention strategies continue to promote marriage as protection enough against the virus. If we are to help protect the health of married women, we must take their needs and situation into consideration. "Married people are at risk like anyone else," said Luyanda Ngonyama, Gauteng coordinator for the Treatment Action Campaign. "Although we claim to have broad and comprehensive strategies, our strategies tend to target the youth because we want them to be the future of the country. We aren't targeting specific groups like married people."

"Even if both partners know their status at the beginning to be negative, there is no guarantee that they will stay negative. There is this idea that once I am married, I'm safe," Ngonyama added. Certain faith-based and governmental bodies continue to propagate the myth of marriage as safe. George W Bush's President' s Emergency Plan for AIDS Relief (PEPFAR) is among one of the most influential initiatives still preaching abstinence. In 2006, PEPFAR's budget allocated 22 percent of its 3, 263 million USD funding to treatment. Of this 22 percent, 7 percent went to abstinence/"be faithful" activities.

Condom distribution received 6 percent of allocated prevention funding, while prevention of Mother-to-Child Transmission (PMTCT) was allocated 5 percent. A story told in percentage points, the misconceptions and values underlying Bush's prevention push have very real and very visible effects. At the country-specific level, PEPFAR officials in the field are required to spend half of prevention funds on sexual transmission prevention and two-thirds of those funds on abstinence/faithfulness activities. Struggling to meet such requirements, country officials are forced to reduce or cut funding for other prevention programmes such as condom education, according to a 2006 report issued by the U.S. Government Accountability Office.

The same report ultimately advocates PEPFAR re-evaluate its abstinence focus. Meanwhile, HIV/AIDS continues to pose a threat to the lives of individuals and stability of states in Sub-Saharan Africa. The life expectancy in Zimbabwe has dropped by more than 20 years since the start of the HIV/AIDS epidemic, according to figures from the World Health Organisation. In South Africa, life expectancy is below 50 years in three provinces-the Eastern Cape, Free State and KwaZulu-Natal, according to the latest UNAIDS report.

Re-thinking the epidemic, what is safe, who is vulnerable and what real prevention means, cannot wait. Over the last several months, the issue of chemical sterilisation of women in India with quinacrine has been a matter of controversy (*Frontline,* May 2, 1997). In West Bengal, where Dr. Biral Mullick admits to having sterilised more than 10,000 women over the past two decades, activists of the Ganatantrik Mahila Samiti led by Professor Malini Bhattacharya forced the West Bengal Government to call a halt to the "trials" and initiate an enquiry into Dr. Mullick's practice.

In Bangalore, where the Contraceptive and Health Innovation Project (CHIP) of Dr. Pravin Kini and Dr. Sita Bhateja hopes to sterilise 25,000 women over the next two years (having so far sterilised close to a thousand), a coalition of health and women's groups have held demonstrations. On May 2, women's groups held a huge demonstration in New Delhi outside the clinic of Dr. J. K. Jain, former member of Parliament of the Bharatiya Janata Party (BJP) and the kingpin of the network for the conduct of these trials in the country. The Government of India denies granting approval to quinacrine as an agent for female sterilisation. In Parliament, in response to questions tabled by Dr. Ashok Mitra, Minister of State for Law Ramakant Khalap stated that the Government was aware that the World Health Organisation (WHO) had specifically recommended that pending further studies, trials with quinacrine on human populations be stopped.

He said: "Approval for clinical trials of quinacrine pellets has not been granted to any investigator by the Drug Controller General of India." He also stated that "no drug manufacturer has been granted licence to manufacture quinacrine and the drug is not imported." Meanwhile, the Indian Council of Medical Research (ICMR), in published statements, condemned the practice. Despite these efforts, some doctors in the private sector and some non-governmental organisations (NGOs) are continuing the trials, which defy accepted international norms for the conduct of clinical trials. Indeed, reports indicate that they are spreading. It is in this context that the All India Democratic Women's Association (AIDWA) and the faculty of the Centre of Social Medicine and Community Health of the Jawaharlal Nehru University approached the Supreme Court with a public interest petition seeking an immediate - and enforced - ban on the trials.

THE EQUIPMENT FOR THEIR INSERTION

The quinacrine trials raise a host of issues regarding the safety of the particular method of sterilisation, the methodology used in assessing this, and above all the ethical issues concerning the trials that have been raised around the world. The sponsors of these trials, which are said to be going on in 19 Third World countries, are two U.S. doctors: Dr. Elton Kessel and Dr. Stephen Mumford. They are funded by a private foundation and same individuals linked with the Federation for American Immigration Reform, a Washington-based group lobbying for restricted immigration into the U.S.

Kessel and Mumford responded to a number of arguments put forward by their critics when they spoke to the Committee for Women, Population and Environment (CWPE) based at Hampshire College, Massachusetts. However, their response left many questions unanswered. One major criticism of quinacrine sterilisation pertains to issues of safety. Kessel maintained that risk-benefit assessment, the cornerstone of clinical trials, "favoured the use of quinacrine sterilisation in populations where maternal mortality was high and contraceptive prevalence low." With reference to the WHO's recommendations observing that quinacrine may be cancer-producing and thus warranted further studies, he argued that toxicologists maintain that the duration of exposure is the most critical element when humans are exposed to carcinogenic or mutagenic substances.

Laboratory tests indicate that quinacrine causes mutations or changes in cells. (While all substances that cause such changes are not cancer-causing, conventional scientific norms dictate that they should be excluded before human trials are undertaken.) Kessel also said that while there is a lack of data on the long-term effects of quinacrine, the small number of insertions minimises exposure. Mumford, on his part, said that quinacrine, as an anti-malarial drug, has been used orally "in higher doses, over a longer period of time, on a larger population" with little deleterious effects.

Similar argument have been put forward by advocates of quinacrine sterilisation in India also. What these arguments miss is that reproductive causes account for only a small proportion of deaths among women in the reproductive age-group in India. Indeed, these causes do not account entirely or even largely for the high maternal mortality rate in the developing countries; the majority of deaths occur owing to diseases of poverty, primarily anaemia, undernutrition and infections and lack of access to health care facilities in the event of complications of pregnancy. Contraception or sterilisation alone thus has an extremely limited role to play in the decline of maternal mortality.

If this were indeed the case, countries such as Brazil and Indonesia (the latter has a particularly aggressive family planning programme), which have witnessed remarkable declines in birth rate, should also have experienced declines in the maternal mortality rate. This has not happened. The argument that quinacrine was used extensively as an anti-malarial drug and that therefore as a sterlising agent it is without danger, is equally specious. Quinacrine was primarily used as an anti-malarial drug only till such time as better alternatives such as chloroquine became available. Further, the extremely high mortality rate for malaria at that time far outweighed the risks due to quinacrine. Unlike the case with malaria then, there are alternative forms of terminal contraception today such as tubectomy for women and vasectomy for men.

Maintaining that sterilisation by the quinacrine method was extremely safe, Dr. Kessel claimed that there were no deaths in the 40-day period following the insertion of quinacrine in 100,000 women. There are, however, a number of problems with such a facile presentation of data. Included in this huge number are presumably the 31,781 women sterilised in Vietnam between 1989 and 1992. Following WHO recommendations the Vietnamese Government called a halt to the trials. The New York-based Association for Voluntary Surgical Contraception (AVSC) found serious scientific flaws in the Vietnamese study. The data on side-effects and failure rates, for instance, were not derived from the full sample of women but from much smaller sub-sets among them. The findings from these varying sub-sets of the study population were then extrapolated to the entire sample.

For instance, failure rates were calculated based on only a third of the total population. Again it is unclear as to how the ectopic pregnancy rate was calculated: in one province, two out of nine pregnancies were ectopic - a hugely unusual occurrence. Yet, according to the AVSC, "this troubling finding is not mentioned in the analysis of ectopic pregnancies." The AVSC thus maintains that "it is not possible to conclude that quinacrine pellets are a safe and effective non-surgical method of female sterilisation." In addition, given the fact that a variety of protocols of dosage, number of insertions and adjuvants have been followed, it is not methodologically legitimate to calculate mortality rates from data obtained by diverse and often unspecified methods pooled together.

Indeed, it has been revealed that three known deaths due to quinacrine sterilisation were not reported in these findings. This further undermines the credibility of the data. Questions have also been raised about the standard cut-off date of 40 days after surgery being used to determine mortality rates in the case of quinacrine sterilisation. Potentially fatal ectopic pregnancy can occur as long as a woman sterilised with quinacrine is in the reproductive age-group. The use of this cut-off date thus does not constitute a long enough period to assess the mortality risks associated with the method.

While Dr. Kessel said that records are being maintained and that cases are followed up long enough to establish mortality rates, Dr. Mumford acknowledged that they have no resources for follow up. Indeed, Dr. Bhuiyan in Bangladesh and Dr. Mullick, in published interviews, admit their failure to follow up cases. Similarly, in Pakistan where women were, according to a participant, "picked off street corners", there were no follow up efforts. It is, therefore, not surprising that the data presented by Kessel are met with scepticism. Kessel stated that government approval for quinacrine sterilisation is "desirable but not essential" since guidelines from the Food and Drug Administration (FDA) of the U.S. "permitted off-label use (that is, the use of drugs approved for another purpose) under medical supervision."

The training literature for quinacrine sterilisation, however, states that one of the advantages of the method is that it "can be provided by many types of trained health care workers, not just doctors." Indeed Dr. Mullick is on record that he has trained "hundreds of health workers" to use quinacrine for sterilisation. The argument that approval for quinacrine for the treatment of other diseases precludes the need for a licence to use it as an agent for female sterilisation is baseless. Under the Drugs and Cosmetics Act of India, a new drug is defined to include "a drug already approved which is now proposed with new claims, namely, indications, dosage form and route of administration."

The Drug Controller of India has only granted approval for the use of quinacrine in tablet form, orally for the treatment of malaria, giardiasis and amoebiasis. The drug is thus not approved for female sterilisation. It has not received this approval from any authority anywhere in the world, including the U.S. The FDA recently issued a warning on the Internet where quinacrine was being promoted as a method of self-sterilisation. The warning noted that the kit advertised "uses pellets of quinacrine hydrochloride, an unapproved drug which can cause ectopic pregnancies, abnormal pregnancies and permanent damage to a woman's reproductive organs."

Despite the blatantly illegal nature of this practice, some of India's leading doctors continue to take part in this dubious enterprise. At the World Congress of Gynaecology and Obstetrics in Copenhagen in August 1997, a special session on quinacrine sterilisation was organised by Dr. Kessel. It was chaired by Dr. J. K. Jain. Prominent doctors from India making presentations included Dr. Biral Mullick, Dr. Ashi Sarin, Dr. Pravin Kini, Dr. Sita Bhateja and Dr. Ajay Ghosh. Given the globalised, liberalised nature of the Indian state today, wherein independent institutions of health research established by the state are being systematically undermined, it is not surprising to witness yet another instance of Third World women being subjected to such experiments.

Notwithstanding the commitments made at the United Nations Conference on Population and Development in Cairo in 1994 to enhance women's health and reproductive rights, the impunity with which U.S.-based NGOs are violating human rights in countries of the South shows up the need to monitor health systems that have been rendered vulnerable by the incorporation of the Indian economy in the global market. It is ironic indeed that this is being done in the context of neo-liberal rhetoric on reproductive health rights. Nirad C. Chaudhuri in his inimitable way once said that the average Indian suffered from the sex-in-mind-fear-at-heart syndrome. If the all-too-frequent cases of rape and abduction of women reported from different parts of India are any indication, it seems the second part of the syndrome is no more valid and the average Indian male is well on his way to becoming a satyr.

Today, the hold of religion and tradition on sexual mores is slowly weakening in most parts of the country. Where it is not so, it may happen sooner than later as we move closer and closer to the concept of a networked global village. To add to the increasingly permissive social trends, sections of our mainstream cinema and the electronic media go on peddling sleaze and soft porn without any kind of let-up. Whether it is

TV ads for selling biscuits or condoms or launch of a new car model or the inaugural ceremony for the Twenty20 World Cup, no promotional activity seems to be complete without somehow bringing in women in scanty clothes to 'sex' things up. As if all these were not enough, to cater to the tastes of the prurient ones among TV audiences, there are people actively working to promote sports like beach volleyball and women's wrestling (the common thread being the scanty clothing of the participants), though ostensibly they do it out of love for these sports.

While the titillating images of women shown in films/ TV cannot be the only reason for the increase in crimes against them, there is no doubt that it does reinforce a certain male view of women which can perceive them only as objects of pleasure. A civilised society needs to ensure that the beast in man is kept in check, not enticed. The starting point could be to ensure that the electronic media/films are not allowed to show images of women which reduce them to mere sex objects. But, one realises that this is a tall order given the fact that such restrictions are likely to get embroiled in legal controversies in our country. A far more effective way would be for women themselves not to associate with any thing or activity which demeans not only them but also their gender as a whole. Whenever any kind of protest is made against 'commodification' of the female body, immediately the protesters are condemned by a section of the mainstream media for trying to do 'moral policing.'

WILLING ACCEPTANCE

If champions of women's rights are really serious about improving the lot of women, they should first do something about the willing acceptance of thousands of women to be reduced to mere objects of pleasure for film and TV viewing males. Side by side, our law needs to be given more teeth to come down heavily on people who commit crimes against women. One recalls Biju Patnaik characteristically recommending castration as punishment for rapists. While Biju babu might have gone just a bit too far, there is no denying that for ensuring the safety of women, the punishment for rapes and other crimes against women needs to be swift and exemplary enough to strike terror in the mind of any potential wrong-doer. In the ultimate analysis, crimes like rape and that typically Indian hobby of "eve teasing" reflect the deeply ingrained male-oriented attitudes of a patriarchal society. Therefore, in the long run, the best way to root out such deviant behaviour is to work on the minds of children when they are in their formative years. Right from when they are young, boys need to be told that girls also have a mind and personality of their own and are as entitled to dignity and freedom of choice as they are. This kind of sensitising the boy child to the other sex is the best way to ensure a safe world for women.

REFUGEE WOMEN AT RISK

"It was not easy for me to decide to leave my homeland. But when I came here, my head was full of the things I learned about America from my school books in Togo. They taught me it was a country that always helped the needy, a country that sent aid to refugees. My teachers told me it was a great land, where people believed in justice. Instead . . . I was taken to prison in shackles and in handcuffs, and I was abused by prison guards. Yet I am not a criminal. I had done nothing wrong. Why was I put in prison? Why was I treated this way?"- Fauziya Kassindja

Fauziya Kassindja fled Togo to escape female genital mutilation. She was 19 years old. She came to the United States seeking refuge, but when she arrived at Newark International Airport, she was handcuffed and shackled. The Immigration and Naturalization Service (INS) detained her for 16 months in prisons and detention centers. Ms. Kassindja was finally released in April 1996-after The New York Times profiled her plight. Her treatment sparked outrage over U.S. detention practices and the legal hurdles faced by women who seek asylum from gender-related violence. Around the world women often suffer persecution because they are female, and experience persecution differently because they are women.

In some countries, laws and social mores dictate gender-specific treatment; in others, women are more vulnerable to violence during wars or ethnic crises because they are often left alone to care for children or elderly family members. Women who are beaten by their husbands, raped with impunity, forcibly sterilized, ritually mutilated, sold into sexual slavery and targeted for death by relatives in the name of family honor, can become refugees when their governments fail to protect them. Some of them flee to the United States in search of safety.

Those women who seek refuge here face significant barriers to gaining the protection they deserve. In fact, since Fauziya Kassindja's ordeal, America's policies toward those who flee here seeking asylum have become even more unfair and inhumane. In 1996, Congress passed-and President Clinton signed-the "Illegal Immigration Reform and Immigrant Responsibility Act of 1996," a package of restrictions that impede the ability of genuine refugees to gain protection in the U.S.

These barriers include:

- Expedited Removal Under expedited removal, INS inspectors at airports and borders are given the power to order the immediate deportation of people who arrive in the U.S. without proper travel documents. While genuine asylum seekers are not supposed to be deported under expedited removal, the process is so hasty and lacking in procedural safeguards that mistakes can and do happen.
- Mandatory Detention The law calls for the mandatory detention of asylum seekers who are subject to expedited removal. Subsequent parole possibilities are woefully deficient because the decision to release an asylum seeker is entrusted to local immigration officials rather than to a judge or other independent authority.
- One-Year Filing Deadline The filing deadline bars asylum claims that are not filed within one year of a refugee's arrival unless the refugee is deemed to satisfy one of two narrow exceptions. As a result of this filing deadline, the asylum claims of many deserving refugees have been rejected or denied.

Women and Asylum There is no way to know exactly how many women affected by the 1996 law were refugees deserving of asylum. But the cases we do know of raise serious concerns about the impact of the 1996 law on refugee women. A woman from the Dominican Republic who fled severe domestic violence was ordered deported under expedited removal.

A rape survivor from Albania was deported to her country of persecution under expedited removal. Women who have fled forced marriages, rape, domestic violence and other gender-related violence have been detained in jails - sometimes for lengthy periods of time, without the opportunity to challenge their detention before an independent authority. Other women who sought asylum based on fears of domestic violence, "honor killings," and other harms have had their asylum claims rejected based on the one-year filing deadline.

Although these barriers have affected all asylum seekers, women-especially those who are fleeing gender-based persecution and traumas-are in some ways particularly vulnerable to the risks these barriers create because:

- Gender-related forms of persecution are often difficult for women to talk about, particularly for women who come from cultures where they would be subject to further persecution or scorn if the nature of their mistreatment became public knowledge.
- Many women, who come from cultures where women have few rights, are uncomfortable - or are unable, in some cases - to talk to men about their experiences. That difficulty tends to be even greater when the experiences relate to sexual violence or mistreatment by male family members.
- Many women refugees may also come from countries where they have been denied access to education and prohibited from interacting with the legal system. Their vulnerability may be compounded by their obligations to care for young children.

UNFAIR LAWS COUNTER U.S. TRADITION OF • PROTECTING REFUGEE WOMEN

The United States has taken important steps to protect refugee women in past years. In 1995, the INS issued guidelines to assist asylum officers in adjudicating women's asylum claims. And in 1996, following the public outcry over the treatment of Fauziya Kassindja, the U.S. Board of Immigration Appeals issued a ground-breaking decision recognizing that asylum could be granted based on fear of female genital mutilation (FGM). In 2001, Attorney General Janet Reno took another critical step towards protecting women refugees when she vacated a 1999 Board of Immigration Appeals decision in Matter of R-A- that would have prohibited a victim of severe domestic violence from receiving asylum.

The Department of Justice had just previously proposed regulatory changes to further confirm that women with gender-based asylum claims may be eligible for asylum. But those regulations have yet to be issued. The U.S. government's leadership in recognizing gender-based asylum claims is crucial in setting an example for many other nations and should be applauded. But this leadership in developing refugee laws to account for gender-based persecution is undercut when women are prevented on procedural grounds from presenting their claims for asylum.

When a woman with a gender-based asylum claim is barred from applying for asylum because of "expedited removal" o:. an unrealistic filing deadline, or when a woman fleeing domestic violence is detained and, in despair, abandons her asylum claim so that her child will not have to endure the lengthy separation caused by that detention, something is significantly wrong with U.S. laws and procedures. The 1996 Law and its Impact on Women I. Expedited Removal When expedited removal went into effect in April 1997, the U.S. fundamentally changed the way it treats many asylum seekers. Prior to that time, only an immigration judge could order the formal deportation of a person who arrived in the United States without valid travel documents.

This was an important safeguard, since many genuine refugees are unable to obtain travel documents from their governments-the very governments that have targeted them for persecution. Before expedited removal, asylum seekers were assured the fundamentals of due process-the right to a hearing before an immigration judge and the right to have a deportation decision reviewed on appeal. Under expedited removal, INS inspectors at U.S. airports and borders are authorized to issue removal orders that can be finalized upon cursory review by a supervisor solely because a person does not have valid travel documents.

The expedited removal order can be executed immediately, and the inspector's determination cannot even be appealed to an immigration judge much less to a federal court judge. While asylum seekers are not supposed to be deported at this stage (they are supposed to be referred for further examination to determine if they have a "credible fear of persecution"), asylum seekers find the process utterly bewildering, and mistakes have been made. Mistakes are in fact inevitable given the summary nature of expedited removal and its lack of procedural safeguards. Expedited removal can have life or death consequences. An on-the-spot decision of a single INS agent can mean safety and freedom, or forced return to face persecution.

How Expedited Removal Affects Women

The INS has not published statistics reporting how many women have been deported under expedited removal. But The Expedited Removal Study, a University of California, Hastings College of Law report released in May of 2000, examined data provided by the U.S. government, and concluded that women were more frequently deported under expedited removal (rather than under regular immigration removal proceedings) than men. The Study offered several possible explanations for this difference, including that expedited removal may be applied in a manner that disfavors women.

Refugee women are particularly vulnerable to the risks

posed by expedited removal for a number of reasons:

- Some women may be afraid to tell an INS Agent why they have fled. Women are often targeted for persecution because they are women, and they may flee forms of persecution in their home countries that are related to their gender, such as female genital mutilation, rape, forced marriage, "honor killings," forced sterilization, and domestic abuse. The personal or social shame experienced by these women can be acute. Disclosing these experiences publicly in an adversarial environment to male strangers may be highly traumatic, particularly for women who, for cultural or religious reasons, would be ostracized if the nature of their harm became known.
- Others, suffering from Post-Traumatic Stress Disorder, may be unable to talk about what has happened to them. For women who are survivors of torture, rape and gender-related traumas, talking about their experiences is often extremely difficult. Experts who work with survivors of torture and trauma say that those who suffer from Post-Traumatic Stress Disorder (PTSD) have difficulty relating information about their mistreatment to U.S. government authorities particularly if they have not had time to recover from their trauma.
- Intimidation magnifies women's difficulties. Asylum seekers have reported misconduct from INS inspectors including insults, taunting, and abusive language-conduct that can create a hostile or intimidating atmosphere, magnifying the difficulty a woman faces in discussing traumatic experiences. As detailed below, "Ms. Koromah," a rape survivor from Sierra Leone, was so intimidated that she was unable to talk about her rape after INS inspectors at the airport accused her of lying and threatened her with deportation. In May 1999, the Women's Commission for Refugee Women and Children reported that it had interviewed dozens of women who had been subjected to the expedited removal process and that these women "universally recount fear, intimidation, and confusion suffered throughout the process."

- Shackling and strip-searches re-traumatize survivors of abuse. Many asylum seekers have reported that officials at the airport have subjected them to strip-searches and invasive body cavity searches-procedures that can be particularly traumatizing for rape survivors. INS policy and written guidelines make clear that handcuffing and shackling are not mandatory, and specifically note that restraints should normally not be used on women. But in practice, these guidelines are not observed. Female asylum seekers are routinely handcuffed, shackled or otherwise restrained. The use of restraints on women who are trauma survivors is especially problematic, as the use of restraints can in effect recreate a prior traumatic experience.
- Women do not know that their persecution can qualify them for asylum. Women who are victims of gender-related abuses may not realize that they may qualify for what is popularly referred to as political asylum, and as a result, they may not realize that they can exercise the right to apply for asylum during expedited removal. This confusion is only compounded by the Board of Immigration Appeal's 1999 decision denying asylum to a victim of severe domestic violence. Although that decision was subsequently vacated, the Bush administration has not indicated whether regulations will be issued governing these claims.
- Failure to recognize gender-based claims. INS inspectors and adjudicators who are entrusted with expedited removal determinations may fail to recognize gender-based asylum claims. When the 1996 immigration law passed, some refugee advocates feared that asylum seekers with non-traditional claims - particularly women with gender-based asylum claims - might be turned away under expedited removal. (This fear was in part based on the fact that, even prior to expedited removal, Fauziya Kassindja's FGM-based asylum claim had initially been rejected by an immigration judge.

Unfortunately, this fear has proved justified. Although the Department of Justice subsequently issued a regulation instructing those who make expedited removal determinations to consider whether the claims are novel or unique, given the expedited nature of these proceedings, it is likely that similar mistakes will continue to occur under the 1996 immigration law asylum seekers are subject to "mandatory detention," and are held in detention facilities and jails. They are technically eligible for parole once they establish that they have a "credible fear of persecution" and meet certain criteria under INS parole guidelines. But the decision to parole an asylum seeker is not made by an independent authority; it is instead entrusted to local INS officials who have wide discretion in applying the parole guidelines. Parole is implemented in an inconsistent and sometimes arbitrary manner.

The problem is so severe that, in December 2000, the INS issued a regulation simply to confirm that the INS Commissioner could exercise authority over local INS parole determinations. As a result of these flawed procedures, many asylum seekers -including survivors of rape, gender-related harms and torture -are detained even when they have family or other community contacts who are willing to house and support them. Parole for asylum seekers, already restrictive in some areas of the U.S., seems to have become even more restrictive in the wake of September 11. Particularly troubling are reports of discriminatory parole practices. The press has documented cases in which asylum seekers from Middle Eastern or Muslim backgrounds, who would previously have been paroled prior to September 11, have been denied parole.

For instance, two Christian women who fled Iraq were denied parole in Miami, even though one of the women had strong community ties, specifically her U.S. citizen sister and legal permanent resident mother. In another case, a thirteen-year old Iraqi girl was detained for over five months as a result of delays in the new security checks affecting asylum seekers from Iraq and other countries. Following the arrival of a boat of Haitian asylum seekers in Florida in December 2001, and a subsequent boat which arrived in late October 2002, the INS has instituted a discriminatory parole policy directed at Haitian asylum seekers.

As a result, Haitian men, women and children have been detained in Florida for prolonged periods of time, even though other asylum seekers are routinely released on parole in Florida. For refugees, it is devastating to be imprisoned like a criminal by the country they turned to for protection. For refugee women-many of whom have suffered unspeakable abuses-detention can be particularly traumatizing. Privacy and dress While detained, women must wear prison-like uniforms, a requirement that can be especially difficult for women who come from cultures where they are required to wear dresses or head-coverings.

The Lawyers Committee recently assisted a Rwandan refugee who felt humiliated and dehumanized when, in addition to all the other indignities that accompanied her imprisonment in a Connecticut jail, her hair was shaved off, without explanation-leaving her with very uneven close-cropped hair instead of the braids she arrived with. At the larger detention facilities, women lack any degree of meaningful privacy as the toilet and shower areas are separated from the general living area by only a partial barrier.

This lack of privacy may be particularly difficult for women who come from cultures where they are required to behave modestly and to keep others from seeing them even partly unclothed. Detention exacerbates depression and trauma. For survivors of torture, rape and other forms of gender-based persecution, detention often exacerbates the symptoms of post-traumatic stress and depression. One Lawyers Committee client-a woman who fled Cameroon after suffering torture and an attempted rape-became extremely depressed after nearly three years in county jails and detention facilities. She said: "I just feel deadened and hopeless.... Often I cannot sleep or eat.

Sometimes I cannot stop crying. I think about the torture that I experienced, and I sit and re-live my experiences in my mind." Experts in treating torture survivors have confirmed that detention can further exacerbate the effects of depression and trauma. Separation from children Women are sometimes separated from children or other family members while detained. The separation of families has been reported across the country-in Florida, Georgia, Minnesota, Illinois, Pennsylvania, New York, California and Texas. The INS has refused to provide some mothers with contact visits, even with young children.

A Peruvian woman, who arrived at the Atlanta airport in December 1999, was handcuffed in front of her 9- year-old daughter and taken to a county jail. Her child-who was already traumatized from the persecution the family had suffered in Peru-was taken away and placed in another institution. When the woman learned that if she wanted to apply for asylum she would be detained and separated from her already traumatized child for longer, she withdrew her request for asylum and returned to Peru-even though she feared for their safety there.

Since the INS detains children, some women have also faced the impossible choice of either letting their children be detained or letting their children return to a country where their lives may be in danger. After INS officers threatened to detain her 8-year-old daughter in a facility in another state, a woman who had fled Peru to escape domestic violence abandoned her asylum claim and returned to an uncertain fate in her home country. Vulnerability to abuse in detention Women in immigration detention are vulnerable to abuse. Many do not speak English, and some have no family or friends in this country in whom they can confide about their experiences in detention.

In October 2000, the Women's Commission for Refugee Women and Children reported "widespread sexual, physical, verbal and emotional abuse of detainees, especially women" at the Krome Service Processing Center, an INS detention center on the outskirts of Miami, Florida. The Justice Department launched an investigation into the conduct of at least 15 INS officers at Krome. One officer was indicted on four charges of sexual assault, and plea bargained to two misdemeanor charges. The female detainees were moved to the Turner Guilford Knight Correctional Center (TGK), a county jail in Florida that was designed for pre-trial detention of criminal offenders.

Last year the Women's Commission and the Florida Immigrant Advocacy Center publicly criticized the treatment of women asylum seekers at the county jail, where women reported strip-searching, deprivation of sleep, and the seizing of rosaries and other personal and religious objects. The transferred women subsequently reported incidents of sexual harassment and molestation by male trustees at TGK. 20 III. The Asylum Filing Deadline The 1996 immigration law imposes a filing deadline on asylum applications.

An asylum seeker in the U.S. must file an asylum application within one year of her arrival or she will be barred from obtaining asylum unless she qualifies for one of two exceptions. An exception is met only in the case of either "changed circumstances that materially affect eligibility" for asylum or "extraordinary circumstances relating to the delay in filing" the application. Since the filing deadline has been in effect, more than 13,000 asylum seekers have had their claims rejected by the INS based on the filing deadline.

An analysis of asylum statistics conducted by two academic experts revealed that the percentage of asylum seekers who are found by the INS to not satisfy the exceptions to the filing deadline actually increased-from 37% in fiscal 1998, to 39% in fiscal 1999, to 42% in fiscal 2000, to 52% in fiscal 2001-indicating that "as rejections of late filers became a bureaucratic routine rather than a new and therefore closely observed procedure, asylum officers may have become more deadened to the injustice of their rejection decisions."

The filing deadline has become a barrier to asylum for many genuine refugees. Refugee women-who may be suffering from the effects of abuse, may be caring for young children, or may not even know that they may be able to seek asylum based on gender-related harms-face some particular challenges as a result of the filing deadline.

- Difficulty seeking legal representation. Many genuine refugees arrive in this country unable to speak English, unfamiliar with our legal system, and unable to afford food and housing, let alone legal counsel. Finding legal representation can be difficult to impossible. A May 2000 report issued by Georgetown University revealed that fewer than one in four asylum applicants are represented at the initial asylum office stage. The difficulty of obtaining legal representation and navigating a legal system in another language is compounded for women who come from cultures where they may have been deprived of educational opportunities or prohibited from interacting with governmental or legal authorities.

- Responsibility for children and basic needs. The difficulties women face in meeting the filing deadline are exacerbated for those who are alone or who bear primary responsibility for young children. Basic needs, such as food, shelter, medical treatment, and stable care for children will often take priority over locating resources needed to approach the legal system.
- Particular difficulty for traumatized women. Many asylum seekers arrive in this country still suffering from the effects of the torture or persecution they have faced. Women who are torture or rape survivors are often traumatized, and as a result may find it difficult to apply for asylum-a process which will require them to revisit in detail the mistreatment they have suffered. Medical experts have confirmed this problem-noting the case of a rape survivor, who still suffered from the effects of her torture several years later, and was only able to discuss her abuse in order to apply for asylum after she had been in therapeutic care. Despite the fact that those who are suffering from the effects of torture should qualify for an exception to the filing deadline, survivors of torture and trauma have been denied asylum as a result of the filing deadline.
- Women may not know they are eligible for asylum. As stated earlier, women with gender- based asylum claims-including claims relating to "honor killings," domestic violence, female genital mutilation and other harms-may be unaware of their potential eligibility for asylum. As a result women with deserving asylum claims-like "Oumou

Amine" who sought asylum based on her fear of FGM-have been denied asylum based on the filing deadline. The United States has had a proud tradition of protecting refugees, and has set an example for other countries in protecting women from gender-related violence.

But U.S. leadership in this area has been undermined by the barriers imposed by the 1996 immigration law. Refugee women who flee from gender-based harm may be particularly vulnerable to these barriers, but the impact of these provisions on all refugees is cause for serious concern. The U.S. should restore fairness to the process so that vulnerable refugees, like the women profiled in this report, are not unfairly denied a safe haven in this country. The Lawyers Committee recommends that the following reforms be made to the expedited removal, detention and filing deadline provisions of U.S. law.

- Limit expedited removal to immigration emergencies. Congress should sharply restrict the use of expedited removal to extraordinary migration situations. It should ensure that additional safeguards are included in those situations where expedited removal is authorized. These safeguards, which should include immigration judge review of all removal orders, will reduce the risk of mistaken deportations.
- Restore due process. The decision to deport an asylum seeker or other individual who arrives with- out proper documents should not be entrusted to immigration enforcement officers at the airport or border. Instead, these decisions should be made by trained immigration judges in fair proceedings that afford individuals the right to legal representation and the opportunity to have decisions reviewed on appeal.
- Improve conduct of secondary inspection. The INS must reform its conduct of secondary inspection and dramatically improve the training of inspectors. Women should generally be interviewed by female officers and female interpreters. The INS should cease the practice of handcuffing and shackling women and other people who do not constitute a risk to others.

- Clarify detention policies. Congress should clarify that the policy of the United States generally is not to detain asylum seekers who pose no risk to the community, and in particular not to detain asylum seekers who have met the "credible fear" standard by establishing a significant possibility of winning asylum. Any exceptions to this general rule should be narrowly tailored. These changes would ensure that U.S. law is consistent with American tradition and international standards.
- Reform parole procedures. The Department of Justice should issue regulations providing for immigration judge review of decisions to detain asylum seekers, and periodic review of detention determinations. These regulations should also specify the criteria to be considered in evaluating decisions to detain, and should make clear that asylum seekers who meet the "credible fear" standard and pose no danger to the community should generally be released. Congress should require that the Department of Justice issue such regulations. The regulations should specifically provide for the parole of women and men who are responsible for the care of children and for the parole of families. The INS should no longer be permitted to issue only guidelines-rather than regulations-on parole of asylum seekers, as this practice has repeatedly proven insufficient to ensure accountability and compliance by local INS districts.
- Alternatives to detention. Asylum seekers should generally not be detained. In those cases in which it is determined that some degree of supervision is needed, the INS should be required to consider alternatives to detention, including supervised release, and for women with children, release to family, friends, or facilities operated by non-profit agencies.
- Improve Detention Conditions. Asylum seekers should not be housed with criminals or in remote county and local jails. The Department of Justice should issue regulations codifying its detention standards. All asylum seekers should be provided with appropriate medical care, including professional counseling for survivors of torture, rape or gender-based persecution. All detention facilities should

be staffed with female officers and with female health care staff. Adequate visitation, including contact visits with children and other family members, should be permitted.

- Eliminate the one-year filing deadline. Congress should eliminate the one-year asylum filing dead-line. At the very least, the filing deadline should be eliminated in affirmative asylum applications, and the fact that an application has been filed more than one year after arrival should be considered a negative discretionary factor, subject to a good-cause exception, in connection with asylum applications filed defensively before immigration judges.

Changes made by the U.S. government in the wake of September 11, including changes to the immigration appellate process, have further eroded the fairness of the U.S. asylum system. The transfer of the INS to the Department of Homeland Security will leave asylum seekers in an even more vulnerable position. Restoring fairness to the asylum process is more important than ever. A fair asylum system is essential to ensure that the U.S. lives up to its obligation to protect the victims of human rights abuses who flee to its shores in search of refuge.

NGO STATEMENT

The NGO community fully supports the proposal for an Executive Committee Conclusion on displaced women and girls at risk and welcomes UNHCR's background discussion paper on issues related to women at risk. We welcome the extensive efforts taken so far by UNHCR in its range of guidelines and policies. We also welcome efforts by States in asylum procedures, and issuance of guidelines or introduction of sex/gender category in national legislation, but note that these approaches are not uniform. We support the proposal of an EXCOM Conclusion, and believe it can translate into the enhanced protection of women and girls by establishing criteria for identification at the field level, and detailing appropriate protection solutions both during displacement and when promoting durable solutions.

We continue to witness a myriad of human rights violations

against displaced women and girls during all stages of displacement - sexual exploitation; harmful traditional practices including early, forced marriage and female genital mutilation; torture; abandonment; involuntary recruitment into militia and armed forces; the denial of rights of women, their spouses or partners including the right to earn livelihoods; abduction and trafficking; the lack of access to humanitarian assistance; and challenges in providing services on an equitable basis - and in matters such as education and livelihoods, lack of access to land and inequitable property rights, especially upon return, and the lack of meaningful participation in decisions affecting their lives.

Displaced women and girls continue to be marginalized and remain amongst the most vulnerable of groups within displaced communities. Moreover, these violations are often cyclical, with a history of repetition throughout all phases of displacement. Many displaced women and girls experience multiple traumatic events, including repeated sexual and gender based violence as a form of persecution, during flight, as IDPs, or in countries of first and subsequent asylum. The impact of each event is compounded by ensuing incidents and further compounded by lack of adequate protection. This creates extreme levels of risk and vulnerability to further abuse and trauma.

The failure of the international protection regime to respond to refugee women and girls at risk has been documented in refugee situations around the world. This includes in protracted refugee and IDP situations across Africa and Asia, and most recently - as documented by the Human Rights Commissioner Loiuse Arbour in her 2005 report - in the ongoing humanitarian emergency in Darfur Chad and Uganda. This systemic failure can lead to further incidences of violence, exploitation, sexual abuse and even death.

While comprehensive statistics are hard to come by, we present the following as an indicative example: in post-conflict Sierra Leone, the Rainbo Centre, which provides holistic services to refugee, IDP and returnee survivors of gender-based violence in Freetown, Koidu, and Kenema, reported the following statistics for the months of May - July 2005:

- 251 sexual assault cases reported during the three month period.
- 84% of the reported cases were rape cases.
- 60% of reported cases were girls between the ages 11-15; an additional 20% were girls between the ages 6-10.

Again, the statistics provided were reported cases. We know that many if not most cases of exploitation go unreported. We also know that these problems are not limited to West Africa but have been acknowledged and reported in refugee and IDP camps, settlements, and impacted urban areas throughout the world from Tanzania through Nepal to Colombia. Recent research has documented statements made by UNHCR staff which supports the widespread nature of rape and sexual abuse of displaced women, such as: "If you can find a woman in this camp who has not been raped I will give you a prize!;" and "But they are all at risk - do you want to resettle every woman in this camp?"

This research has highlighted that although risk is high for all displaced persons, and in particular for women and girls, that in all populations there are some women and girls who face specific risks related to their gender or sex. There is an urgent need to identify and respond to these women on an individual basis as well as collectively. Although resettlement criteria for women at-risk exists, research has demonstrated various problems with its execution including: confusion over the definition; inconsistency between UNHCRs resettlement criteria and the ones various countries are applying; failures in implementation due in part to lack of adequate training of all staff involved in resettlement processes; disregard of rape and sexual abuse as sufficient grounds for resettlement; a culture of distrust of refugees' stories, or a disbelief in the extent of the abuses women and girls are facing; a lack of access to resettlement; lack of access to education; poor quality of physical, social and legal protection available; and slow response time among resettlement countries.

The pervasive denial of the livelihood and movement rights of the 1951 Convention and other international norms is also a factor in dependence and vulnerability to sexual exploitation and sexual and gender based violence in all phases of displacement. This is so not only when states deny women their rights to work, practice professions, run businesses, own property, move about freely, and choose their place of residence; women and girls are also increasingly vulnerable to violence and abuse when states deny men these rights.

Addressing these problems is an international responsibility. Donor countries should direct development aid toward the empowerment of all displaced people, especially women, and the communities that host them to realize their rights. In addition, it must be assured that the existence of a definition of women at risk only in the context of resettlement does not mean that all other protection strategies and durable solutions are not actively pursued for women at risk. As an international community, we have repeatedly failed to offer displaced women and girls effective protection. Clearly better guidance is needed at both the field level and resettlement country level on how to better identify and protect those at most risk.

A Conclusion on Displaced Women and Girls at Risk might articulate and/or lead to the following:

- An identification of risk factors which predispose displaced women and girls to risk, translated to;
- A better understanding amongst UNHCR staff, EXCOM member States and partners, of the risks faced by displaced women and girls in various contexts including prior to and during flight, during displacement, upon return and in resettlement;
- The development of tools to better identify, assess and monitor the situation of displaced women and girls at risk, including the development of obligatory case management systems;
- The full participation of displaced women and girls in identifying their protection needs and implementing solutions,
- The engagement of men and boys in the promotion of and understanding of women' and girls' concerns;

- The promotion of gender sensitive interviewing techniques, and interpretation for displaced women and girls including the use of same-sex interviewers and separate interviews from accompanying male family members when UNHCR and states undertake refugee status determination and resettlement interviews;
- The promotion of early and simultaneous pursuit of durable solutions including early identification of women or girls at risk who have legitimate reasons for not wishing to integrate locally or return to their home or communities of origin;
- More timely, effective and responsive resettlement programs for displaced women and girls at risk;
- The empowerment of women to engage in livelihoods and support themselves with the rights to work, practice professions, run businesses, own property, and freedom of movement and the special vulnerability of women and girls to dependency, exploitation, and abuse even when men are denied these rights.
- The provision of education as key preventive element for physical, psychological and cognitive protection;
- A reiteration of specific and often unique social service needs for this population upon resettlement including schooling, counseling and psycho-social support;
- The development and implementation, in partnership with displaced women, girls and their communities, of viable, timely and effective protection solutions for women and girls at risk during displacement. This should include a range of short and medium term measures which would include access to safe houses, Safe spaces and Safe shelters in and outside camps, boarding schools or schools outside camps and relocation to another camp.
- Enhanced organizational accountability for the protection of displaced women and girls at risk.

In practice, community involvement in risk identification, prevention, and intervention are the most successful means of reducing the protection risks faced by displaced women and girls. Women and girls must be involved in their own protection and their communities, including the men, must be similarly engaged. Moreover, in terms of community-based involvement and in order to fully participate in decisions affecting their lives, in identifying their protection needs and solutions, women and girls should have access to good quality education services and vocational training.

Education is not only a durable solution but also a protection tool that needs to be also addressed in situations of emergencies, and throughout the displacement circle. For enhanced effectiveness, these community-based responses should be supported by additional interventions, such as the provision of security personnel, the presence of female staff, and the availability of requisite health services and livelihood opportunities. It is, however, only through individual assessments and individualized responses that we can adequately address the unique protection concerns facing women and girls.

We, therefore, advocate for a strong Executive Committee Conclusion that provides specific risk factors to aid the identification of women and girls at risk, promotes mechanisms for robust monitoring of those at risk, emphasizes the role of the community in their own protection, and proposes urgent and longer term protection solutions that are practical - including expanded resettlement for this group.

THE EMPOWERMENT OF INDIAN WOMEN

From time immemorial, the women in this land of ours were treated as a sort of thing. Her placing in the society was not at par with other human being. She has no rights. She cannot move nor do anything at her will. In Hindu Shastras, she has been branded just like animals. From the verses of Ramayan as written by Mr. Tulsi Das, " Dhol, ganwar, shudra, pashu, naari- Ye sab tadan ke adhikari," one may easily draw inferences as to what status has been granted to our mothers. Similarly, we can understand that of Dropadi of *Mahabharata* was reduced to the status of a bitch, as she was the wife of five husbands (Pandwas). She was not only, the wife of five husbands; she put at stake in gambling by none else than the so called Dharmraj Yudhishthar! In 'Manusmrati' the ancient Hindu Code-book, the status granted to women is quite visible and she was put to the lowest rug of humanity as she was treated at par with the animals and slave by the proprietors of Hindu Dharma. Such was the placement earmarked to our mothers, sisters and even great grand mothers that the heads of humanity bend upon down with shame!

That is why Dr. Ambedkar was of the firm opinion that until or unless, by applying dynamite, the Hindu Dharma-shastras are not blown up, nothing is going to happen. In the name *sanskaras,* the Hindu women are tied up with the bondage of superstitions, which they carry till their death. They are also responsible for inculcating these wrong notions learnt by them through baseless traditions and preaching of the Shastras in the budding minds of their offspring. Otherwise also the women in India have remained a matter of joy and a source of amusement as such she was used and misused by men just to serve their evil ends. She has been used just like a machine for procreation. It has also been mentioned in Hindu Shastras that the woman is the bond slave of her father when she was young, to her husband when she is middle aged and to her son when she is a mother. Of course, all the epigrams, aphorisms, proverbs, platitudes and truisms bear necked truth about the stature of women in India.

It does not mean that no efforts have been made in the past to bring dignity to women. As in Europe, Christianity inaugurated the Era of equality, liberty and fraternity by preaching that a prince and pauper are equal in the eyes of God. There is also a very long tradition of social reforms by our saints and other social reformers. But the proprietors of the orthodoxy thwarted these efforts. In the absence of any legal sanction or authority, these efforts could not sustain. In this direction Dr. B.R. Ambedkar has tried to brake down the barriers in the way of advancement of women in India. He laid down the foundation of concrete and sincere efforts by codifying the common Civil Code for the Hindus and the principle is capable of extension to other sections of the Indian society. Prior to these efforts of Dr. Ambedkar, the destiny of the Indian women depended upon the wrong notions and perceptions chalked out by the proprietors of orthodoxy.

The prevailing two schools of Hindu Law viz. 'Mitakshara' and 'Dayabhag, created and sustained inequality. According to 'Mitakshara' the property of a Hindu is not his individual property. It belongs to what is called coparcenary, which consists of father, son, grandsons and great grandsons by reason of birth. The property passed under Mitakshara by survivorship to the members of coparcenary who remain behind, and does not pass to the heirs of the deceased. Whereas Dayabhag recognised the property held by the heir as his personal property with an absolute right to dispose it of either by gift or by will or any other manner that he chooses. The chaotic conditions of the Hindu law were reduced to eat propositions in the form of judicial pronouncements and codification was the legislative recognition of the judge made law. Dr. Ambedkar himself had explained lucidly the reasons for consolidation and codification.

Article 25 of the Indian Constitution permits all the freedom. The reforms introduced by Dr. Ambedkar through "Hindu Code-bill" have been adhered to and have been accepted by and large. He, by codifying Hindu Law in respect of marriage, divorce and succession, rationalized and restored the dignity to women. Prior to the Hindu Succession Act, 1956 and Hindu Marriage Act, 1955, the Hindu Law was uncodifyed in a large measure, though Hindu Women's Right to Property Act, 1937 was the subject legislative intervention. The Sharda Act is also worth mentioning. It has set the seal of authority upon that piece of social reforms, which the heads of orthodoxy were, imposing and impending.

In Hindu Code Bill, the principles of codification covered:

1. Right to property,
2. Order of succession to property,
3. Maintenance, marriage, divorce, adoption, minority and guardianship.

Needless to say, the Bill was a part of social engineering via law. It was by any standard of any time a revolutionary measure. It was really a first step towards the recognition and empowerment of women in India. Under these revolutionary measures, a woman will have property in her own right and be able to dispose of her property. The Hindu Code Bill introduced by Dr. B. R. Ambedkar in the Constituent Assembly on 11th April 1947. A debate on this bill continued for more than four years and still remains inconclusive. Here once again, the orthodoxy prevailed upon the reforms. In the words of Dr. Ambedkar, it was killed and died unset and unsung. He felt that the then government led by Pt. Jawaharlal Nehru was not eager to clear the Hindu Code Bill. He, therefore, tendered his resignation but continued to participate in the Parliamentary debates on the request of the Prime Minister.

Sharp criticism of this Bill in and outside Parliament led many to believe that it might inflict heavy damages on the Hindu society. Even the President Dr. Rajendra Prasad got scared and issued a threat that he would withhold his assent even if it had been passed by the Parliament. But the efforts of Baba Saheb Ambedkar were lauded also like anything. The Times of India on 26th December 1950 carried a statement of Dr. Ambedkar in which he said that the Bill aimed at removing the legal obstacles in the social advancement of women. Justice P.B. Gajendra Gadkar while congratulating Dr. Ambedkar for the role he had played in drafting and piloting the Bill said, "If Dr. Ambedkar gives us Hindus our Code, his achievement would go down in history as a very eloquent piece of poetic justice indeed."

In recent past, a lot hue and cry is being made over 'Women's Reservation Bill' by the different sections of the Indian society, different political or apolitical organizations but nobody seems to be honest in its perspectives. The political empowerment is a must for the all round development of the women, but as in the case of *dalit* politicians and legislators, our efforts may prove futile. We must concentrate on imparting social education before giving any concrete shape to their political empowerment to the women. Without academic and social education, the political empowerment of women in certain parts of the country had proved futile. In Panchayat Raj set up in U.P. and elsewhere in the country, the uneducated women are subjected to exploitation at the hands of government machinery.

It will not be prudent on our part to restore the rights of the women belonging to the affluent section of the society only. Therefore, our efforts should be directed towards all round development of each and every section of Indian women by giving their due share. It is a must to maintain and protect chastity, dignity and modesty of women. It is the need of the hour to give due share to each and every section of the Indian women. I am sure, without removing social stigma, no progress or development could be achieved. Now the question arises as what sort of empowerment our women needed prior to restarting their equal property rights? There are lot of nodal agencies including the national Commission for Women said to have been working for the welfare of the women apart from governmental efforts. Where does they reach in this direction? Leaving a meager number of urban and suburban women, the Indian women are still crying for simple justice.

Which is not even allowed to have been accessed to them. With their age, no bar, they have been raped, kicked, killed, subdued & humiliated almost daily. Why? Because of our indifferent attitude towards them. This indifferent attitude and approach of our crops up at the time of the birth of female child. They are subjected to rebuke and ignored so far as their education and other facilities are concerned which are required for their proper and healthy growth/development. The male child is given preference over the female child? With this attitude of our own, we use to suppress and remained unfair towards the fair sex. First of all we must try to treat our female child as par our female child as par with our male ones and thenceforth restore equality amongst them. No restoration of property right would be meaningful without making her mentally strong. We must allow them to think breathe and act independently and bring her out of the shackles of slavery. Do not impose the filthy rites, rituals and superstition citing the examples from our dated SHASTRAS. Don't treat women your slave or servant who has come to this world just to cook your food, wash your dirty clothes, and fulfill your other needs.

Please mined it that they are your mothers, sisters, wife (Life partners). If we able to mend our ways, the restoration of their property rights to them would be meaningful. Let us be a little bit honest to diagnose the illness by taking into consideration all the aspects and aspirations in changed scenario, circumstances and atmosphere. Only then we could have a perfect planning to achieve our cherished aim that is empowerment of Indian women and could be able to restore their property and other rights in order to bring her at par with other human beings. This could be achieved only if we are able to blow up the heinous Hindu-shastras by using dynamite as affirmed by none else than Dr. B.R. Ambedkar, the emancipator of the millions including Indian women.

Looking at the history of social movements in the 20th Century, one realizes that increasingly women service the various social and economic movements mostly as workers and volunteers but not as its leaders. In the next phase which, I believe, is the human rights revolution, women must lead and set the agenda of this movement. Women must lead the revolution with a new holistic vision of the universality and indivisibility of human rights for all. Men must realize that they are narrowing the agenda and inhibiting true social change toward peace and democratization when they keep women out of leadership positions. On the way to assuming leadership, human rights education is one of the imperatives that women must adopt.

To learning about human rights, men must join women in promoting and protecting women's human rights as part of the larger agenda of social change. As leaders, women need to adopt the notion of human rights as fully comprehensive. The understanding that social, economic, environmental, medical, and cultural injustices are human rights violations and that the promotion of human rights is at the heart of what human rights education can offer to these new leaders, by which they can be setting the political agenda of human rights, and thus the future of humanity. The two years of preparation for the 4WCW evoked a difficult, yet revolutionary dialogue worldwide.

Even though not fully acknowledged as such, the hard questions and the many debates that lead to closing and opening brackets, to rejecting and accepting ideas, issues and concerns, the agreements, contradictions and even the co-optation were all about human rights of women and thus about human rights of humanity. Beijing and the vibrant discussions at the NGO Forum and between governments made it very clear that women must understand that all injustices to women are human rights violations, and that the presence of justice is human rights in action. The Vienna Conference on Human Rights, in 1993, underscored that women's rights are human rights and more important that human rights are universal, indivisible and interconnected; by itself a revolutionary special agreement.

Unfortunately the Beijing "Process" did not go further to the necessary understanding that "human rights is the right to be human" as said so eloquently by Professor Upendra Baxi, the Indian philosopher. Understanding that Human rights is a value system by which we need to live with one another is recognizing that women working to prevent injustice are working to eradicate and prevent human rights violations against humanity as a whole. The challenge is now to find a place, carve a space for humanity to enjoys human rights as the right to be human, regardless of whether we are women, men or children, young or old, and of whatever color, religious belief, culture, or historic memories and commitments. The sanctity of life, the basis of all human solidarity, needs to be affirmed and reaffirmed by all. In Professor Baxi's word: "no single phrase in recent human history has been privileged to bear the mission of human destiny than human rights..." as developed in the last fifty years.

When finally, we know that "we were all born equal in dignity", to use Eleanor Roosevelt's words, then the revolution will get its momentum and our demands for equality will become meaningful to women and men alike. The time has come for women to demand: Equality Now!! Women must organize to declare in tandem, no matter what their immediate concern, that human rights are universal and indivisible, and that the violation of even one single human right of women is a violation against humanity. We can no longer allow men to patronize us by being "good" to us and thus obscuring the real issue of equality and dignity. Their "kindness" in setting quotas, creating ministries to attend to our issues, allowing special conditions and concessions, these are not good enough, and in the long run neither are they in the interest of men.

Women must themselves lead the discussions. Sadly, some men want us to wait patiently till we achieve full equality, as proclaimed in the recent court decision on affirmative action for women. This court was a court of 16 men. They have the "wisdom' and the power while we women must carry the burden of inequality and be grateful for their "Charity." While we need to acknowledge that serious dialogue is taking place on women's human rights, this will only be meaningful and productive when we develop the arguments that equality of women is in the interests of men as well and therefore of society as a whole. This means to grant all of humanity its human rights-to let the energy of women flow throughout society, join the energy of men and take part in the struggle against globalization, poverty, war and arms dealing, nuclear proliferation and the obscure future of our children.

We need to recognize that there are three basic constituencies in the world today playing a crucial historic role as social justice movements on major global issues. These are: women, the human rights professionals, and the development workers; and all concerned with bettering the human condition. However, the great tragedy is that these various groups are not working together as full partners in order to achieve without compromise the integration of gender, human rights and development challenges, as their common goal. The task ahead is full collaboration, enhancing and strengthening the international movement for social justice of women and men alike. We believe that human rights education is the process by which this can be achieved.

Lets examine the differences and commonalities of these three constituencies:

Women as full participants in repairing the world. Yet, there are many women's movements,- the feminist movement, the women's health movement, the movements: to protect the girl child, to fight for a better work place, to save women sold in the market place; to mention just a few of them.

Women's groups exist to fight every injustice against women. Some of these groups have identified their issues as human rights issues, but many have not yet responded to the call from Vienna. Human rights are universal, interdependent and indivisible. The refusal by many groups to recognize their issues as human rights issues is for fear that it will weaken their arguments, confine them to the issues of violence, deem them confrontational, narrow their mandate, or box them into the legal paradigm. But, until all women's groups, whether they are fighting against hunger, poverty, violence or for education, clean water or healthcare, for example, must realize their connectedness through human rights and become indivisible in their pursuit for social justice.

Let's remember: women are the largest and most powerful force in the world today. And let's face it, men are tired. The labor movement, largely a men's movement, is almost dead, being killed by trade agreements and consumerism. Women, moving out of various forms of oppression are the energy of today, and the promise of the social revolution of tomorrow. The second important constituency is the excellent and devoted group of human rights professionals. These are advocates for human rights who define human rights abuses, develop international laws to protect humanity against human rights violations, regulate, set and interpret standards and norms and call attention to the potential human rights infringements.

However, rarely do they take into account the suffering of women as the suffering of people. Those who do are usually women. Yes, we have CEDAW, which demands all of women's needs, but, as long as the issues of gender are not fully integrated as a matter of fact in the totality of human rights, then, what we call the "human rights of women" in many cases becomes what is known as gender issues. I find the approach of many human rights experts extremely patriarchal with very little sensitivity to women as full members of society.

These men contribute to the rich thinking about human rights but have relegated women to a separate Convention that keeps our concerns apart. They speak of a "Men's" world and then tell us that the word "women" is included in the word "men." The tragedy is compounded by human rights experts which are not gender sensitive, not realizing that if you do not integrate holistically women's human rights into human rights in general, one cannot begin to address the real challenges of human rights for humanity. It is perfectly legitimate for the experts to focus on a specific human rights concern.

But, whatever the human rights concern, both men and women must are always be part of it. I do not mean to say that there are no differences between men and women. But, despite these differences the experts must learn that in international law men and women should not be dealt with as separate entities. Last but not least, the third constituency: the many groups active with development concerns. For the most part they take actions that will determine how we will live in the 21st century. What is typical of these group's policies is "growth for the sake of growth." They advocate multi disciplinary, multi national theories of "trickling" - "up" or "down" depending on their greed or sentimental ideologies, micro enterprise and the development of a middle class, market economies and trade agreements... in short, globalization "to meet the needs of humanity" unfortunately with little compassion and care.

These groups in the most part disregard women and human rights. They posit their position with full conviction while neglecting the issue of human dignity. They believe that as long as people have more income people's lives will be improved. Certainly more income is important, but it will not make people's lives and their children's lives better. These groups must accept the conditionalities of human rights and the understanding that women must be equal partners in the development of their communities based on a human rights civil, cultural, economic, political and social contract. Human rights violations will increase; clinics will not be built, children will not be educated, women will not become major participants sharing the economic power as long as there is no commitment to a human rights culture.

However, both human rights experts and women's groups must acknowledge "development as a human right", as proclaimed in the Vienna Declaration and in many international documents. But we must stress again that without a holistic understanding of human rights, which maintains the parameters of development within a human rights framework, the "growth for the sake of growth" approach may raise economic indicators higher, but will not better people's lives. If these three powerful constituencies pursue their agendas without a humble appreciation for the need of cooperation with each other, women, men, girl child, boy child, will not realize their full human potential and the gap of dignity will be widened.

Development must be gender sensitive, law must fully include women, and women must understand human rights as relevant to their daily lives and their family's daily lives. Women must move from the private to the public sphere and participate in weaving a viable economic future for their communities in which they have full say. This is imperative! The Beijing conference was a women's conference and a human rights conference. The resultant Platform for Action is a blueprint for human rights education as it points out all the concerns of human rights of women and of humanity as a whole. The Platform maps out all the injustices, human rights violations that affect women in their daily lives and the strategies eradicate human rights violations which are specifically perpetrated against women because they are women.

Women must lead the human rights revolution! We women have the energy and insight for changing the world with the men who wish to join us as equals. Right here in Vienna, in 1993, the obstacles to accept women's human rights were conceptually removed when the world recognized women's rights as human rights. We all worked for Vienna, for Cairo, for Copenhagen and for Beijing. We have pushed ourselves and our governments to work hard on these issues. We cannot stop now. We have studied the platform of action again and again. We all know what is written in it by heart. We know its little strength and many faults ... and by now we can write our own platform of action to transcend co-optation and the politics of "equity" and "equality." But, we must go further and deeper within the richness of our energy. Our task now is to educate and infuse our movements with the understanding that all social justice work is human rights work and that human rights are indivisible and for all!

Furthermore, there are no human rights without economic rights and economic development must be within the human rights conditionalities. And lastly, women are central to development and must be fully included in all the decision making processes. Each of us must become a human rights educator... We women need to recognize that our issues are indeed political issues. Thus, human rights education must include political education. We must introduce our human rights goals into the political discussion of our communities.

We must make it an imperative for the politicians we elect to deal with these issues. This is what politics are all about. We will be able to do so if we all become human rights literate, learning to speak the human rights language which informs our aspiration and hopes. We cannot leave this language to the academicians or the developers. We must deeply understand how human rights are relevant to our lives, and ensure that politicians make our concerns their concerns. Human rights education will give us the language to remove political dogma and empower us with a viable human rights analysis. It is us women who must lead this human rights revolution for the benefit of society as a whole, claiming our human rights to be human and to be women.

Bibliography

Afkhami, Mahnaz, ed. (1995) *Faith and Freedom: Women's Human Rights in the Muslim World.* Syracuse: Syracuse University Press.

Americas Watch (1991) *Criminal Injustice: Violence Against Women in Brazil.* New York: Human Rights Watch.

Amnesty International (1995) *Human Rights Are Women's Right.* New York, New York: Amnesty International.

Askin, Kelly D. And Doreen M. Koenig, eds. (1999) *Women and International Human Rights Law.* Ardsley, New York: Transnational.

Beneria, L. and S. Feldman, eds. (1992) *Unequal Burden: Economic Crises, Persistent Poverty and Women's Work.* Boulder, Colorado: Westview Press.

Bunch, Charlotte (1990) Women's Rights as Human Rights: Toward a Re-Vision of Human Rights. *Human Rights Quarterly* 12(4):486-498.

Charlton, Sue Ellen M. (1984) *Women in Third World Development.* Boulder, Colorado: Westview Press.

Cook, Rebecca J. (1994) *Women's Health and Human Rights: The Promotion and Protection of Women's Health Through International Human Rights Law.* Geneva: World Health Organisation.

Cook, Rebecca J., ed. (1994) *Human Rights of Women: National and International Perspectives.* Philadelphia, Pennsylvania: University of Pennsylvania Press.

Forbes Martin, S. (1992) *Refugee Women.* London: Zed Books.

Fraser, Arvonne S. (1999) Becoming Human: The Origins and Development of Women's Human Rights. *Human Rights Quarterly* 21:853-906.

Henever, N. (1983) *International Law and the Status of Women*. Boulder and London: Westview Press.

Human Rights Watch (1995) *The Human Rights Watch Global Report on Women's Human Rights*. New York and Washington: Human Rights Watch.

Maraskin, Roslyn (1999) *Women and Justice: Development of an International Policy*. Amsterdam: Gordon and Breach.

Moser, Caroline O.N. (1993) *Gender Planning and Development: Theory, Practice and Training*. London: Routledge.

O'Hare, Ursala A. (1999) Realizing Human Rights for Women. *Human Rights Quarterly* 21(2):364-402.

Overseas Development Institute (1995) *Making Aid Work For Women*. London. ODI.

Peters, Julie and Andrea Wolper, eds. (1995) *Women's Rights, Human Rights: International Feminist Perspectives*. New York: Routledge.

Peterson, V. Spike and Anne Sisson Runyan (1993) *Global Gender Issues*. Boulder, Colorado: Westview Press.

Sadasivam, Bharati (1997) The Impact of Structural Adjustment on Women: A Governance and Human Rights Agenda. *Human Rights Quarterly* 19(3):630-665.

Shiva, Vandana (1989) *Staying Alive: Women, Ecology, and Development*. London: Zed Books.

Stiglmayer, Alexandra, ed. (1994) *Mass Rape: The War Against Women in Bosnia-Herzegovina*. Lincoln: University of Nebraska Press.

Tomasevski, Katarina (1993) *Women and Human Rights*. London: Zed Books.

United Nations High Commissioner for Refugees (1995) *Sexual Violence Against Refugees: Guidelines on Prevention and Response*. Geneva: UNHCR.

Vickers, Jeanne (1993) *Women and War.* London: Zed Books.

Vinding, Diana, ed. (1998) *Indigenous Women: The Right to a Voice.* Copenhagen, Denmark: International Work Group for Indigenous Affairs.

Von Achterburg, Angeline, ed. (1998) *Out of the Shadows: The First African Indigenous Women's Conference.* Amsterdam: The Netherlands Center for Indigenous Peoples.

Wetzel, Janice Wood (1993) *The World of Women: In Pursuit of Human Rights.* New York: New York University Press.

Index